To Write
Like a
Woman

To Write
ESSAYS IN FEMINISM
Like a
AND SCIENCE FICTION
Woman

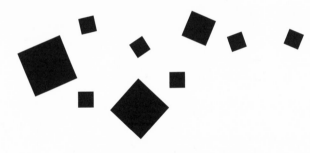

Joanna Russ

*Indiana
University* BLOOMINGTON AND INDIANAPOLIS
Press

The paper used in this publication meets the minimum requirements of American National Standard for Information Sciences—Permanence of Paper for Printed Library Materials, ANSI Z39.48-1984.

Manufactured in the United States of America

Library of Congress Cataloging-in-Publication Data

Russ, Joanna, date
      To write like a woman : essays in feminism and science fiction /
Joanna Russ.
           p. cm.
      Includes bibliographical references and index.
      ISBN 0-253-32914-0 (cloth : alk. paper). — ISBN 0-253-20983-8 (pbk. : alk. paper)
      1. American literature—Women authors—History and criticism—Theory, etc. 2. English literature—Women authors—History and criticism—Theory, etc. 3. Science fiction—History and criticism—Theory, etc. 4. Gender identity in literature. 5. Authorship—Sex differences. 6. Feminism and literature. 7. Sex role in literature. 8. Women and literature. I. Title
PS147R87 1995
810.9'9287—dc20   95-3576

1 2 3 4 5 00 99 98 97 96 95

CONTENTS

 Introduction by Sarah Lefanu

How many people read literary critics for pleasure? Or perhaps the question should be put another way: how many literary critics are there who can be read for pleasure? If you read books about books—and these are the books that literary critics write—and read them for pleasure, what form does the pleasure take? What is it that you want when you read books about books?

There are lots of things you may want: you may wish to gain new insights into the books (or films or stories or TV series); you may wish to have your own opinions confirmed, or your not-quite-fully-formed thoughts articulated; you may want to be stimulated to read books you haven't read, or to reread books you have read; you may want to be provoked, or challenged, or enraged. Or you may want to be made to laugh. Probably, you want illumination of one kind or another, and probably you want to be entertained. I know that I always want these last two: pleasure is to be found in illumination and in entertainment. Joanna Russ is both illuminating and entertaining: these two qualities are inextricably linked to her belief that there is, that indeed there must be, a relationship between the written word, or the televisual image, and life, and that this relationship is of constant and intriguing interest.

My purpose in this introduction is not to suggest to academics why and how these essays—gathered here together for the first time— should be read. What I hope to show is that this book is of more than professional interest, although to those involved professionally, as either students or teachers in science fiction studies or in women's studies, it goes without saying that it is wonderful to have at long last gathered in one volume a collection of essays that have previously been available only in specialist, or small circulation, publications. It is also— and I would say more importantly—a book for the general reader; not just for the general reader of science fiction, or for the general reader of women's fiction; but for the reader who reads for pleasure, that is both for entertainment, and there is plenty to amuse and entertain in these essays, and for illumination.

In an introductory essay it is perhaps more conventional to start with what someone is writing about than with the way in which they say it, but in the case of Joanna Russ it is difficult to separate the two. In the essays collected here, essays written over the last twenty-five years, it is possible to discern a thread that runs through them all, however different their actual subject matter. That thread is Russ's interest in knowledge: in How Things Work, in how we know the world in which we live, and how that knowledge is reflected in the books that we read and write, and in the films that we watch and make. How is knowledge fictionalized? How is knowledge imparted? What ways into knowing the world are handed down in the myths and stories of western culture?

These are large, general concepts, but Joanna Russ tackles them through the particular. In a moment I will describe some of these particulars, but the point I want to make now is that how you impart knowledge is as important a part of that communication as the subject of scrutiny. The way that Joanna Russ writes about her chosen subjects is as important as what those subjects are. This is what makes her an entertaining as well as an illuminating writer; this is what suggests, to me, comparisons with a writer to whom she makes reference every so often in these essays, a writer who, like her, is scholarly without being abstruse, who like her, is passionately interested in what she calls, in her preface, the "multiform nature of the universe": Stephen Jay Gould. Joanna Russ's field is literature rather than Gould's natural world; the desire she brings to her field is that of all scientists: to find out How Things Work.

What then is Joanna Russ's subject matter? The subjects of these essays range from science fiction through science, technology, politics, popular culture, that is, genre writing such as modern Gothic, horror and ghost stories, politics, women writers, sexuality, utopian writing, Mary Shelley, Star Trek and Star Wars, politics, Willa Cather, Charlotte Perkins Gilman, politics. I have repeated "politics": Russ's interest lies in the relation of the written word to life: to the life of the writer and to the life of the reader. She is interested in the economic, sexual, and social position of those who write and of those who read, she is interested in cultural traditions and how they are passed on, or refused, or transformed, or assimilated by those who write and by those who read. The questions she asks of a book, say Mary Shelley's *Frankenstein*, or Monique Wittig's *Les Guérillères*, or of a story, of any one of the ten sex war stories in the essay *"Amor Vincit Foeminam,"* or of a film like *Star Wars*, or of a genre like the modern Gothic; the questions are: what does this book (or story or film) say to us? how does it say this to us? what assumptions does it draw on? why is it saying this? what is its relation to life? These are political questions. They may also be literary or aesthetic questions, but it is the relation of art and culture, and in most of these essays the written word in particular, to the lives of women and men, that make these political questions.

Some of the answers Joanna Russ offers seem so simple, so obvious, that you say "of course," but in fact they haven't been obvious until she has pointed them out. Her role as a critic, in pursuit of the knowledge of how things work, is to demystify, to pick apart, to deconstruct. Take her analysis of the plots and characters of six modern Gothic novels in the brilliantly funny essay "Somebody's Trying to Kill Me and I Think It's My Husband." Russ picks her way through the incredibly tortuous plots of these popular novels, commenting on the strangely ubiquitous characters of the handsome, sarcastic, clever but cold Older Man, and the (also older but fatherly) Other Man with the gentle smile and crinkly eyes (she defines them, respectively, as the Super-Male and the Shadow-Male), drawing our attention meanwhile to the strangely passionless descriptions of food, decor, and clothes, and to our heroine's relationship with the younger female of the household, and shows us that behind the action-packed surface—smuggling, attempted murder, and, in general, criminal activity on a scale almost unheard of in real life—behind this, or rather at the center of it, is a completely passive heroine, a young woman who "does nothing except worry." There is no dreary housework or childcare in these books, and why? The answer is obvious when Joanna Russ articulates it: "Occupation: Housewife" she says, "is simultaneously avoided, glamorized and vindicated."

Throughout these essays Russ reminds the reader that, as often as not, there is no more to something than meets the eye. If you know how to look, that is. Clarity of vision, looking at what is there rather than what might be a hidden agenda: in "Recent Feminist Utopias" she talks about how, in the books under review, war is portrayed as social collapse and natural disaster. And casually, in parentheses, she comments on the fact that this is indeed the way that most women do experience war, as something out there, something that they are not actively involved in, but that has huge repercussions on their lives and families. This simple aside suggests an answer to that old complaint, "why don't women write about important things?" (the glories of war, the intricacies of the military hierarchy). The answer being that what women experience as important is not necessarily the same as what men experience as important; or the importance of a phenomenon is experienced in different ways. Joanna Russ is a great demystifier, and her contempt for obfuscation, whether such obfuscation arises through ignorance or shoddy thinking on the part of the writer, or whether it is a deliberate strategy for excluding the reader from the inner sanctum of knowledge, is a constant thread that runs through these essays. In 1977 her target is the mystification of technology (in this coruscating essay she uses a delightfully convincing model of physical addiction to help explain the constant occurrence in endless conferences of "non-discourse" about this "non-subject"); later it is literary theory and its hideous offspring. Joanna Russ writes in a way that is informal and lucid. Her style does not require of her readers a Ph.D. in Higher Reading. In this she is not unlike the literary critic Phyllis Rose, another scholar who is driven by a passion for exploring the twisted threads that link literature to life.

Russ enjoys parentheses, the elegant aside casually dropped. As often as not, it is in these asides that she targets mystifying practices. Indeed, tucked away in a postscript to the final essay in the book—an essay that takes issue with the obscurantism surrounding psychoanalytic criticism and in which she comments wryly that Freudians "get this weird idea that Freud knew everything"—in the postscript she reminds us that "All theories are merely models." Of course. But there are a lot of people who think that theories are the truth.

It is perhaps here—where scientific analysis and the pleasure of postscript writing meet—that we find an example of the happy relationship there can be between what is entertaining and what is illuminating. Clarity of style goes hand in hand with clarity of thought, for lucid prose allows no swamp for mystification to breed. These essays are both rigorous and subtle in their analysis of literary form and literary endeavor. Russ is not afraid to take an idea and run with it to see how far it will go. She takes up, for example, Darko Suvin's suggested view of science fiction as being "quasi-medieval" and pursues it down various paths, investigating the didactic content of science fiction and using an analogy with the relation between medieval Christianity and medieval literature to illuminate her argument, which is that a reader or critic of science fiction must have, in order to read properly, a passionate belief in reality and the importance of scientific knowledge. Assumptions and form dovetail, she argues, so that knowledge itself, the process of finding out, is in science fiction a crucial good. Science fiction is a primary concern of Joanna Russ's. She argues eloquently and persuasively for the importance and the originality of science fiction, for its difference from other forms of literature. It is obvious from these essays that here is a critic who knows, understands, and practices the art that she is writing about.

Her other primary concern is women's writing, and, with the essays collected here, the reader can see the links between these two concerns. They do not merge seamlessly but rather set up interesting resonances with each other. In the essay on Mary Wollstonecraft Shelley, for example, Russ questions the place assigned to Mary Shelley in the canon of women's writing, for as a novelist, Russ argues, Shelley is "half-bad," and no more deserving of a place in that canon than various other women writers who have been denied it. As a mythmaker, however, it is a different story. And what form do those myths take? They take a science fictional form. Russ's fine-honed skill at deconstructing myths and stories allows us to see how it was that Mary Shelley created in literary form two of the central myths of modern industrialism, that is, the creation of non-organic life (*Frankenstein*) and the end of the world seen as a natural rather than a supernatural catastrophe (*The Last Man*) (this last being, as Joanna Russ points out, one of the most stubbornly ubiquitous plots in SF, and now surely common currency). Mary Shelley, contends Russ, was not, as a writer, just avoiding realism, but was in full flight from an almost unbearable reality.

Whatever the subject matter, Joanna Russ is saying, whether it is science fiction or horror fiction, or nineteenth-century women's novels, or much-admired stories by Ernest Hemingway, look at what is there. Look at Mary Shelley's life, at her miscarriages, her dead babies, her dead husband. Look at, to take another example, what kind of a story Charlotte Perkins Gilman's *The Yellow Wallpaper* is: it is a ghost story. If you don't appreciate that it is a ghost story, then you can get into a fine old tangle as to what it is all about. In this particular essay on *The Yellow Wallpaper* Russ criticizes a type of feminist psychoanalytic literary theory that prioritizes speech and silence as *the* feminist issues (there is a marvelous parenthesis in this essay on "the silliness possible to those who consider the pun the major agency in human thought"), but at the same time the essay refers back to her earlier work on SF and its associated forms. She insists on the importance of genre writings, seeing "paraliterary" genres, such as ghost stories, as able to express what can't be expressed in a high culture dominated—still dominated—by realism.

Look at Willa Cather's life, says Russ. Look at what it means to be a lesbian at a time, post–Krafft-Ebing and post–Havelock Ellis, when romantic friendships between women, such as those enjoyed by Sarah Orne Jewett, were no longer possible, when, instead, romantic friendships were morbidified, made unhealthy and criminal. And then look at Willa Cather's writing, and see the sense in her "masquerade" of writing as a man. This essay, published in 1986, looks back to one of the earliest essays collected here, "What Can a Heroine Do? or Why Women Can't Write," in which Russ asks how women writers have dealt with, and continue to deal with, the structures and myths that are available for them to work with in a male-dominated culture. In this essay she writes about Virginia Woolf and Charlotte Bronte. Her analysis of the literary canon is informed and enriched by her deconstruction of other literary forms. Her reading of what are considered by others to be marginal texts—science fiction, fantasy, horror, for example—feeds into an understanding of how other women's work, that of Woolf, Bronte, Cather, Gilman, has been, and continues to be, read in a partial, selective way.

Literary forms, paraliterary forms, genre writing, women's writing: those readers who favor science fiction will have their understanding enriched by what Russ has to say about women's writing. Those readers who know Russ for her work on women's writing will be amazed by their recognition of the importance of knowing what science fiction is about for an understanding of other literary forms. But there is another kind of reader, the gentle, general reader, who may be a student or teacher, but who may simply read widely and intelligently without the benefits or otherwise of courses or credits or training or tenure.

All of these readers will find in these essays: wit, humor, anger, passion, a love of books, a love of knowledge, a belief in the importance of the pursuit of knowledge, leaps of the critical imagination that throw light on a subject in totally unexpected ways (I would single out as an example the revealing comparison made between the portrayal of the morality of King Shahriyar in *The Thousand and One Nights* and that of the boy in Ellison's *A Boy and His Dog*). They will find points closely argued; they will find threads unraveled and followed carefully back to their beginning. What Joanna Russ has to say is always sensible (although sometimes it is shocking); the way she says it is always elegant. Some literary criticism makes the reader feel excluded and therefore stupid. Such work is never sensible, nor is it elegant. Joanna Russ, by contrast, aims to include the reader. She aims to show the way into the books and stories she's talking about. Reading, she believes, must be related to living; Russ invites her readers to read alongside her, and like her, to bring their own experiences to bear on what they read. Why else, indeed, would you wish to read?

 Author's Introduction

So what's to introduce?

George Bernard Shaw once said in old age that he would not feel justified in changing anything he'd written years before any more than he'd feel justified in changing another writer's work. That is, the young Shaw and the old one were not the same person. I feel the same way about my own earlier work—and yet, looking back through these essays, I find that there is a continuity all the same.

If any theme runs through all my work, it is what Adrienne Rich once called "re-vision," i.e., the re-perceiving of experience, not because our experience is complex or subtle or hard to understand (though it is sometimes all three) but because so much of what's presented to us as "the real world" or "the way it is" is so obviously untrue that a great deal of social energy must be mobilized to hide that gross and ghastly fact. As a theatre critic (whose name I'm afraid I've forgotten) once put it, "There's less there than meets the eye." Hence, my love for science fiction, which analyzes reality by changing it. Mundane, realistic fiction often carries its meaning *behind* the action, *underneath* the action, underneath the *ostensible* action. Science fiction cancels this process by making what is usually a literary metaphor into a literal identity. Thus its absolutely literal use of language, in any form from the obvious joke (like Theodore Sturgeon's story title, "The Girl Had Guts") to witty details (like Olaf Stapledon's invention in *Last and First Men* of a religion of music whose martyrs "sang, even in the flames") to a story like Isaac Asimov's "Nightfall," which takes two of the commonest linked metaphors in English (light as knowledge and light as reality) and literalizes them in a story in which the one real metaphor (which links both) occurs only at the very end of the tale. If science fiction cancels the relation between ostensible, surface action and "hidden" meaning, fantasy turns this relation inside-out. There, the "hidden" meaning *is* the surface, projected outward as if on a movie screen, while the realistic or mundane equivalent is under that surface, behind the story, only an implication (as in Shirley Jackson's reverse-Modern Gothic, *The Haunting of Hill House*). Here the supernatural is explicit, its natural counterpart only implicit.

I write science fiction. I write fantasy. I read both.

There are certain pleasures that do not occur in realistic literature. Thus I will always remember, from *2001*, the spectacle of the Earth and the Moon circling around a common center (to wittily appropriate music) and realizing with a shock of delight that primary and satellite do indeed move around one another in this way, very much like the dancers evoked by the music. Similarly, I will never forget (in Ursula Le Guin's *The Dispossessed*) a horse's face suggesting to the protagonist that of a distorted human being—phylogenetically speaking, he's correct. Nor (in Susan Palwick's "Ever After") the story of Cinderella becoming—with little or no alteration—that of a vampire. Parody, with its particular transformations of reality, is the only realistic genre that can distort itself in anything like this way in the service of truth. (I write parodies, too.)

The kind of temperament that enjoys these inversions is, I think, the kind of mind that enjoys taking things apart to see how they work. Such taking apart is a kind of mental topology, the study of which is another subject I find fascinating. One must have a taste for abstract analysis to write science fiction or fantasy or parody . . . or criticism. Long, long ago, in the 1960s, I heard Alan Watts saying on WBAI-FM in New York that there were two temperaments in the world: "the goo people," who conceptualize reality as a kind of featureless unity of substance, and "the prickle people," who do so in terms of structure. I knew at once to which group I belonged.

Just the other day, watching clearly delimited cloud shadows move over the Santa Catalinas here in southern Arizona, I became aware of what I had missed for so many years in cloud-covered Seattle: *edges*. How multiform the universe is, how branching, how structured, how crystalline! Mountain ranges, clouds, trees, human relations, human literary inventions—how fractal they all are!

Part One

1

Towards an Aesthetic of Science Fiction

*T*he following essay was published in Science-fiction Studies *in 1975. Having read science fiction since 1951 and having written (and published) it since 1959 (the date of my first story's appearance in* The Magazine of Fantasy and Science Fiction*), I had gotten very tired of the usual reaction such behavior got from academic literary critics. It still happens. Tell one of them you write/read s.f. and the reaction is apt to be two steps backward, an instant judgment that you are a very strange person indeed, and a feeble (or hearty) "Oh, you mean that Buck Rogers stuff." (Those who say, "Oh, that Ray Bradbury stuff," are usually more tolerant.) Such were the reactions that led me to write this essay.*

Is science fiction literature?

Yes.

Can it be judged by the usual literary criteria?

No.

Such a statement requires not only justification but considerable elaboration. Written science fiction is, of course, literature, although science fiction in other media (films, drama, perhaps even painting or sculpture) must be judged by standards other than those applied to the written word.[1] Concentrating on science fiction as literature, primarily as prose fiction, this paper will attempt to indicate some of the limitations critics encounter in trying to apply traditional literary criticism to science fiction. To be brief, the access of academic interest in science fiction that has occurred during the last few years has led to considerable difficulty. Not only do academic critics find themselves imprisoned by habitual (and unreflecting) condescension in dealing with this particular genre; quite often their critical tools, however finely honed, are simply not applicable to a body of work that—despite its superficial resemblance to realistic or naturalistic twentieth-century fiction—is fundamentally a drastically different form of literary art.

Fine beginnings have been made in the typology of science fiction by Darko Suvin[2] of McGill University, who builds on the parameters prescribed for the genre by the Polish writer and critic, Stanislaw Lem.[3] Samuel Delany, a science-fiction writer and theorist, has dealt with the same matters in a recent paper concerned largely with problems of definition.[4]

One very important point which emerges in the work of all three critics is that standards of plausibility—as one may apply them to science fiction—must be derived not only from the observation of life as it is or has been lived, but also, rigorously and systematically, from science. And in this context "science" must include disciplines ranging from mathematics (which is formally empty) through the "hard" sciences (physics, astronomy, chemistry) through the "soft" sciences (ethology, psychology, sociology) all the way to disciplines which as yet exist only in the descriptive or speculative state (history, for example, or political theory).

Science fiction is not fantasy, for the standards of plausibility of fantasy derive not from science, but from the observation of life as it is— inner life, perhaps, in this case. Mistakes in scientific possibility do not turn science fiction into fantasy. They are merely mistakes. Nor does the outdating of scientific theory transform the science fiction of the past into fantasy.[5] Error-free science fiction is an ideal as impossible of achievement as the nineteenth-century ideal of an "objective," realistic novel. Not that in either case the author can be excused for not trying; unreachability is, after all, what ideals are for. But only God can know enough to write either kind of book perfectly.

For the purposes of the aesthetics of science fiction, a remark of Professor Suvin's made casually at the 1968 annual meeting of the Modern Language Association seems to me extremely fruitful. Science fiction, said Suvin, is "quasi-medieval." Professor Suvin has not elaborated on this insight, as he seems at the moment more concerned with the nature of science fiction's cognitive relation to what he calls the "zero world" of "empirically verifiable properties around the author."[6]

To me the phrase "quasi-medieval" suggests considerable insight, particularly into the reasons why critical tools developed with an entirely different literature in mind often do not work when applied to science fiction. I should like to propose the following:

That science fiction, like much medieval literature, is *didactic.*

That, despite superficial similarities to naturalistic (or other) modern fiction, the protagonists of science fiction are always collective, never individual persons (although individuals often appear as exemplary or representative figures).

That science fiction's emphasis is always on *phenomena*—to the point where reviewers and critics can commonly use such phrases as "the idea as hero."

That science fiction is not only didactic, but very often awed, worshipful, and *religious* in tone. Damon Knight's famous phrase for this is "the sense of wonder."[7] To substantiate this last, one needs only a head-count of Messiahs in recent science fiction novels, the abrupt changes of scale (either spatial or temporal) used to induce cosmic awe in such works as Olaf Stapledon's *Last and First Men,* James Blish's *Surface Tension,* stories like Isaac Asimov's "Nightfall" and "The Last Question," Arthur C. Clarke's "Nine Billion Names of God," and the change of tone at the end of Clarke's *Childhood's End* or Philip José Farmer's story "Sail On! Sail On!" (The film *2001* is another case in point.)

The emphasis on phenomena, often at the complete expense of human character, needs no citation; it is apparent to anyone who has any acquaintance with the field. Even in pulp science fiction populated by grim-jawed heroes, the human protagonist, if not Everyman, is a glamorized version of Super-everyman. That science fiction is didactic hardly needs proof, either. The pleasure science fiction writers take in explaining physics, thirtieth-century jurisprudence, the mechanics of teleportation, patent law, four-dimensional geometry, or whatever happens to be on the tapis, lies open in any book that has not degenerated into outright adventure story with science-fiction frills.[8] Science fiction even has its favorite piece of theology. Just as contemporary psychoanalytic writers cannot seem to write anything without explaining the Oedipus complex at least once, so science fiction writers dwell lovingly on the time dilation consequent to travel at near light-speed. Science is to science fiction (by analogy) what medieval Christianity was to deliberately didactic medieval fiction.

I would like to propose that contemporary literary criticism (not having been developed to handle such material) is not the ideal tool for dealing with fiction that is explicitly, deliberately, and baldly *didactic*. (Modern criticism appears to experience the same difficulty in handling the eighteenth-century *contes philosophiques* Professor Suvin cites as among the precursors of science fiction.) Certainly if one is to analyze didactic literature, one must first know what system of beliefs or ideas constitutes the substance of the didacticism. A modern critic attempting to understand science fiction without understanding modern science is in the position of a medievalist attempting to read *Piers Plowman* without any but the haziest ideas about medieval Catholicism. (Or, possibly, like a modern critic attempting to understand Bertolt Brecht without any knowledge of Marxist economic analysis beyond a vague and uninformed distrust.)

An eminent critic (who knows better now) once asked me during a discussion of a novel of Kurt Vonnegut's, "But when you get to the science, don't you just make it up?" The answer, of course, is no. Science fiction must not offend against what is known. Only in areas where nothing is known—or knowledge is uncertain—is it permissible to just "make it up." (Even then, what is made up must be systematic, plausible, rigorously logical, and must avoid offending against what is known to be known.)

Of course, didactic fiction does not always tell people something new; often it tells them what they already know, and the retelling becomes a reverent ritual, very gratifying to all concerned. There is some of this in science fiction, although (unlike the situation obtaining in medieval Christianity) this state of affairs is considered neither necessary nor desirable by many readers. There is science fiction that concentrates on the very edges of what is known. There is even science fiction that ignores what is known. The latter is bad science fiction.[9]

How can a criticism developed to treat a post-medieval literature of individual destinies, secular concerns, and the representation of what is (rather than what might be) illuminate science fiction?

Science fiction presents an eerie echo of the attitudes and interests of a pre-industrial, pre-Renaissance, pre-secular, pre-individualistic culture. It has been my experience that medievalists take easily and kindly to science fiction, that they are often attracted to it, that its didacticism presents them with no problems, and that they enjoy this literature much more than do students of later literary periods.[10] So, in fact, do city planners, architects, archaeologists, engineers, rock musicians, anthropologists, and nearly everybody except most English professors.

Without knowledge of or appreciation of the "theology" of science fiction—that is, science—what kind of criticism will be practiced on particular science fiction works?

Often critics may use their knowledge of the recurrent and important themes of Western culture to misperceive what is actually in a science-fiction story. For example, recognizable themes or patterns of imagery can be insisted on far beyond their actual importance in the work simply because they are familiar to the critic. Or the symbolic importance of certain material can be misread because the significance of the material in the cultural tradition that science fiction comes from (which is overwhelmingly that of science, not literature) is simply not known to the critic. Sometimes material may be ignored because it is not part of the critic's cognitive universe.

For example, in H. G. Wells's magnificent novella, *The Time Machine,* a trip into the 8000th century presents us with a world that appears to be directly reminiscent of Eden, a "weedless garden" full of warm sunlight, untended but beautiful flowers, and effortless innocence. Wells even has his Time Traveler call the happy inhabitants of this garden "Eloi" (from the Hebrew "Elohim"). Certainly the derivation of these details is obvious. Nor can one mistake the counter-world popu-lated by bleached monsters. But the critic may make too much of all this. For example, Bernard Bergonzi (I suspect his behavior would be fairly typical) overweights Wells's heavenly/demonic imagery.[11] Certainly *The Time Machine*'s pastoral future does echo a great deal of material impor-tant in the Western literary tradition, but it is a mistake to think of these (very obtrusive) clusters of Edenic-pastoral/hellish imagery as the "hid-den" meaning of Wells's Social Darwinism. On the contrary, it is the worlds of the Eloi and the Morlocks that are put in the employ of the Social Darwinism, which is itself only an example of mindless evolution, of the cruelty of material determinism, and of the tragic mindlessness of all physical process. The real center of Wells's story is not even in his ironic reversal of the doctrine of the fortunate fall (evolution, in Wells's view in *The Time Machine,* inevitably produces what one might call the unfortunate rise—the very production of intelligence, of mind, is what must, sooner or later, destroy mind). Even the human devolution pictured in the story is only a special case of the iron physical law that constitutes the true center of the book and the true agony of Wells's vision. This vision is easy to overlook, not because it is subtle, indirect, or hidden, but because it is so blatantly hammered home in all the Time Traveler's speculations about evolution and—above all—in a chapter explicitly entitled "The Farther Vision." As Eric Bentley once remarked, "clarity is the first requisite of didacticism."[12] Didactic art must, so to speak, wear its meaning on its sleeve. *The Time Machine* is not about a lost Eden; it is—passionately and tragically—about the Three Laws of Thermodynamics, especially the second. The slow cooling of the sun in "The Farther Vision" foreshadows the heat-death of the universe. In fact, the novella is a series of deaths: individual death (as exemplified by Weena's presumed death and the threat to the Time Traveler himself from the Morlocks) is bad enough; the "wilderness of rotting paper" in the Palace of Green Porcelain, an abandoned museum, is perhaps worse; the complete disappearance of mind in humanity's remote descendents (the kangaroo-like animals) is horrible; but the death of absolutely everything, the physical degradation of the entire universe, is a Gotterdämmerung earlier views of the nature of the universe could hardly conceive—*let alone prove.* As the Time Traveler says after leaving "that remote and awful twilight," "I'm sorry to have brought you out here in the cold."

Unless a critic can bring to *The Time Machine* not only a knowledge of the science that stands behind it, but the passionate belief that such knowledge is real and that it matters, the critic had better stay away from science fiction. Persons to whom the findings of science seem only bizarre, fanciful, or irrelevant to everyday life, have no business with science fiction—or with science for that matter—although they may deal perfectly well with fiction that ignores both science and the scientific view of reality.

For example, a short story by Ursula K. Le Guin, "The Masters" (in *Fantastic,* Feb. 1963), has as its emotional center the rediscovery of the duodecimal system. To criticize this story properly one must know about three things: the Arabic invention of the zero, the astounding importance of this invention for mathematics (and hence the sciences), and the fact that one may count with any base. In fact, the duodecimal system, with its base of 12, is far superior for some uses to our decimal system with its base of 10.

A third example of ways science fiction can be mis-read can be provided by Hal Clement's novel, *Close to Critical.* The story treats of an alien species inhabiting a planet much like Jupiter. Some psychoanalytic critic, whose name I have unfortunately forgotten, once treated material like this (the story was, I think, Milton Rothman's "Heavy Planet") as psychoneurotic, i.e., the projection of repressed infantile fears. And certainly a Jovian or Jovian-like landscape would be extremely bizarre. Clement's invented world, with its atmosphere three thousand times as dense as ours, its gravity three times ours, its total darkness, its pine-cone-shaped inhabitants, its hundred-foot-wide "raindrops" that condense at night and evaporate each morning, can easily be perceived by the scientifically ignorant as a series of grotesque morbidities. In such a view, *Close to Critical* is merely nightmarish. But to decide this is to ignore the evidence. Clement's gas-giant is neither nightmarish nor grotesque, but merely accurate. In fact, Mr. Clement is the soberest of science fiction writers, and his characters are always rational, humane, and highly likeable. The final effect of the novel is exactly the opposite of nightmare; it is affectionate familiarity. The Jovian-like world is a real world. One understands and appreciates it. It is, to its inhabitants, no worse and no better than our own. It is, finally, beautiful—in the same way and for the same reasons that Earth is beautiful. *Close to Critical* evokes Knight's "sense of wonder" because it describes a genuinely possible place, indeed a place that is highly likely according to what we know of the universe. The probability of the setting is what makes the book elegant—in the mathematical sense, that is: aesthetically satisfying. If there is anything grotesque in Clement's work, it is in the strain caused by the split between idea-as-hero (which is superbly handled) and the human protagonists, who are neither interesting, probable, nor necessary, and whose appearance in the book at all is undoubtedly due to the American pulp tradition out of which American science fiction arose after World War I. The book suffers from serious confusion of form.

Science fiction, like medieval painting, addresses itself to the mind, not the eye. We are not presented with a representation of what we know to be true through direct experience; rather, we are given what we know to be true through other means—or in the case of science fiction, what we know to be at least possible. Thus the science-fiction writer can portray Jupiter as easily as the medieval painter can portray Heaven; neither of them has been there, but that doesn't matter. To turn from other modern fiction to science fiction is oddly like turning from Renaissance painting, with all that flesh and foreshortening, to the clarity and luminousness of painters who paint ideas. For this reason, science fiction, like much medieval art, can deal with transcendental events. Hence the tendency of science fiction towards wonder, awe, and a religious or quasi-religious attitude towards the universe.

Persons who consider science untrue, or irrelevant to what really matters, or inimical to humane values, can hardly be expected to be interested in science fiction. Nor can one study science fiction as some medievalists (presumably) might study their material—that is, by finding equivalents for a system of beliefs they cannot accept in literal form. To treat medieval Catholicism as irrelevant to medieval literature is bad scholarship; to treat it as somebody else's silly but interesting superstitions is likewise extremely damaging to any consideration of the literature itself. But nonscientific equivalents for the Second Law of Thermodynamics or the intricacies of genetics—or whatever a particular science fiction story is about—will not do, either. Science bears too heavily on all our lives for that. All of us—willy-nilly—must live as if we believed the body of modern science to be true. Moreover, science itself contains methods for determining what about it is true—not metaphorically true, or metaphysically true, or emotionally true, but simply, plainly, physically, literally true.

If the critic believes that scientific truth is unreal, or irrelevant to his (the critic's) business, then science fiction becomes only a series of very odd metaphors for "the human condition" (which is taken to be different from or unconnected to any scientific truths about the universe). Why should an artist draw metaphors from such a peculiar and totally extra-literary source? Especially when there are so many more intelligent (and intelligible) statements of the human condition that already exist—in our (non-science-fiction) literary tradition? Are writers of science fiction merely kinky? Or perverse? Or stubborn? One can imagine what C.P. Snow would have to say about this split between the two cultures.

One thing he might say is that science fiction bridges the two cultures. It draws its beliefs, its material, its great organizing metaphors, its very attitudes, from a culture that could not exist before the industrial revolution, before science became both an autonomous activity and a way of looking at the world. In short, science fiction is *not* derived from traditional Western literary culture, and critics of traditional Western literature have good reason to regard science fiction as a changeling in the literary cradle.

Perhaps science fiction is one symptom of a change in sensibility (and culture) as profound as that of the Renaissance. Despite its ultra-American, individualistic muscle-flexing, science fiction (largely American in origins and influence)[13] is collective in outlook, didactic, materialist, and, paradoxically, often intensely religious or mystical. Such a cluster of traits reminds one not only of medieval culture, but, possibly, of tendencies in our own, post-industrial culture. It may be no accident that elaborate modern statements of the aesthetic of the *didactic* are to be found in places like Brecht's "A Short Organum for the Theatre."[14] Of course, didactic art does not necessarily mean propaganda or political Leftism. But there are similarities between Samuel Delany's insistence that modern literature must be concerned not with passion, but with perception,[15] Suvin's definition of science fiction as a literature of "cognitive estrangement,"[16] George Bernard Shaw's insistence on art as didactic, Brecht's definition of art as a kind of experiment, and descriptions of science fiction as "thought experiments."[17] It is as if literary and dramatic art were being asked to perform tasks of analysis and teaching as a means of dealing with some drastic change in the conditions of human life.

Science fiction is the only modern literature to take work as its central and characteristic concern.

Except for some modern fantasy (e.g., the novels of Charles Williams), science fiction is the only kind of modern narrative literature to deal directly (often awkwardly) with religion as process, not as doctrine, i.e., the ground of feeling and experience from which religion springs.

Like much "post-modern" literature (Nabokov, Borges), science fiction deals commonly, typically, and often insistently, with epistemology.

It is unlikely that science fiction will ever become a major form of literature. Life-as-it-is (however glamorized or falsified) is more interesting to most people than the science-fictional life-as-it-might-be. Moreover, the second depends on an understanding and appreciation of the first. In a sense, science fiction includes (or is parasitic on, depending on your point of view) non-science fiction.

However, there is one realm in which science fiction will remain extremely important. It is the only modern literature that attempts to assimilate imaginatively scientific knowledge about reality and the scientific method, as distinct from the merely practical changes science has made in our lives. The latter are important and sometimes overwhelming, but they can be dealt with imaginatively in exactly the same way a Londoner could have dealt with the Great Plague of 1665 ("Life is full of troubles") or the way we characteristically deal with our failures in social organization ("Man is alienated"). Science fiction is also the only modern literary form (with the possible exception of the detective

puzzle) that embodies in its basic assumptions the conviction that
finding out, or knowing about something—however impractical the
knowledge—is itself a crucial good. Science fiction is a positive response
to the post-industrial world, not always in its content (there is plenty of
nostalgia for the past and dislike of change in science fiction), but in its
very assumptions, its very form.

Criticism of science fiction cannot possibly look like the criticism we
are used to. It will—perforce—employ an aesthetic in which the el-
egance, rigorousness, and systematic coherence of explicit ideas is of
great importance.[18] It will therefore appear to stray into all sorts of
extraliterary fields: metaphysics, politics, philosophy, physics, biology,
psychology, topology, mathematics, history, and so on. The relations of
foreground and background that we are so used to after a century and
a half of realism will not obtain. Indeed, they may be reversed. Science-
fiction criticism will discover themes and structures (like those of Olaf
Stapledon's *Last and First Men*) that may seem recondite, extra-literary,
or plain ridiculous. Themes we customarily regard as emotionally
neutral will be charged with emotion. Traditionally "human" concerns
will be absent; protagonists may be all but unrecognizable as such. What
in other fiction would be marvelous will here be merely accurate or
plain; what in other fiction would be ordinary or mundane will here be
astonishing, complex, wonderful. (For example, allusions to the death
of God will be trivial jokes, while metaphors involving the differences
between telephone switchboards and radio stations will be poignantly
tragic. Stories ostensibly about persons will really be about topology.
Erotics will be intracranial, mechanical [literally], and moving.)[19]

Science fiction is, of course, about human concerns. It is written and
read by human beings. But the culture from which it comes—the
experiences, attitudes, knowledge, and learning that one must bring to
it—these are not at all what we are used to as proper to literature. They
may, however, be increasingly proper to human life. According to
Professor Suvin, the last century has seen a sharp rise in the popularity
of science fiction in all the leading industrial nations of the world.[20]
There will, in all probability, be more and more science fiction written
and, therefore, more and more of a need for its explication and criticism.

Such criticism will not be easy. The task of a modern critic of science
fiction might be compared to the difficulties of studying Shakespeare's
works armed only with a vast, miscellaneous mass of Elizabethan and
Jacobean plays, a few remarks of Ben Jonson's, some scattered eulogies

on Richard Burbage, Rowe's comments on *Othello,* and a set of literary standards derived exclusively from the Greek and Latin classics—which, somehow, do not quite fit.

Some beginnings have been made in outlining an aesthetics of science fiction, particularly in the work of Lem and Suvin, but much remains to be done. Perhaps the very first task lies in discovering that we are indeed dealing with a new and different literature. Applying the standards and methods one is used to can have only three results: the dismissal of all science fiction as non-literature, a preference for certain narrow kinds of science fiction (because they can be understood at least partly in the usual way), or a misconceiving and misperception of the very texts one is trying to understand. The first reaction seems to be the most common. In the second category one might place the odd phenomenon that critics inexperienced in the field seem to find two kinds of fiction easy to deal with: seventeenth-century flights to the moon and dystopias. Thus *Brave New World* and *1984* have received much more critical attention than, say, Shaw's late plays or Stapledon's work. The third category has hitherto been rare because academic consideration of science fiction has been rare, but it could become all too common if the increasing popularity of college courses in the subject is not accompanied by criticism proper to the subject. Futurologists, physicists, and sociologists may use science fiction in extra-literary ways, but they are not literary critics. If the literary critics misperceive or misconceive their material, the results will be to discourage readers, discourage science-fiction writers (who are as serious about their work as any other writers), destroy the academic importance of the subject itself, and thus impoverish the whole realm of literature, of which science fiction is a new—but a vigorous and growing—province.

NOTES

This essay was originally published in *Science-Fiction Studies* #6, Volume 2, Part 2, July 1975.

1. "Environments" and similar examples of contemporary art seem to lend themselves to science fiction. For example, as of this writing, an "archeological" exhibit of the fictional Civilization of Llhuros is visiting our local museum. Strictly speaking, the exhibit is fantasy and not science fiction, since the creator (Professor Norman Daly of Cornell University) makes no attempt to place this imaginary country in either a known, a future, or an extraterrene history.

2. See particularly "On the Poetics of the Science Fiction Genre," *College English* 34(1972):372–82.

3. For example, "On the Structural Analysis of Science Fiction," *SFS* 1(1973): 26–33.

4. "About Five Thousand One Hundred and Seventy-Five Words," *Extrapolation* 10(1969):52–66.

5. At least not immediately. Major changes in scientific theory may lead to major reevaluation of the fiction, but most science fiction hasn't been around long enough for that. I would agree with George Bernard Shaw that didactic literature does (at least in part) wear out with time, but most science fiction can still rest on the Scottish verdict of "not proven."

6. Suvin (note 2), p. 377.

7. Damon Knight, *In Search of Wonder* (2d ed., 1967). The phrase is used throughout.

8. From time to time what might even be called quasi-essays appear, e.g., Larry Niven, "The Theory and Practice of Teleportation," *Galaxy*, March 1969.

9. A dictum attributed to Theodore Sturgeon, science-fiction writer, is that 90 percent of anything is bad.

10. As of this writing, SUNY Binghamton is presenting a summer course in science fiction taught by a graduate student who is—a medievalist.

11. Bernard Bergonzi, *The Early H. G. Wells* (Manchester, 1961), p. 52ff.

12. Eric Bentley, *The Playwright as Thinker* (New York 1967), p. 224.

13. Kingsley Amis emphasizes that twentieth-century science fiction is predominantly an American phenomenon: *New Maps of Hell* (New York, 1960), p. 17 (or Ballantine Books ed., p. 17), q.v.

14. In *Brecht on Theatre,* trans. John Willett (New York, 1962), pp. 179–205.

15. In a talk given at the MLA seminar on science fiction, December 1968, in New York.

16. Suvin (note 2), p. 372.

17. This phrase has been used so widely in the field that original attribution is impossible.

18. Suvin (note 2), p. 381, as follows: "The consistency of extrapolation, precision of analogy, and width of reference in such a cognitive discussion turn into aesthetic factors . . . a cognitive—*in most cases strictly scientific—element becomes a measure of aesthetic quality."*

19. In turn, James Blish's *Black Easter* (which I take to be about Manicheanism), Stapledon's *Last and First Men* (the Martian invasion), A. J. Deutsch's "A Subway Named Moebius" (frequently anthologized), and George Zebrowski's "Starcrossed" (in *Eros in Orbit,* ed. Joseph Elder, 1973).

20. Suvin (note 2), p. 372.

2

Speculations: The Subjunctivity of Science Fiction

his essay predates the first by two years, having been printed in 1973 in Extrapolation, *then a Johnny-come-lately journal, now (along with* S.-F. Studies) *a staid old veteran of the field. The early 1970s saw the establishment of much of the fundamentals of s.f. criticism, of which the following is a part. The explosion in undergraduate (and eventually graduate) courses in the field came a little later. It was an exciting time. I still think some of the insights below are worth noting, though in general it seems less important to me now to describe the techniques of s.f. than it did to the young woman who wrote the following. Artists know them, whether or not critics do; that's what counts. Nonetheless it was great fun to pin down such ideas as the zero world of empirically verifiable reality (Darko Suvin's idea) or Delany's delicately precise sorting-out of all the tenses English doesn't quite have. I think I was quite accurate in describing below the intellectual athleticism good s.f. insists on in the reader; anyone who wants to test the following assertions should read, say, Philip José Farmer's "Sail On! Sail On!" and try to figure out in the first few pages what's really going on, or Kipling's "Night Mail" (an indirect, marvelously detailed piece of utopian fiction pretending to be future journalism and a classic in the field).*

I

At the 1968 meeting of the MLA Seminar, science-fiction writer Samuel Delany offered a definition of the subjunctivity of prose narrative and in so doing constructed a new definition of science fiction, perhaps the first to be proposed in several decades:

> Subjunctivity is the tension on the thread of meaning that runs
> between word and object. [For] a piece of reportage, a blanket indicative
> tension informs the whole series: *this happened*. . . . The subjunctivity for
> a series of words labeled naturalistic fiction is defined by: *could have
> happened*. . . . Fantasy takes the subjunctivity of naturalistic fiction and
> throws it in reverse . . . *could not have happened*. And immediately [this
> level of subjunctivity] informs all the words in the series. . . . [In] SF the
> subjunctivity level is changed once more . . . *have not happened*.
>
> *Events that have not happened* are very different from the fictional *events that
> could have happened,* or the fantastic *events that could not have happened*. . . .
>
> *Events that have not happened* include those *events that might happen:*
> these are your . . . predictive tales. They include *events that will not happen:*
> these are your science-fantasy stories. They include *events that have not
> happened yet*. . . . These are your cautionary dystopias. . . . [They] include
> past events as well as future ones. *Events that have not happened in the past*
> compose that SF specialty, the parallel-world story.[1]

Delany has here gone beyond the usual concept of science fiction as
predictive; and what is more useful, he has uncovered a distinction
between fantasy and science fiction that does not depend on estimates
of the author's intentions or his scientific accuracy.

Fantasy, according to the above description, embodies a "negative
subjunctivity"—that is, fantasy is fantasy because it contravenes the real
and violates it. The actual world is constantly implicit in fantasy, by
negation. In Delany's words, fantasy is *what could not have happened;* i.e.,
what *cannot* happen, what *cannot* exist. And I would submit that the
negative subjunctivity, the *cannot* or *could not,* constitutes in fact the chief
pleasure of fantasy. Fantasy violates the real, contravenes it, denies it,
and insists on this denial throughout.

Science fiction, however, writes about *what has not happened.* Its
connection with actuality, with possibility, is one of its chief pleasures.
Whenever some scientific or technological advance becomes known, SF
writers search the literature to find out who predicted it and when and
how close he got; apparently *what has not happened* and *what could not
have happened* (or *what cannot happen*) are not the same.

So science fiction concerns itself with what has not happened; that is,
its subject matter does not exist. The subject matter of naturalistic fiction
is understood to be in some way characteristic or typical of what does
exist (*this could have happened*); fantasy is understood to bear a reverse
relation to what exists (*this could not have happened*). What is the relation
of science fiction to what exists? That is, how can one write seriously
about nonexistent subject matter? I pose this question not in practical

terms, for readers and writers of science fiction are familiar with practical solutions, but as a question of definition and description. Certainly, many literary critics do not seem able to conceive of fiction that neither contravenes reality nor represents it; they usually treat science fiction as if it were fantasy plain and simple. Their criticism suffers accordingly.

I I

What is science fiction?

Common answers are:

(1) Prophecy or Extrapolation;

(2) Allegory;

(3) Satire and Utopian Fiction.

Unfortunately, none of these labels will identify more than a small minority of the stories in the field. *Prophecy or Extrapolation* assumes that science fiction is trying for the subjunctivity of reportage (that is, a description of actual events), but that science-fiction writers work under the extraordinary handicap of reporting events that haven't yet happened—so that the story may prove to be good reportage (when the event happens) or bad reportage (when the event happens at another time than predicted or in another way or is proved impossible). Aside from the difficulty of understanding why such reportage should be presented in short stories and novels rather than in straightforward essay form, a good part of the field cannot possibly be covered by the predictive label: for example, the dystopia—which the author, by writing about it, hopes to prevent—or any parallel-universe or parallel-past-universe story.

And there is the problem of how to define science fiction that has in fact been proved incorrect (almost all the past work in the field)—does this fiction become fantasy? Does it become fantasy *only after* it is proved wrong? How many people must know of its failure before it can be considered fantasy? And so on. Few readers or writers of science fiction think consciously and explicitly that science fiction is in the prophecy business, but this rather simple-minded assumption does persist in back of a good deal of criticism of the field.

Nor does *allegory* cover the field. If all science fiction is allegory, some stories are clearly more allegorical than others. If R. A. Lafferty's *Fourth Mansions* is allegorical, what is Isaac Asimov's *I, Robot?* If *I, Robot* is considered allegory, the term must be extended to cover all fiction, and if all fiction (or all fiction with a clear moral tendency) is allegorical, then the term "allegory" becomes useless.

Many academic critics are comfortable with science fiction that is satiric or utopian and uncomfortable with any other kind. There remains the fact that a great deal of science fiction (e.g., Samuel Delany's *Babel-17*) has nothing to do with utopian fiction; nor does Alfred Bester's *The Stars My Destination;* nor Ursula Le Guin's *The Left Hand of Darkness*. These novels are neither satire, utopia, dystopia, nor allegory. Nor are they predictive.

Unfortunately most science fiction that becomes known outside the field *is* satiric and/or utopian—usually a parable of moral or political disaster. Dystopias, for whatever reason, are much more popular than utopias; we have *Brave New World, 1984, This Perfect Day,* and so on. Perhaps the popularity of SF satire is due to its simplicity: satire proposes or embodies a very simple relation between actuality and what has been called "the secondary universe"; that is, the fictional universe. Satire directly distorts and exaggerates what we all know to be true (straight-line extrapolation also tends toward simple exaggeration) for the purposes of explicit criticism. The subjunctivity of science fiction satire is that of science fiction in general—*this has not happened*—but the relation of the strange or bizarre or futuristic matter in the story to actuality is very plain. Satire in which this relation is *not* plain is satire without point.

The question remains: if science fiction can be either allegorical, predictive, satiric, utopian, or *something else*—what is the *something else?*

I I I

The willing suspension of disbelief of which Coleridge spoke can apply both to fantasy and to "naturalism" (as Delany uses the word). Sometimes it's assumed that a reader has a harder time suspending his disbelief when he reads fantasy than when he reads fiction about what *could have happened;* in fact, fantasy is probably easier not-to-disbelieve. It makes fewer claims to being plausible or faithful to actuality (since it *could not have happened*).

To return to satire, one does not suspend one's disbelief while reading satire—or, more accurately, any suspension of disbelief that occurs is a much more complex matter. The keenest pleasures of satire may be the moments at which one *dis*believes—keenly, explicitly, and acutely.

Certainly the effect of satire is not to convince a reader that the satirically exaggerated is plausible, accurate, actual, or like the real. To the contrary, one's reaction is more often: this is ridiculous, this is exaggerated, this is impossible. But the material that provokes such a reaction is in fact only an exaggeration (if the satire is a good one) of what the reader already believes in, for the very good reason that *it already exists in the actual world.* So we come up against a peculiar situation in which fictional material is disbelieved because it is real or, more accurately, disbelieved only to be believed; believed only to be disbelieved. One believes because the detail is in the book, disbelieves because it is satirically exaggerated and hence absurd, believes because it is "only" an exaggeration of what, after all, does exist. This is very close to Brecht's *verfremdungseffekt.* What is familiar is made strange—one disbelieves; however, it is rooted in the familiar—one believes (or rather stops disbelieving); yet it is absurd or comic—one begins to question the piece of actuality that has been used as a model for the satire.

This is not a mixed reaction but the perception of a kind of paradox: the comedy of the satirical exaggeration "spills over" onto its model in actuality and one feels about the model as one felt about its comic extension.

I would submit here that science fiction stands in some kind of paradoxical relation to both fantasy and naturalism in much the same way that satire stands in relation to both fantasy (the exaggeration) and actuality (the model). Certainly, most science fiction is naturalistic in style; yet there is the oddest kind of play between the sober literalness of tone of such fiction and its implicit ties to actuality. Critics outside the field, who assimilate science fiction to fantasy, tend to neglect both the straightforward realism of most science fiction (I'm talking about style, remember) and the oddities that such realistic matter-of-factness produces. It is the hardest thing in the world to get academic critics (especially New-Critical symbol hunters) to understand that *events in a science-fiction story are first and foremost What Happened,* that they are to be taken as literally true in the same sense that the events in any naturalistic novel are to be taken as literally true. Science fiction developed as popular literature in the tradition of realism and has only recently begun to play with the avant-garde toys of the 1920s, but most literary people (not only professors) insist on taking science fiction as symbol first, story second. Psychoanalytic critics, if they read science fiction at all, are horrified—such grotesquerie *must* be sick. That is, both camps insist that any literature that is not naturalism (in Delany's sense) *must be fantasy*. They entirely miss the difference in subjunctivity between science fiction and fantasy and hence treat as bizarre symbolism what often has a solid scientific base. There is, for example, scarcely a writer of classic science fiction who has not been attracted by the conditions prevailing on the surface of the different planets of the solar system; an academic critic who does not know anything about the chemistry or the temperature and pressure of Jupiter's surface may conclude that a story like Hal Clement's "Critical Point" intends to be nightmarish. It doesn't and it isn't.

I V

Fantasy usually carries a frame of some sort about it; science fiction usually does not.

Fantasy very often starts in what Alexei Panshin calls "The Village" (the "real" world) and moves slowly into the fantastic "World Beyond the Hill."[2] Science fiction does not.

That is, fantasy very often imitates the structure of the pastoral; one escapes from the familiar into the strange or fantastic only to return to the familiar at the end of the story. Or, as in most nineteenth-century horror stories, one gradually becomes aware that one's familiar world contains the fantastic or horrible. Fantasy is usually a loop with two ends; the two ends are either rooted in the familiar world, The Village, or one end is rooted in The Village and the other end has been cut, as in Sheridan LeFanu's "Green Tea." Very seldom is the protagonist left facing the horrible or fantastic; in some manner the story conducts us back to the familiar and safe—either the protagonist so returns, or he dies and *we* return.

Science fiction usually begins *in medias res;* we are plunged instantly into a strange world and we never return from it. A common pattern in science fiction is The Dislocated Protagonist—that is, the protagonist who finds himself in a strange place or a strange world *at the beginning of the story* with no knowledge of how he got there. He usually does find out how he got there, but he also stays there. An even commoner pattern is The Dislocated Reader—that is, the story begins *as if it were a naturalistic story,* and the reader must find his own way through the strange world: to the characters in the story, of course, it's not a strange world at all.

The frame of fantasy indicates the relation between fantasy and actuality: actuality is the frame, fantasy (*what could not have happened*) exists inside the frame. We begin in actuality and move into fantasy; the segment or segments of "realism" exist in the story as a standard by which to measure the fantasy (for example, the elaborate preface to J. R. R. Tolkien's *Lord of the Rings*).

In science fiction the frame is sometimes in evidence but more often not. A reader judges the science-fictional-ness of what happens by what he himself knows of the actual world; that is, *the reader carries his frame with him*. What, in naturalism, would be the frame—the most "real" part of the story (future histories, quotations from encyclopedias, newspaper reports, and so on)—becomes the most bizarre and the least believable. Such elements are pure Brechtian alienation: they are *not so* and they pretend extra-hard to be so. Furthermore, they are science-fictionally *not-so;* that is, they are not related to actuality by negative subjunctivity, but by some other kind of subjunctivity. Like satire, science fiction proposes a dialectical relation between the model and the fictional exaggeration/extrapolation/whatever. Consider, for example, the effect of referring to "the barbarism of the twentieth century"; or more drastically still, "the pastoral peacefulness of the twentieth century." Such phrases are not "framed" by naturalism; they are dropped into a totally strange context, a strange world; there is no represented real world in the science-fiction novel against which to measure "the pastoral peacefulness of the twentieth century." The little shock such a phrase gives a reader comes from the reader's own knowledge of the twentieth century and from nowhere else. Of course, the science-fiction writer assumes that his readers will have such knowledge.

In science fiction the relation between the "secondary universe" of fiction and the actual universe is both implicit and intermittently more or less perceivable. It consists not of what is on the page but in the relation between that and the reader's knowledge of actuality. It is always shifting.

One does not suspend one's disbelief in reading science fiction—the suspension of disbelief (complex to begin with, as it is with satire) fluctuates constantly. That is, the relation with actuality—what Delany would call the subjunctivity of the story—fluctuates constantly.

In this, science fiction resembles much contemporary fiction, what has been called post-realistic fiction. It makes sense to ask which part of a fantasy (*could not happen*) or a naturalistic tale (*could happen*) is real and which part isn't—that is, which part of the story is meant to be objectively true and which part is the subjective imagining of one of the characters. But one cannot ask this of *Pale Fire.* Writers like Genet and Nabokov thrive on paradox, e.g., fake narratives, framing devices that turn inside out as one watches—all sorts of trick effects that make the work deliberately slippery. This slipperiness is the varying tension between the work's existence as artifact and its existence as a coherent "secondary universe"—states that would be ideally constant in naturalistic fiction. One is momentarily pulled into a work like *Our Lady of the Flowers* (suspension of disbelief) only to be pushed out or pushed into what turns into a further suspension of disbelief and so on.

These vanishing perspectives and trick mirrors are the stock-in-trade of the post-realistic novelist. The story moves constantly along the line stretched taut between the work-as-artifact (an extreme form of the kind of alienation practiced by satire) and the-work-as-secondary-universe. By the time one reaches a writer like Barthelme, one cannot even be fooled any more—asking what really happened and what the characters or the narrator imagined would make absolutely no sense in his constructs. The point of the whole exercise lies in the paradox. One can neither suspend one's disbelief nor avoid suspending it. The relation of this kind of mimesis to actuality is very different from anything we are used to, possibly because the post-realistic novelists conceive of the relation between the subjective and the objective, the inside and the outside of the human mind, very differently from the authors we are used to.

Science fiction writers conceive of the relation between possibility and impossibility very differently than the writers we are used to. Their work has an analogous shifting, paradoxical quality. Science fiction, as I mentioned before, writes about what is neither impossible *nor possible;* the fact is that, when the question of possibility comes up in science fiction, the author can only reply that nobody knows. We haven't been there yet. We haven't discovered that yet. Science fiction *hasn't happened.* A novel like Ursula Le Guin's *The Left Hand of Darkness* is certainly a science-fiction novel. Yet one cannot say that the hermaphroditic humans it describes are either possible or impossible. We don't know. To write about what is already possible takes us out of the realm of science fiction altogether, something few people outside the field have realized.

As Samuel Delany has said, science fiction avoids offending against what is known to be known (ideally science fiction would avoid offending against what is known, but none of us is perfect). This limbo, this no-man's-land of not-possible, not-impossible inheres in the least sophisticated science fiction—a very different matter from fantasy, in which the impossibility is both clear and insisted upon (*what cannot happen*).

V

In any fiction a sequence of words may be simultaneously a real person, a character, a mood, a structural element, a figure (as in a painted landscape), and an allegorical or political or social idea (for example, part of an abstract didactic statement). Modern fiction is obviously so—and in modern fiction the structural element may contradict the figure, the figure may contradict the character, and so on.

The key is "simultaneously"—these are not levels of meaning with the literal level "first" and the others coming under it or after it. In fact, the symbolism can come "first" (that is, one reacts to it first) and can conceal the literal concreteness of the event or person. Nabokov often sets things up this way, as with Lolita herself. In Genet the daydreamlikeness of the events, the obviousness of the book-as-artifact, as a record of the psychological processes of its creator (though that, too, is fictional) obscure the particularity of events and situations. Both writers beguile the reader with overinterpretation and then, so to speak, hit him across the nose with facts. Much of *Lolita*, much of *Pale Fire*, all of Genet's novels, are actually *simpler* than they appear to be—although the impression of mysterious complexity is also part of the book, and one can't get rid of that, either.

I would contend that in science fiction the reader himself performs the paradoxical movement into and out of the work. Aesthetic distance fluctuates constantly, and so does the constantly varying factor of "science-fictionalness" (divergence from the representation of actuality). Science fiction practices the alienation effect: sometimes straightforwardly, sometimes inside out, as it were. For example, the effect of a reference to "Asimov, one of the great writers of the twentieth century" is a kind of triple alienation. First of all, the future in the story is not the real future (about which none of us can know anything) but a fictional future. Second, the reference looks back from the fictional future not to the real past but to a *fictional past*. Third, this fictional past is not our present but a kind of fictional present coexisting with our present.

As modern fiction often uses the devices of comedy (discontinuity, automatism, and so on) but not for comic effect, so science fiction often uses the devices of satire (mostly distancing devices) but not for satiric effect. What is at first bizarre turns out to have hidden in it the familiar, but this perception of the familiar causes the familiar to be seen from an odd perspective that makes it, in turn, bizarre.

A post-realistic tale that succeeds in being altogether incoherent is not comprehensible. A post-realistic tale that succeeds in being altogether comprehensible is not post-realistic. A science fiction story that succeeds in being altogether strange is not comprehensible. One that succeeds in being altogether familiar is not science fiction. That is, without any points of reference that connect straightforwardly with actuality, the work falls apart. But with every point of reference clearly and directly related to actuality, the work loses its science-fictionalness, the suspension of disbelief is complete, and one has "straight" fiction. To put it another way: science fiction must be neither impossible nor possible.

Science fiction occupies a paradoxical or dialectical position between fantasy and naturalism. The term "science fiction" belongs in the same class as "black comedy" and "post-realism."

To ask of fiction the questions one might ask of actuality makes sense to us only because we have two centuries or more of realistic writing behind us; we have begun to believe it's the only kind of writing there is. But science fiction—like post-realistic fiction—does not stand in any such simple relation to actuality. Fiction is a highly overdetermined verbal construct, "polyphonic" in Ehrenzweig's sense.[3] A story is closer to the interaction of magnetic fields than to what we think of as life. And perhaps life is, too.

NOTES

This paper was presented at the third annual meeting of the Popular Culture Association in Indianapolis, April 13, 1973. The essay first appeared in *Extrapolation: A Journal of Science Fiction and Fantasy*, Volume 15, No. 1, December 1973.

1. Samuel L. Delany, "About Five Thousand One Hundred and Seventy Five Words," in *Extrapolation* 10 (May 1970): 52–66; reprinted in Thomas D. Clareson, *SF: The Other Side of Realism* (Bowling Green, Ohio: Bowling Green University Popular Press, 1971), pp. 130–46.

   2. Alexei Panshin, "The Nature of Creative Fantasy," *Fantastic* 20 (February 1971), 100–106.

   3. Anton Ehrenzweig, *The Hidden Order of Art* (Berkeley: The University of California Press, 1967).

SF and Technology as Mystification

*T*he 1970s were also notable in academia for a prolif-
eration of conferences and books about "technology,"
if "notable" is the word. I prefer "disgusting" or
possibly "infamous." Like "excellence" (another
non-subject I remember with considerable pain), "technology" allowed a lot of folks to go through the motions of thought and
scholarship without ever touching such unpleasant and disturbing
subjects as what we all have to do to make a living. Academics are
still trying to be ladies and gentlemen, and while our salaries are still
inadequate, respect for our subjects ditto, and the destructiveness of
big business considerable, I don't think the way to fix this is to ignore
the whole subject of money and what we must do to get even a little
of it, let alone what a lot of other people have to go through to get any.
The subject has, I hope, faded away, although psychoanalysis may
have replaced it as the intellectually hot property of—well, English
departments at least. Everything I say here can, I think, apply as well
to Star Trek spin-offs as it did to the original TV show, except that
The Next Generation strikes me as even more conservative, given
its context, than the original Star Trek, given its. But then TV was in
a dreadful state in the 1960s when S.T. first appeared. (Those who
know the original essay may notice that the reference to "lunacy"
and "idiocy," attributed in first publication to Ellmann, was actually
to Rebecca West. A colleague persuaded me to suppress this fact on the
grounds that West was a fascist. Having read West's early feminist
writings in the last few years and thoroughly enjoyed them, I have
returned the reference to its original state, in honor of some of the
funniest, sharpest feminist humor ever written—West's in the early
twentieth century.)

Talk about technology, long familiar to science-fiction readers and writers, is getting popular in Academia too. Particularly interesting to humanists is the connection between technology and whatever their own particular subject happens to be; I've attended three such formal symposia in the last five years, six, including SF conventions, and including informal discussions among students, in writing classes, SF classes, and elsewhere, somewhere between fifty and sixty.

Technology is a *non-subject.*

That is, "technology," as it finds its way into almost all the discussions of it I have been unfortunate enough to participate in in the last five years, is the sexy rock star of the academic humanities and, like the rock star, is a consolation for and an obfuscation of something else.

Talk about technology is an *addiction.*

The model of addiction I wish to use in this connection is hyper-insulinism, better known as hypoglycemia. It's a clear model and without social stigma. Like all addictions, hypoglycemia is probably extremely rare without the presence of a specific supernormal stimulus, and these occur rarely in nature. The supernormal stimulus at fault in the case of hypoglycemia (according to the medical theory I'm following here) is refined white sugar, or sucrose, and even sugar cane itself was pretty rare, say, fifty thousand—or even fifty—years ago, while Twinkies and Mallomars abound not in nature, but in supermarkets, that is to say, in culture.

Refined sugar tastes sweet. Refined sugar and refined starch also have the virtue of lasting longer on supermarket shelves than the unrefined sugars and starches found in vegetables, fruit, and unrefined grain. People buy the stuff because it tastes good and manufacturers like it because it makes food last; put the two together and we seem to have found a chemical angel. But heroin was also thought to be a chemical angel, as its discoverer thought he had found a cure for morphine addiction; hence the name. Sucrose turns out to be another angel of the same sort.

People who eat large quantities of sucrose over long periods of time (and modern Americans consume phenomenal amounts of sugar) are eating a sugar whose chemical structure makes it very quickly digested. Only glucose, or blood sugar itself, goes from stomach to bloodstream quicker than sucrose. Moreover, it's possible to ingest enormous quantities of the stuff while having to deal with very little bulk (or protein); people who try to get an equal fix on apples or wheat sprouts will probably be stopped by indigestion before they reach anywhere near the amount of sugar used in glucose-tolerance tests—an "insult" dose equivalent to about two candy bars.

Thus the theory goes; caught in the toils of the supernormal stimulus, the victim eats too much of it, too often. The victim's blood sugar rises too fast, too often. Too often and too fast this poor soul's pancreas is called upon to send out large quantities of insulin to metabolize all this sugar. Eventually, the prodded pancreas goes into a sort of organic tizzy; even a moderate rise in blood sugar triggers off too much insulin, the person's blood sugar drops steeply, he or she feels ravenous, and disdaining unrefined sugar and starch (which by now no longer taste potent enough) she or he gobbles more strawberry shortcake or another Mr. Goodbar and the whole business starts all over again.

Presumably if the process continues and the person is susceptible enough, the highs become briefer, the lows worse; eventually you have someone exhibiting the effects of mild insulin shock: sweating, flushing, headache, irritability, exhaustion, and, by a more complicated organic process, terror, rage, adrenalin exhaustion, trembling, and, in extreme cases, greying-out.

What price yummies!

Notice: this model is a true physiological addiction. If the word addiction is to make sense at all, it cannot label simply the state of needing something intensely or needing it all the time. Such a definition could apply to the human need for oxygen. An addiction is a situation of constantly escalating need—in short, of insatiability. Not only that, but the cause of the escalation is the satisfier of the need. Addiction is what people call a vicious circle—really an increasing spiral. The more you need, the more you get; the more you get, the more you have; the more you have, the more you need, and so on.

This model of addiction may be over-simple or questionable when dealing with hyperinsulinism, but applied (by analogy) to certain economic and social phenomena, two things become strikingly apparent.

First, the addict is the ideal customer.

Second, addiction is a beautiful and effective method of social control. It is especially good at obfuscating and confusing—in political terms, *mystifying*—what it is that the addict really needs.

From the point of view of profits, the perfect stimulus is one which satisfies a human need only briefly or partially, and at the same time exacerbates the need. If the stimulus didn't satisfy the need at all, the customer would quit buying it out of frustration and disgust. If the stimulus fully satisfied the need, the customer would buy no more. (Certainly not beyond the recurrent biological demands of hunger, for example.)

That such stimuli abound in modern industrial society is an open secret. So is the fact that large numbers of people are paid large sums of money for inventing them and spreading them about. In the physiological realm we are presumably protected against this by the Food and Drug Administration (save for sugar, nicotine, alcohol, and caffeine, anyway) but in the cultural realm it's *sauve qui peut* and watch out for flying best-sellers.

Consider, for example, *Star Wars*. I was dragged to see this film past a bookstore displaying the sword-and-sorcery novel a friend of mine has rather unkindly nicknamed *The Sword of Sha Na Na*. What is important about coupling these two in one sentence (and one event) is not that the film is as bad as the book, but that both are bad in exactly the same way. This is not to say that either is without some interesting or seductive elements. For no addictive stimulus is simply bad or dull; if it were, nobody would want it at all. What such artifacts do is follow the formula for physiological addiction in the psychic, cultural realm: they satisfy a need partially, and at the same time they exacerbate it. Publishers' and movie-makers' formulas for a "real hit" are obviously those of an addiction: not just enjoyment or desire but *intense* craving (lines stretching around the block), not just intense craving but *sudden intense craving that must be satisfied at once (opening in sixteen million theatres tomorrow, at a theatre near you!)*, not just sudden intense craving but *insatiable* craving; thus people see the film many times and —this is a dead giveaway—*a minor industry grows up about the film:* Buttons, sweatshirts, TV programs about how the film was made, TV programs about how the first TV programs about the film were made, and so on. These are what the trade calls "spin-offs."

Please note that addictive culture is not identical with what we like to call "escapist culture." Perhaps there is no way of escaping in art from one's society, as any social product will of necessity embody the society's values and pressures, and the less these values or pressures are confronted and examined in the work, the more in force they will be. Thus *Star Wars*—which is being sold to the public as "fun"—is, in fact, racist, grossly sexist, not apolitical in the least but authoritarian and morally imbecile, all of this both denied and enforced by the opportunism of camp (which the youngsters in the audience cannot spot, by the way) and spiced up by technical wonders and marvels, some of which are interesting, many of which are old hat to those used to science fiction. Addictive culture, to succeed, can't be all bad. (Perhaps somebody, sometime, will cotton to the fact that the most interesting film form for SF is the travelogue—although even travelogues cannot be made without moral and political assumptions.)[1]

Let us for a moment compare *Star Wars* with *Star Trek*. The latter has certainly generated an immense paraphernalia around itself, but the minor industry around *Star Wars* is part of a commercial advertising campaign. That around *Star Trek* originated in the audience itself, and commercial exploitation of the paraphernalia came later, probably when the reruns (shown earlier and earlier in the day) attracted an audience much younger than the original one.[2]

Why the difference? I suspect that, although *Star Trek* is addictive (to judge from its audience and my own experience), it is also, relative to *Star Wars*, politically liberal, morally serious, and in its best episodes so much less addictive than most of the TV competition that the idea-men of the industry—the front office producers—almost instinctively distrusted it. Those hooked on the show not only wanted to watch it; they also wanted to talk about it and think about it. In "The Russian Point of View," Virginia Woolf writes of a passage in Tolstoy "which so conveys the feeling of intense happiness that we shut the book to feel it better."[3] At times even the most addicted Trekkies "shut the book to feel it better" (at least the grown-up ones). At times *Star Trek* generated not a desire to see more, but a desire to sit still and contemplate, to sit still and be moved—to my mind, sure signs of non-addictive culture.

What adult person, after seeing *Star Wars*, wants to sit still and be moved? *Star Wars* generates only one desire—the desire for a sequel—for which purpose large pieces of the plot were left hanging in mid-air at the end of the film. Indeed, even as this is being written, the current issue of *Locus* arrives with the following information:

> Leigh Brackett is writing the script for the sequel which will start pre-production this coming fall for a January 1980 release. . . . The question among SF fans is not "Have you seen *Star Wars?*" but, "How many times have you seen *Star Wars?*" . . . The novelization . . . sold 3-1/2 million copies. . . . The calendars, blueprints, portfolios, toys, etc. are still selling phenomenally well.[4]

One might draw from the contrast of *Star Wars* and *Star Trek* a definition of the stimulus and the cravings involved in cultural addiction: addictive culture deals with issues people feel to be crucial in their lives, but instead of confronting these issues, addictive art merely reconfirms the values and internalized pressures that produced the issues in the first place. Addictive art is briefly palliating; the relief lasts only as long as the art does and one is left more needy than before, i.e., the cravings that were promised relief are now worse.

Star Wars, I think, addresses itself to a dim but powerful desire for "fun," i.e., excitement and self-importance. These are human desires and not bad ones, but the film satisfies them by simplifying morality, politics, and human personality to the point where they can all safely be ignored in the interests of the "fun." However, morality, politics, and human personality are most of the world and the film cannot actually do without them without renouncing drama altogether. Thus we have a work in which the result of the simplification isn't to banish morality, politics, and human personality (which is impossible) but to present them in their most reactionary—and dullest—form. Thus monarchies are better than republics, slavery is noble (the machines are conscious personalities endowed with emotions and free will but it is still unquestionably right to own them), everyone human in the film is white (with the possible exception of one extra in one scene), and after the hero's mother (disguised as his aunt to avoid the real parenticidal wishes no doubt present in the teenagers in the audience) dies, there is only one woman left in the entire universe. This universe then goes into terrific plot convulsions to aid, nurture, and glorify one very ordinary white, heterosexual, male, bucktoothed virgin. To judge by the film's last scene, which is modeled on Leni Reifenstahl's *Triumph of the Will* (a Nazi propaganda film made of the Nazi Party Congress held in Nuremberg), the director intended *Star Wars* as a half-hearted comment on the whole genre. I believe that his recent allegation on television that the film is "wholesome" is simply dishonest. Of necessity addictive art must be bad art, or at least half-bad art; that is, in order to concentrate on the adventures and special effects, we simplify politics, economics, history, personality, morality, and human relations (which otherwise tend to get rather badly in the way, just as they do in life). But drama—and fiction—is what happens to people, i.e., fiction is politics, economics, history, personality, morality, and human relations.

Star Trek addresses itself to different desires, ones often explicitly stated in the series itself. They are: worthwhile goals, a clear conscience, peers whom one can respect, love, and be loyal to, a chance to exercise one's skills, self-respect, a code of conduct that can be followed without disaster—and excitement and self-importance. All these good things are to be gained by self-control and adherence to a morality that, although fairly simple, still transcends the official code handed down by Starship Command. I believe that the issue of ego control is central to the series; time and again the crew's fragile but valuable system of command and self-command is undermined by something coming from outside the ship, only to be reestablished by somebody's heroic personal efforts (often Captain Kirk's) just before the drama ends. It is noteworthy that the show's special effects were few and (in comparison with SF in feature films) often unconvincing (probably because of the economics of series television), the best of them being imaginative but physically simple like the "beam transporter" and the automatic sliding doors.[5] The moments fans cite with greatest pleasure are not special effects, but rather moments of character revelation, especially moments of deep emotion between the characters. The series was mildly liberal, mildly feminist (within narrower limits than producer Gene Roddenberry wished, if one can trust the pilot film, which was incorporated into the series as a two-part show set in the past), international, with at least some non-white characters (e.g., Uhura and Sulu), and it presented its characters as adults with explicitly limited powers, not fourteen-year-olds presented as rulers of the universe. Unsurprisingly, *Star Wars* began life as the subject of a large advertising campaign, and *Star Trek*—if gossip is to be trusted—was disliked by the front office, which changed its director/producer in its third (and final) year in order to get rid of the show.

Addictiveness is probably a matter of degree. It may be impossible to create a work of art that fully confronts the issues that make people miserable. On the other hand, there is a real difference between, say, the modern Gothic romance, which mystifies, reconfirms, and thereby exploits the situation of women in a sexist society, Charlotte Brontë's *Villette*, which confronts and analyzes it, and George Eliot's *Mill on the Floss*, which partly does so and partly shrinks from the pain and immorality of doing so. We feel the difference as a difference in complexity or dramatic value, or a difference in the riskiness of the work, or the difference in the amount of work demanded of us as readers, but the fundamental difference is the thoroughness with which the work deals with certain crucial issues.

What does all this have to do with talk about technology?

In the physiological model of addiction there is an increasing spiral of physical need; in the cultural model, an increasing spiral of what I shall call (for want of a better term) emotional need. In hypoglycemia the need is for an elevated blood sugar, but the means used to achieve it (refined sugar) only leads to a less elevated blood sugar. In *Star Wars* the need is for self-worth and pleasure (I believe this is what the "fun" represents). The means used to achieve these are, roughly, sexism, racism, heterosexism, competition, and macho privilege. But this kind of privilege is exactly what is producing a world in which most of the viewers of *Star Wars* do not have the self-worth and the access to excitement and pleasure that they need. In *Star Trek* the need is for community and morality; the means offered to achieve these ends are self-control and adherence to a fairly simple established morality. Anybody looking at the real world can tell that these means do not work (I have heard the show called "Civics 101"). Viewers know it; otherwise they would not have to keep watching the same (inadequate) solution played out again and again. *Star Trek* is a very muddled and partial utopia. Yet is is utopian and I believe that, if anything lifts the show out of the class of purely addictive culture, it is the series' utopian longing and the consequent sense of profound tragedy that hovers just under the surface of that longing. In this connection I would like to mention Alice Sheldon's story "Beam Us Home," a poignant short story about *Star Trek* and the only Trekkie spin-off I know of that achieves the status of non-addictive art. "Beam Us Home" may make you want to weep, but the last thing it will make you want is a sequel.[6]

Talk about technology is cognitive addiction. That is, such talk (like much in academia) purports to satisfy certain cognitive cravings that spring from issues central to all of us in our own lives, but it does not do so. Instead, it follows the pattern of brief palliation followed by increasing dissatisfaction and—usually—the academic equivalent of spin-offs: books proliferate, papers are given, journals are edited, other symposia are planned, but somehow nothing gets settled and eventually people drift on to other concerns—not because the subject has been exhausted, but because it has somehow disappeared.

Twenty years ago the "history of ideas" was the sexy subject in the humanities. It seems to have quietly faded away. Yet I remember the scholars who talked about that were intelligent people; and certainly, when I recall my three experiences with formal symposia on "Technology And" (usually the humanities or literature), nobody involved in those was stupid. Yet what is striking about the formal and informal occasions alike is the exclusion of both subject-matter and people: there was no economics, there was little sociology, there was little real history, there was no political analysis of any kind. There were almost no women and there were few references to works by women, literary or scientific, and no references at all to women's work. And, as in *Star Wars,* there were practically no non-white faces.

I believe these exclusions have a good deal to do with the choice of "technology" as a subject and the way in which non-discourse about this non-subject keeps occurring. That is, in all these discussions the conversation occurs as if we were in a heaven of abstract discourse in which ideas develop autonomously and influence other ideas without the slightest connection with the real conditions of the lives of the people who are having the ideas, in short without economic class or sex caste or racial caste. It is what I think Marx would call ahistorical talk. It is certainly talk that pretends to be apolitical. And, of course, the one thing left out of all these discussions is real technology. I remember one symposium that digressed into "standards of excellence" until the one Marxist present quietly vanished, another in which most of those present deviated into attempts to find a watertight definition of "technology," Talmudic bogglings that could have continued until the maximization of entropy. I should add quickly that at that occasion the organizer of the event did not do so, being a man notably free from nonsense, and that the only other two people present who fretted were myself and the only other woman in the group, a poet. I think it was no accident that two of the three of us were women. Lunacy, as Rebecca West speaks of it,[7] is masculine, and when you insist on talking about a non-subject, you're bound to end in academic lunacy.

By "lunacy" I mean the attitude of those who consider abstractions apart from the specific conditions of people's lives. Lunatics do this because they are insulated from the solid, practical details of their own lives by other people's labor; they therefore begin their thinking about life by either leaving such practical details out or assuming that they are trivial. West also labels a corresponding feminine defect as "idiocy." Idiocy is the refusal to go beyond the specific details to any larger pattern. Idiocy is what happens to those who have been told that it's their God-given mission to mend socks, clean toilets, or work in the fields, and nobody will ever let you make the real decisions, anyway. Idiocy debars people from entering academia. Lunacy is a qualification. To be blunt, lunatics do not have to clean up after themselves, either materially or in the realm of emotions and social relations, and their views of life are, therefore, bound to be a playing with false abstractions. In a sexist, racist society the people who clean up not only after themselves but after others are exactly those people remarkable by their absence from *Star Wars* and most of the discussions about technology it has ever been my misfortune to get trapped in. Middle-class white men are not the only people capable of producing political mystifications about the world, but they do seem to have something of a corner on the process.

What is technology?

My own definition is on the modest side. I mean by "technology" a rational, systematic, taught, learned, and replicable way of materially controlling the material world, or parts of it. This does not include animal technologies, except as metaphor; that's stretching the word (though a few species, like chimpanzees, may have a few kinds of simple behavior that might be looked at this way). This use of technology likewise excludes the control or organization of the non-material world; if language, for example, is talked about as "a technology," the word becomes meaningless and can be applied to anything.

In this modest definition, every known human society has a technology; there's the digging-stick technology, the animal-domestication technology, basket-weaving, pottery, and so on.

Most people who talk about technology don't talk this way.

First of all, they mean something *modern;* the Xerox copier or the railroad is technology; the hand loom or the potter's wheel is not. Modernity appears to be located during or after the Industrial Revolution.

Second, they mean something *ubiquitous.* Technology is all around us. One statement I can find about "technology" says "technology is in our time almost indistinguishable from the urban environment of Western countries."[8] In my definition of the word, such a statement would be absurd, since it would imply that the urban or village environment of non-Western countries is non-technological, i.e., something that arose spontaneously from nature. The use of "technology" here is clearly not mine.

Third, technology is not only everywhere; it's *autonomous. It* acts. *It* threatens our promises. *It* influences. *It* transforms.

Fourth, technology is often spoken of as *uncontrollable.* "Things are in the saddle and ride mankind." It controls us and is dangerous; it can threaten change or destruction.

What is this entity that began during the Industrial Revolution and continued thereafter, that is uncontrollable, autonomous, all around us, and both threatening and promising?

Hiding greyly behind that sexy rock star, technology, is a much more sinister and powerful figure. It is the entire social system that surrounds us; hence the sense of being at the mercy of an all-encompassing, autonomous process that we cannot control. If you add the monster's location in time (during and after the Industrial Revolution), I think you can see what is being discussed when most people say "technology." They are politically mystifying a much bigger monster: capitalism in its advanced, industrial phase. Such mystification is easy to spot when silly people do it; I recall a student of mine who said that technology was evil and then hastily excepted his stereo set. When intelligent people do it, the mystification is harder to see. Yet technology, so used, is a non-subject and talk about it is bound to be non-discourse. Either the talk becomes digressive and serves as a pretext for everyone displaying his or her academic specialty (the most harmless form non-discourse can take), or it is downright false. For example, one cannot make connections between technology and literature because neither exists as an autonomous force. Artists, like other people, respond to the day-to-day, moment-to-moment specificities of life that they, like everyone else, must live out. Nor can talk about such topics as "sensibility" (long a favorite in literature classes) be anything but trivial without reference to the social and economic system that surrounds us and is inside us, as the fish is in the sea and the sea is in the fish. Nobody responds to an abstract view of the universe, whether in physics or theology, unless that abstract view metaphorically embodies a social reality with which the responder is intimately familiar. But avoiding social and political realities by the appeal to false universals is an old habit of the humanities. One of my students recently expressed surpise when I mentioned that George Bernard Shaw was a socialist. He told me that he had studied *Major Barbara* in another literature class and never received that information. I asked the student, rather baffled, what the class had made of the discussions of poverty and class that abound in the play and was told, "Our professor said that didn't matter because the play was really about people." I also have a dim but horrible memory of hearing the same kind of thing from another student about, of all people, Bertolt Brecht.

It is because technology is a mystification for something else that it becomes a kind of autonomous deity, one that can promise both salvation and damnation and there are at least two reasons "technology" is substituted for political realities in academic discussion. One is common to both sexes. Money is such a frightening subject for most of us that we have to pretend it doesn't exist. In the nineteenth century not talking about money was supposed to be a sign of gentility; nowadays it's a sign of intellectual pretension and academic respectability. Academics become symposiaddicts and conventionmaniacs not only to get tenure; at conventions and symposia we can feel like the free intellectuals we want to be instead of the petty bureaucrats we unfortunately are so much of the time. The wealthy (I suppose) can afford to think clearly about money, at least can't afford to ignore it. Middle-class people, the people who largely populate academia, are both frightened enough to want to ignore the subject and relatively secure enough to be able to pretend to—at least once in a while.

The second reason is masculine. Both technophilia and technophobia are owner's attitudes. In the first case you think that you have either power or the ear of the powerful, and in the second case, although you may feel you have lost power, you at least feel entitled to it. Hence the scapegoating of modern industrial society, which ought to be controllable (by you) and knowable (ditto) and is neither. Those who believe themselves powerless (and are so)—women, non-whites, the poor—do not become technophiles. But they do not become technophobes, either. I think it no accident that our great modern literary technophobes—Norman Mailer, D. H. Lawrence, Ken Kesey—go beyond institutionalized sexism into the personal bigotry of gynophobia (and in Mailer's case, attempted gynocide). Men like Gandhi and Tolstoy also combine disapproval of the industrial world, an advocacy of a return to pre-industrial virtues, and the hatred and fear of women, whom Tolstoy saw as embodying sexuality, i.e., *his own* sexuality. Technophiles, on the other hand, according to French critic Gérard Klein, tend to be upwardly mobile members of the lower middle class who believe that their knowledge of "science" and technology will give them the ear of those in power.[9] Klein's classic example is H. G. Wells, but his thesis fits too many of our famous American SF writers to be a comfortable one. Klein argues that the earlier technophiles (before the 1960s) and the pessimists of the post-1960s—in short, the entire science-fiction community—is a subgroup of the middle class, excluding "the ruling classes (middle and high bourgeoisie) and the working classes (industrial, farm, office workers, and similar)," which is distinguished by its "scientific and technical culture." Klein mentions one "Black writer" (though not by name) as evidence of the limits of this class subgroup.[10] He mentions only one woman, Ursula Le Guin, and although she is mentioned as an exception to specific tendencies, Klein's excellent article never states explicitly that the group of which he speaks enjoys not only relative social privilege as middle-class people, but relative social privilege as men. Interestingly, the descent of SF into pessimism, as Klein calls it, is not shared by a recent group of works (beginning in 1971): classless feminist utopias, all written by women.[11] As Klein argues, the expression of anxiety is a result of "the absence of any utopia, any social project."[12] Both technophobes and technophiles demonstrate, to my mind, a kind of megalomania: the imperial nature of capitalism, the desire to own and control everything, whether in its ascendant or disappointed phase. The technophiles certainly embody the fallacy that more is better and the thingification of people and social relations.

Talking about technology is asking the wrong questions. An example comes to mind for which I cannot find the reference, but no doubt readers can recall examples of their own. Some years ago I read a technophilic book in which the author speculated delightedly about how many sex organs human beings might acquire via surgery. The writer was, of course (and I mean that "of course"), male. He was even "daring" enough (his own word) to propose that men be given female organs and women male organs. The male friend of mine who had recommended the book (another technophile) thought this an excellent idea; in this way men and women would understand one another better, he said. Now to believe that the misunderstandings that occur between men and women occur because men's penises and women's clitorises are shaped differently or because fucking feels different for each sex is the grossest kind of mystification. It is certainly clear to me (and any other feminist) that men's and women's misunderstandings of one another, far from being due to the differences in their sexual organs or their experiences in sexual intercourse *per se,* are carefully cultivated in the service of sex-caste positions in a very nasty hierarchy, and that one cannot dissolve the hierarchy by giving people double and triple sexual equipment, even if we could get over the anatomical problem of where to place the extra goodies. Tinkering with the genitalia when the social structure is the problem is like the common science-fictional device of "solving" the quality of life by giving people immortality (e.g., Heinlein's *Time Enough for Love* and *I Will Fear No Evil*, Blish's *Cities in Flight* series, Anderson's *Tau Zero*, or Niven's *Ringworld*). Another one is the New World of I-mucked-this-one-up-so-give-me-another approach (e.g., Bradbury's *The Martian Chronicles* or Heinlein's *Tunnel in the Sky*).

If talk about technology is an addiction, how do we cure it? I would go back to the physiological analogy. What the hypoglycemic craves is refined sugar; what the hypoglycemic must avoid at all costs is refined sugar.

The technology-obsessed must give up talking about technology when it is economics and politics that are at issue. But the addict cannot simply be left bereft; a sugar addict so treated would starve in short order. Instead, just as the offending addictive is taken out of the victim's diet, something else is put in—in this case protein, which is digested slowly and therefore slowly metabolized. In the case of technology, I suggest that politics and economics take the place of the kicked technology-habit until the victims' intellectual taste buds recover and they find themselves capable of thinking in more practical terms, especially about money and power. When they do this, they will find interesting historical evidence pointing to the non-autonomy of technology and its subordination to economic and political uses. For example, in Japan the ruling classes banned and then for several centuries successfully ignored that extremely seductive machine, the gun, because they realized that the maintenance of their class position depended on its non-use. This is a lovely example of how particular people, with particular interests of their own at stake, can pick up and drop technology as they please. There is also the illuminating fact (if it is a fact) that "the atom bomb was in manufacture before the first automatic washing machine."[13]

Just as the hypoglycemic, under stress, may find the fascinations of the chocolate bar returning, so the technology-obsessed, under conditions of cognitive confusion, may find that they begin again to yearn for the evasive gyrations of that sexy intellectual rock star, technology. The cure is similar. The hypoglycemic listens to the little voice that says, "Eat a little protein. You'll feel better." The technology-obsessed—including those who read, write, and study SF—must cultivate a similar little voice: "Eat a little economics. Eat a little political analysis. You'll think better."

NOTES

This essay first appeared in *Science-Fiction Studies*, Volume 5 (1978).

1. In "The Lost Continent," a piece on documentary films in Roland Barthes's *Mythologies* (U.S., 1975), pp. 94ff, Barthes deals with just such questions.

2. To give one example, the "tribbles," little furry creatures sold in various SF bookstores, were made by the writer of the "tribble" episode, a popular one in the *Star Trek* series. The amateur status of many of the creators of blueprints, etc. is one of the most endearing things about the whole Trekkie craze.

3. Virginia Woolf, *The Common Reader* (1923–48; here New York: 1953), p. 186.

4. *Locus* 10, x (Dec. 1977), 1.

5. They are explained in *The Making of Star Trek*, by Stephen E. Whitfield and Gene Roddenberry (New York: Ballantine, 1968), the "beam" (matte shot), p. 372; the doors, pp. 199–200. The sliding doors, which produced a letter of admiring inquiry from an apartment-complex builder, were simply worked by off-camera stage-hands.

6. James Tiptree, Jr. (pseud. for Alice Sheldon), *Ten Thousand Light-years from Home* (New York: Ace, 1973).

7. Rebecca West, cited in *Thinking About Women* (U.S., 1968), p. 108.

8. Prospectus for the MLA forum on "Technology and the Literary Mind," April 25, 1977. The forum was held in December 1977. This paper, in altered form, was presented there.

9. Gérard Klein, "Discontent in American Science Fiction," *SFS* 4 (1977):3–13.

10. Ibid., pp. 5–6.

11. The earliest of the group in Monique Wittig's *Les Guérillères*, translated into English in 1971; the most recent, as of this writing, is Suzy McKee Charnas's *Motherlines*, to be published by Putnam's in 1978.

12. Klein (see note 11), p. 12.

13. Tillie Olsen, "Women Who Are Writers in Our Century: One out of Twelve," *College English* 34 (1972):13.

4

Amor Vincit Foeminam: The Battle of the Sexes in Science Fiction

A *s the following attests, the same post* did *bring Bamberger's and Cooper's work simultaneously in the late 1970s. (The following saw publication in 1980.) I saw red. Green, blue, whatever. So I went looking for others, in order to stamp out the whole tribe. Samuel Delany told me the stories were too idiotic to bother with, but they would not leave me alone until I gave them their place in the sun. Their crudity and silliness were worse than my representation of them, honestly; they were terrible. But it was fun. As a critic, a reviewer, and a teacher, I have spent my life reading a huge amount of extraordinarily bad fiction; sometimes the only way to discharge the emotion aroused by the incessant production of gurry is to beat the gurry to death, especially when it's as marvelously foolish as this was. I should add that when I first noticed James Tiptree, Jr.'s difference from the other authors treated herein, I did not know who (or what) "Tiptree" was. That came later. "Mama Come Home" was Alice Sheldon's first written story, or close to it and, in the whole canon of her work, quite crude and thin. Still it was fundamentally rational in its assumptions, unlike the other imaginings treated below. Those interested in the feminist utopias mentioned here can read the essay after this one ("Recent Feminist Utopias") to find more interesting and better-written fiction. Many of these novels and stories are still in print.*

That the same post should bring Parley J. Cooper's SF novel *The Feminists* and Joan Bamberger's "The Myth of Matriarchy" is not surprising[1]: modern feminist or anti-feminist concerns both turn predictably to role reversals in the group relations between the sexes; and literal sex war, from civil war to secret cabal to street riots, does indeed appear in modern SF. What is surprising is that the myth of the matriarchy Bamberger describes as current among aboriginal South American tribal societies is the same myth given flesh by Pinnacle Books in 1971. Since it is highly unlikely that Cooper has been reading Bamberger (or vice versa), one must conclude that similarly sexist societies produce similar fantasies. As Bamberger puts it:

> . . . the secret object belonging to men (masks, trumpet, ritual lodge songs, and the like) . . . are badges of authority, permitting one sex to dominate the other. However begun, the myths invariably end with the men in power. Either the men have taken from the women the symbols of authority or have installed themselves as the rightful owners of the ceremony. . . . In no versions do women win. (p. 274)

Surprisingly, however, "concerns with female reproduction distinctions are nowhere in evidence. . . . The mythical message . . . stresses moral laxity and an abuse of power rather than any physical weakness or disability" (p. 279). According to Bamberger, the "ideological thrust" of the South American myths is "the justification . . . for male dominance through the evocation of a vision of a catastrophic alternative" (p. 279).

To summarize: the men's Sacred Objects—the badge of authority and means of domination over others—are stolen or contaminated by women, who then become dominant over men. (Or the story begins with the women dominant.) Women lose because they abuse this power or are immoral (in various ways, e.g., incest), whereupon the men seize or reclaim the Sacred Objects, sometimes with supernatural aid. The purpose of the story is to show that women cannot handle power, ought not to have it, and cannot keep it. This is the natural order of things. It is also extremely precarious. According to Bamberger, throughout the Amazon area women are punished by gang rape and sometimes by death for such misdemeanors as viewing the sacred male paraphernalia (p. 275).

In my subsequent remarks, I will be discussing the following ten tales from 1926 to 1973, all by male writers, as well as one tale by "Tiptree":

Thomas Berger, *Regiment of Women*. New York: Simon & Schuster, 1973.
Nelson S. Bond, "The Priestess Who Rebelled," in *When Women Rule*, ed. Sam Moskowitz. New York: Walker, 1972. (Originally in *Amazing Stories*, October 1939.)

Edmund Cooper, *Gender Genocide*. New York: Ace Books, 1972.
(Originally published in the U.K. as *Who Needs Men?*, Hodder &
Stoughton, 1972.)

Parley J. Cooper, *The Feminists*. New York: Pinnacle, 1971.

Thomas S. Gardner, "The Last Woman," in *When Women Rule*.
(Originally in *Wonder Stories*, April 1932.)

David H. Keller, M.D., "The Feminine Metamorphosis," in *When
Women Rule*. (Originally in *Science Wonder Stories*, August 1929.)

Keith Laumer, "War against the Yukks," *Galaxy*, April 1965.

Bruce McAllister, "Ecce Femina!" *Fantasy and Science Fiction*, February 1972.

Booth Tarkington, "The Veiled Feminists of Atlantis," in *When
Women Rule*. (Originally in *The Forum*, March 1926.)

James Tiptree, Jr., "Mama Come Home," in *Ten Thousand Light-
years from Home*. New York: Ace, 1973. (Originally in *If* in 1968,
under the title "The Mother Ship.")

Wallace G. West, "The Last Man," in *When Women Rule*. (Originally
in *Amazing Stories*, February 1929.)

The modern SF writers, disregarding their South American brothers' indifference to biological distinctions, make biology itself the
guardian of the Sacred Object: they install the Sacred Object on their
own persons. All the stories to be discussed (with the possible exception of James Tiptree's "Mama Come Home") use as their Sacred
Objects the male genitalia; possession thereof guarantees victory in
the battle of the sexes. This victory is therefore a victory of nature, and
so the battle may be won without intelligence, character, humanity,
humility, foresight, courage, planning, sense, technology, or even
responsibility. So "natural" is male victory that most of the stories
cannot offer a plausible explanation of how the women could have
rebelled in the first place. In three of the ten stories, women are not
actively engaged in fighting men; they have merely withdrawn from
men's company—but the challenge to male domination is seen as
identical. The conflict is resolved—either for all women or for an
exemplary woman—by some form of phallic display, and the men's
victory (which is identical with the women's defeat) is not a military or
political event but a quasi-religious conversion of the women. Although women in these stories constantly plan to do away with men,
men (it seems) are not willing to do away with women—that is, do

without women. But they certainly do not want angry, defeated
women who might secretly plan how to start the conflict all over
again. Unfortunately the illogicality of the solution requires reliance
on mystified biology, which makes hay of real biology. Every human
motive becomes a sexual motive, and the authors are forced to falsify
their characters, especially the men. Since a likable man might be liked
(by a woman) for his likableness and not for his Sacred Object, the
men in these stories (with perhaps one exception) are either sadistic
supermen, who incarnate the power of the penis, or lackwits who
have nothing but their penises to offer. A human reacting to a human
would ruin the whole business; the only pure test case is a vagina
acknowledging a godlike phallus, which is attached to nobody. In the
overdetermined world of the Sex War, economics do not exist, everything everybody does is sexually motivated, promiscuity is frigidity
and vice versa, and the cure for rape is rape. As we move from the
1920s and '30s to the modern versions (*The Feminists, Gender Genocide,*
and "Ecce Femina!"), overt violence increases and coherence de-
creases, the men are more and more on the defensive, and in two
("Ecce Femina!" and *Gender Genocide*) the men win individual victories
but are doomed as a group. But the story remains the same story.

The first question one might ask about The Rule of Women, as
Bamberger puts it, is how it began. The stories' answers are uniformly
meager. For example, the only explanation offered by *The Feminists* (it is
the longest of any) is:

> It was a quirk of fate. . . . Women did not intend to take total control.
> Their takeover is the fault of the passive male. He allowed himself to be
> controlled for the price of sex and then emasculated. . . . Women . . .
> originally wanted only equality, but when they realized the ease with
> which they achieved it, they broadened their goals. (pp. 20–21)

The Feminists is a very badly written book, and for that reason the baldest
example of the myth in the whole collection. In the world of 1992,
which has no futuristic details whatever, "the poison of the atmosphere
had completely destroyed the vegetation" (p. 8), the subways have
collapsed in New York City, the buses run infrequently, there is no
snow-clearing equipment, and the United States has become a police
state with military rule and curfews. All women (including army
soldiers) wear skirts; sex without permission of "The Committee" is
punishable by death; and the gynocracy is pure high-society matriarchy. The hero, a member of the masculinist underground, is

wounded in the *thigh* and feels great pain "shoot up . . . *into his groin*" (p. 118; italics added). He is captured by a tall soldier with "a masculine swagger to her walk" and "bushy eyebrows" (p. 129) who is witness to the first explicitly phallic display in the novel:

> Instinctively he had covered his naked loins with his hands but now, realizing that she was laughing at his modesty, he removed his hands and boldly thrust his loins forward.
> She continued to smile, but he knew the gesture annoyed her. (p. 129)

Bushy-browed Captain Luttrell ("I want to see if you disprove my theory of the male's inferiority. . . . The foundation [of it] may already have begun to crack" [p. 154]) sends him back to New York City, where the mayor wants to use him as a scapegoat. So threatening (but fascinating) is his mere photograph that she has dreamed up a special execution for him; he finds himself facing "the gigantic blade of a guillotine" (p. 179). This symbolic castration is averted by the mayor's discovery that he is in reality her long-lost son. She faces the mob herself. The mayor's loyal aide explains: "The mayor discovered that she possessed *the major feminine weakness* she despised in others. *Before she was a Feminist, she was a Mother!*" (p. 187). Italics spent, the book goes on to tell us that the regime is crumbling and that the men will win.

The incoherence of *The Feminists* is right on the surface. Yet the Sex War myth produces some degree of nonsense in all the stories: centrally, the collapse of a gynocracy that is both impressively powerful and totally incompetent, before what might most politely be called the Sacred Object. (*The Feminists* is the only story in which the hero converts to normality not a potential sweetheart but his own mother.)

Keith Laumer's picture of the Rule of Women, "War against the Yukks," is intentional comedy. The two heroes are a scatterbrained professor called Elton and a British game warden called Boyd. The two stumble upon, and are kidnapped by, an 8,000-year-old space module directed by a Lunar Battle Computer buried under the moon's Mount Tycho, which adapts itself to their language within seconds and takes them to an automatically run dome on Callisto populated solely by women. Those are the remnants of an ancient sex war, started (as Elton says) by "some idiotic feminist movement somewhere" (p. 185), presumably the same idiots who built the Lunar Battle Computer. However, memory of the ancient war has degenerated into religion, as one Girl explains:

> The terrible power they [the men, i.e., the Yukks] had was that they
> made perfectly nice Girls want them to do . . . Strange Things. Even now,
> there's always the danger that a Girl will fall into Strange Ways—like
> dreaming about a Yukk chasing her, with all six hands reaching for her. . . .
> That's what makes the Yukks so terrible. (p. 183)

As in *The Feminists*, there is no masturbation or lesbianism among the
Girls; instead there is perpetual blushing at the idea of Strange Thoughts
and comic, innocent suggestions to sleep, bathe, or wrestle with the new
"girls." But despite the Girls' naiveté, nature wins again; the two Girls'
Strange Thoughts become uncontrollable, and all four try unsuccess-
fully to escape in a spaceship. Just as Mother is about to despatch them,
we learn that the installation's frozen sperm providentially ran out
twenty years before, and our heroes subside into a harem fantasy. "It
should take us a year or so to work our way through, and then start
over" (p. 194).

The oddest thing about "Yukks" is that atmosphere of super-heated
sexuality among the Girls, with (simultaneous) total passivity. Whatever Strange Thoughts women may have, they can only wait (blushing
and taking cold baths for 8,200 years) for the bearers of the Sacred
Object to come along and start something.

Nelson Bond's "The Priestess Who Rebelled" is tragic in tone, and the
heroine lives in a primitive matriarchy (in the year 3482 A.D., after WW
III). The biology is badly mystified—e.g., in this society modeled on bees
and termites (a common pattern for matriarchies in SF) not only have
the Men gone hairless, high-voiced, and soft (moulting, perhaps) but
the Warrior-class women have "tiny thwarted breasts, flat and hard"
and the Mother-women are "full-lipped," with soft, white skins and
humid eyes "washed barren of all expression by desires too oft aroused,
too often sated" (pp. 108–109). Since all women choose which caste to
enter after puberty, it is hard to understand why the warriors' breasts
have become thwarted—or why often-pregnant women develop full
lips, or why they spend a lot of time in sexual intercourse, or why a lot
of sexual intercourse makes your eyes blank.

The story begins when Meg, who has become a priestess and is
therefore vowed to virginity, undertakes a pilgrimage to what the reader
soon recognizes as Mount Rushmore (the tribes' gods are Jarg, Ibrim,
Taamuz, and Tedhi). Matriarchal woman meets patriarchal man when
Meg is rescued from a "Wild One" (a homeless male) by Daiv. "'You,'
said the man-thing . . . 'talk too much.'" His next words: "'You women!'

he spat. 'Bah! You do not know how to train a horse. . . .'" And his next:
"'You talk too much!' repeated the man-thing wearily" (pp. 208–209).

He propositions her casually; she refuses but is forced to his campfire
to get food. "Priestess" has the most coherent (and morally respectable)
account of the rise of the matriarchy of any of these tales; it was, we are
told, a women's revolt against men's endless war-making. Finally the
women become settled city-dwellers and the men homeless Wild Ones.
How the Wild Ones generate more Wild Ones all by themselves is never
explained. There is considerable quarreling over whether the "Gods"
are male or female, which ends in "a mating custom which you do not
know" (says Daiv) and the obligatory phallic display, here a kiss:

> She struggled and tried to cry out, but his mouth bruised hers. . . .
> Suddenly her veins were running with liquid fire. Her heart beat upon
> rising, panting breasts like something captive that would be free. . . . A
> vast and terrible weakness trembled through Meg. She knew, fearfully,
> that if Daiv sought to mate with her, not all the priestessdom of the Gods
> could save her. There was a body-hunger throbbing within her that hated
> his Manness . . . but cried for it! (p. 216)

Meg proceeds to Mt. Rushmore and receives the final blow:

> The Gods—were men!
> . . . Even the curls could not conceal the inherent masculinity of Jarg
> and Taamuz. And Tedhi's lip was covered with Man-hair. . . . (p. 219)

Against the psychedelic kiss, the discovery that God is male, and the
attraction of a life that consists mainly of being told she talks too much,
Meg's friends, family, her lifelong loyalties, her own traditions and her
religion, count as nothing. The Sacred Object triumphs again—with a
little help from the gods.

The defeat of the rebellious women in "The Feminine Metamorphosis" is due entirely to God, who invents for the purpose a special strain
of syphilis that afflicts only Chinese, does not show up on Wassermann
tests, and ends up driving into terminal paresis 5,000 American businesswomen who have masculinized themselves with Chinese andro-
gens in an attempt to take over the world. At first the women's
complaints look sensible:

> "I cannot understand why I was not promoted!. . . I am more
> competent than the man you appointed to that position, and . . . I have
> been in full charge of the department during the illness of the late
> occupant."
> "You were not promoted because you were a woman. . . ." (p. 149).

This explanation of female rebellion quickly segues into the plot described above, with the Sacred Object taking on an erratic, wandering life of its own, and smiting down the female thieves who have attempted to appropriate it. With fewer and fewer boy babies born (due to the machinations of the women) and parthenogenesis in the offing ("in Government laboratories and nurseries" [p. 187]), it is time to bring out the heavy artillery. As the detective hero says: ". . . you forgot God. He had certain plans for the human race. . . . You took five thousand of our best women, girls who would have made loving wives and wonderful mothers . . . and . . . you have changed them into five thousand insane women" (pp. 195–96).

Although the five thousand were dedicated businesswomen when the story began (many with "bachelor apartments," p. 152), the moral is clear: women not subjugated *in vivo* ("loving wives and wonderful mothers") will be raped *in vitro* and will die of venereal disease. And nobody human is responsible.

Bruce McAllister's "Ecce Femina!" is a story of women in motorcycle gangs; they shoot up "Vitamin E9—the 'ultravitamin that isn't really a vitamin'" (p. 119), thus endowing themselves with superhuman strength and sadism. Their favorite pastime is castrating and killing men, episodes commemorated by jacket patches of the female symbol with a skull placed inside the circle (p. 121). There are "hundreds of chapters" of "The Women's League" in California (p. 119); and, although Vitamin E9 may explain how the Rule of Women began (is the echo of "estrogen" intentional?), why it persists is a mystery:

> Soon I had him telling me about his wife, about how he had gotten sick and tired of supporting her—her bike, her E9, her arrogance, her appetite, her perversions [unnamed]. . . . He, like thousands of husbands each day, had found himself a weapon and gone nomad, traveling solo from tract to tract. . . . *The police never did anything. The courts never did anything. No one ever foreclosed* (p. 133; italics added).

The biggest, toughest woman of all, known as "Ripper Jack" [*sic*] because she has killed 200 men (p. 142), nurses a wounded man back to health, defends him against the gang, and finally flees with him. Here is Jack before her conversion, as the narrator, who has been *wounded in the leg* in Cambodia, sees her:

> She was a tower of strength. . . . Her boots were like hooves. Her levis . . . were like the tough, weathered hide. Her legs were like those of a buffalo. Her chest bulged like a truck's cab. Her arms were like swollen

pistons and her long-sleeve Pendleton was like steel wool. . . . She was a
god. From the waist down she was a bull; from the waist up, a man. (p. 132)

After the flight with the man she has come to love (because he is the
only man she tries to fight who will not fight back—love is more
effective in taking the zing out of these Amazons than any number of
battles) the narrator receives a snapshot of Jack with her man and her
baby. Jack now looks like this:

> . . . a heavyset woman, her muscle gone to fat, her breasts flabby under
> her flowerprint blouse. In her lap her big hands are cradling a baby, which
> is so young it's still pink.
> . . . And you can't tell whether she's smiling or not.
> But then you never could. (p. 144)

In short, a Hell's Angel turns into Mona Lisa in only one year, and the
reason is biology; not only is Jack a mother, but, of all the women, only
she never shot up Big E. Again we have the degradation of men, the lack
of an explanation for the women's dominance (the explanation given is
magic, considering the absolute lack of resistance to what are, after all,
only motorcycle gangs), the view of the narrator as "emasculated"
because he is terrified by a group of superhumanly strong, sadistic
persons who are determined to torment him, the insistence that women's domination of men is unnatural (though presumably the pre–Big
E situation was not), and the final redemption by heterosexual love.
There is also, as in all these stories, the lack of any other kind of love or sex.

If the author of "Ecce Femina!" merely stumbled on the myth,
Edmund Cooper, in *Gender Genocide,* is doggedly insistent about it. In this
world set 250 years in the future, an all-female, technologically advanced society occupies southern England and periodically sends exter-
minators north to kill the primitive survivals of patriarchy in northern
Scotland. Cooper knows what started the Rule of Women: present-day
feminists, who are trying to build a world in which women kill men to
enter adulthood and, if they are especially brave, are awarded the Silver
Nipple. (Cooper's London contains a monument called "Germaine's
Needle.") Cooper allows female homosexuality into his future world
only to spend 195 pages denying that it's any fun; the story suffers even
more than most from the usual contradiction: if love conquers women
so automatically and dependably, how did the Amazon state ever come
into existence? Indeed, Rura (the heroine) is a traitor to her nation, her
upbringing, and her comrades by page 20; on her first expedition to kill
"pigs" (and their "sows" and "piglets") she finds she cannot do it, and

even bandages the wounds of the man whose wife and child were killed by her now-dead comrades.

> Why was she doing this for a pig whose sow had just killed Moryn? She did not know. Perhaps it was because sunlight and death were incongruous. . . . She did not know.
> "You were trained to kill, yet you do not. Why is this?"
> "I don't know." (p. 21)

The man (not some knock-kneed little crofter, mind you, but Mac-Diarmid, the leader of the entire rebellion) then knocks her down, spares her life, and, announcing his determination to make a traitor of her, kisses her: "It was like no other kiss she had ever known. It was humiliating, it was degrading, it was disturbing. It drained strength from her limbs, filled her head with nightmares" (p. 25).

The kiss is followed by a meeting back in the south with an old woman whose story unsettles Rura completely. As usual, the reliance on mystical biology includes the most extraordinary nonsense: that rape is impossible, that first intercourse in the missionary position (after having been bruised and beaten) invariably produces ecstasy, that a woman can feel a man's semen enter her, that a vagina is a womb, and that clitorises are inferior in sensitivity to cervixes:

> No woman—particularly an exterminator—who is conscious and uninjured can be raped. . . . The revulsion and feeling of sickness just sort of died. And the weight on top of me seemed to be—well, interesting. And when he pinioned my arms and bit my throat and dug his fingers into my breast, it all hurt like hell but it aroused me. . . . So I let him enter. . . . I tell you, I never knew what a climax was until that red-haired animal squirted his semen into my womb. (p. 49)

A long period of inner conflict follows. Even the rewriting of history does not avail against nature, and when Rura goes out on another mission, and again can't fire her gun, she is gang-raped, called "hell-bitch" and "screwmeat" (p. 77), taken to MacDiarmid, claimed by him to replace his dead wife, ordered to be quiet (some authors seem to think this is standard wooing procedure), slapped, and told: "You have entered a man's world. You have much to learn" (p. 84).

After a feeble attempt to kill him, she collapses into his arms with the words: "I love you" (p. 92). The next day, with his original wound still unhealed, suffering from stab wounds he got in a fight with a follower the day before, and with Rura only twenty-four hours away from having been gang-banged into insensibility, he teaches her "what it is like to be a woman" (p. 91).

> It was not like the rape of the previous day. It was not like lying with
> women. It was not like anything she had ever known.
> It was warm, it was disturbing, it was exciting, it was humiliating, it
> was proud. . . . A man—this man by her side—had washed away twenty
> years of conditioning. He had loved her; and . . . semen had pulsed
> excruciatingly, wonderfully, through her vagina. (pp. 114–16)

Rura's conversion occupies the first half of the book; the second half
is an idyllic honeymoon, threatened constantly by "hellbitches." One of
the most instructive omissions in the novel is the absence of social
relations between the primitive Highlanders; men are rivals or subordi-
nates in the feudal hierarchy (the way in which the men vie for power
by dueling to the death with one another is hardly efficient for a
community threatened by extinction), and social relations between
women don't exist. In fact, there are no women except Rura.

What remains is to confirm Rura's conversion before the lovers die in
a final *liebestod,* thus avoiding the question of what will happen to their
idyll after Rura has had her baby and must, perforce, pay less attention
to the Laird than to his son (both characters discuss the coming baby on
the absolute presumption that it will be a boy)—or, God forbid, when
she meets other Highlanders and finds out that heterosexuality does not
necessarily mean monogamy. Cooper's novel is one long proof that, for
women, heterosexuality is so much physically pleasanter than lesbianism that it binds a woman not only to sexual pleasure but to one man in
particular and to a whole ideology of male dominance. Other possible
alternatives—promiscuity, for one—are simply unthinkable.

I think it is clear by now that these stories are not only not written for
women; they are not written about women. To quote Michael Korda, in
Male Chauvinism: "[Men] don't as a rule hate [women]. . . . They just
don't want to know anything about them."[2]

Elsewhere Korda says that men make women play roles "in a
psychodrama that isn't even theirs" (p. 225). Perhaps the psychodrama
of the Sacred Object is intended less to keep women down than to keep
men up. (Sorry!) Penis worship *solus* is a lonely business and unconvincing. In this secular religion one cannot find another man to worship
one's penis—he, after all, has got one of his own and is looking for a
worshipper himself. (About the relation of homosexual men to the
myth, I do not know and therefore cannot speak.) So women are drafted
as a permanent class of worshippers. Under the hatred and fear of
women evident in the myth, there is, I believe, a desperate appeal for
collusion—the male victory, in every one of these fictions, is abjectly

dependent on the female reaction. Without the women's adoration, the men's genitals are not sacred or impressive but only a means to male sensual enjoyment, a self-indulgence strikingly absent in these tales. *Gender Genocide* describes Rura's passion at length but not the Laird's; "Priestess" (at the moment of conversion) describes Meg's arousal, which is taken as defeat. (For Daiv to be similarly disturbed would be a defeat and so cannot happen—he might then be converted to matriarchy.) Only in the comic stories can men be sexually aroused, but there it is the women who become overwhelmed and lose their heads, while the men (as in "Yukks") coolly exploit the women's excitement.

You'd think these authors had been reading Ti-Grace Atkinson. They certainly agree with her that heterosexual love is an institution designed by men to subjugate women. What they add is that it anesthetizes men.[3] And inculcates in them an intense fear of expendability—perhaps the reason why these stories simply and flatly equate an all-female world with female domination of men. The remedy in both cases is to link heterosexual pleasure inextricably to female subjugation.

In the fictional worlds in which the women have refused this equation there is no sexual pleasure at all and the world is in decay, as in West's "The Last Man," one of the stories in Sam Moskowitz's *When Women Rule.* "The Last Man," published in 1929, portrays a world of decaying technology and devolving intellect; the atavistic couple in the story flee into the wilderness and survive, the woman tempting the man with fruit (her name is Eve). Although there is no present-day Sex War in "The Last Man," there was one in the past, the woman's world is tyrannical and sexless, and the real woman—a throwback—initiates natural love and the couple's subsequent flight because she can't stand the all-female society's lack of liveliness and love. An interesting answer to the story, written in 1932, is "The Last Woman," by Thomas S. Gardner, in which the atavistic couple (led by the man; the woman is passive and beautiful) is recaptured and executed. The all-female world is given as the creation of the class of all women; the all-male world is carefully presented as the creation of one abnormal man. The all-female world is decaying and inept, and had to be produced by radical biological changes that are irreversible; the all-male world is scientifically brilliant, powerful, and productive, and has been produced by the action of a drug whose results are temporary and reversible. The asymmetry of the stories is striking. It is hard to escape the conclusion that these "worlds" are really portraits of the two sexes as seen by the two authors.

In "The Veiled Feminists of Atlantis" Booth Tarkington presses the familiar charge that women will not be content with equality but will desire superiority. After wheedling the secrets of magic out of their benevolent men, the ruling-class women of Atlantis become the men's superiors. The women's unjust insistence on retaining the veil (symbol of mysterious sexual power) produces a battle of magic, which sinks the island. Only the "uninitiated populace" (p. 103) survives. The great question, says the story, is who won, but considering that the Atlanteans' descendents are patriarchal (that the women go unveiled among neighboring tribes is a red herring), the "great question" seems deliberately mystificatory, especially in view of an earlier, very striking, image: "One might say that a Kabyle woman's eyes are the eyes of a woman who has seen her grandmother beaten to death, but has not been tamed by the spectacle" (p. 100).

Under the occult details and exotic atmosphere, one discerns the familiar charges: that the rule of women over men is unjust (but the rule of men over women was benevolent), and that women's use of power will be immoral and destructive. Tarkington does not defeat his women with the Sacred Object; rather he assumes it by predicting that feminists cannot have sexual power. He takes from his women what he sees as their Sacred Object—the veil—thus implicitly rendering them unattractive. The condescending mystification of "Who won?" is the comment of a gentleman (one European gentleman tells the story to another *about* a primitive tribe) fairly sure of his privileges. He does not, it seems, need the reassurance of a Sacred Object, except implicitly.

Thomas Berger's *Regiment of Women,* a role-reversal world in which women bind their breasts and rape men anally with dildoes, is cheery and inane, a world of diesel dykes and screaming faggots (all imagined by a very naive writer). It has hardly more overall coherence than *The Feminists,* although it is infinitely better written in its single scenes. The book betrays the conviction that a woman cannot dominate a man unless she has a penis somewhere about her (even is she keeps it in her bureau drawer) and that a man cannot be subjugated unless he acquires breasts, for which purpose silicone implants will do perfectly well. The year is 2047 but the clothes and props are late 1960s. The transvestism and artificial breasts seem to be in the service of rewritten history, although when the hero has his breasts removed late in the book, an army sergeant (female) only comments, "You boys! . . . cosmetic surgery has a tough time keeping up to date" (p. 146). Embryos are brought to

term in artificial wombs, although the book doesn't say who raises the
children, a very betraying omission. The biology and sociology are zany:
men who are totally anorgasmic and have never masturbated can be
forced to ejaculate by machines, women rape men artificially, and the
gynocracy, as usual, is totally in control and extremely incompetent,
kneeing men in the groin or castrating them in adulthood, which ruins
their minds and makes them fat and will-less. Men's Liberation is a
single underground organization which cannot attract young men but
only old ones, and the gynocracy triumphed because "men once had
power but lost it through pity for women" (the only explanation ever
given [p. 175]). In short, we are back in the usual world in which the
rule of women is sexless and tyrannical, and all this with a literalness
that destroys the role-reversal intention. The story ends with a misfit
couple fleeing to the wilderness, where the heroine makes the hero into
a man by teaching him to drive, running down her own accomplish-
ments, insisting he hold up a gas station, and telling him nature meant
him to dominate because his penis is shaped like a weapon. Their final
love-making is engineered by little Harriet (who seems to shrink constantly during the last few chapters as George realizes more and more
how tiny she is) but the author, who has the sophistication to see that
Georgie needs collusion, cannot imagine that Harriet might actively
make love to Georgie. She can only taunt him into making love to her,
an act he experiences as both rape and murder.

Berger calls the relation they eventually settle into "a reciprocal
arrangement" (p. 345), but here is the end of the book:

> She tried to stay on top. "You're too damned heavy!"
> But he easily rolled her over.
> "It's time I caught the rain," he said. And he inserted himself this time.
> If he was going to be a builder and a killer, he could be boss once in a
> while.
> Also, he was the one with the protuberant organ. (p. 349)

One of the few attempts to write thoughtfully about the Sex War that
I can find is "Mama Come Home" by James Tiptree, Jr. Although the
story contains eight-foot-tall women, they are part of a race from
Capella of which we are a neotenic mutation; in its "mature" (i.e.,
Capellan) form, the women of the human race are two feet taller than
men and dominate them, partly because they have the ability to rape
men, which they do on Earth in parks and other deserted places, also

murdering their victims afterwards. When we learn that with their super-technology the Capellans "plan to turn off the sun a little. As they leave" (p. 68) in order to "kick us back to the ice age" (p. 69), it becomes clear that these ladies are very bad indeed: "The men of Capella were slaves. . . . A cargo of exotic human males was worth a good deal more than ore" (p. 68).

So far we are strictly in Sex-War Land. But the author (unlike others treated in this paper) explicitly observes: "The Capellans overturned our psychic scenery, our view of ourselves. . . . Look at their threat to our male-dominant structure" (p. 71). Then, pushing the myth rather far, the hero himself is raped.

> The navigator leaned down and said something in a velvety contralto. I didn't need a translator—I'd seen enough old flicks. . . . She casually twisted my arm until things broke. . . . The ensuing minutes I make a point of not remembering except when I forget not to wake up screaming. . . . I was discovering some nasty facts about Capellan physiology through a blaze of pain. (Ever think about being attacked by a *musth* vacuum cleaner?) . . . Presently there was, blessedly, nothing. (p. 65)

Still, in "Mama Come Home" the real struggle is not between Earth men and Capellan giantesses. One of the hero's CIA colleagues is Tillie, a woman under five feet in height who happens to look exactly like a Capellan, and whose impersonation of one is what saves Earth.

The real struggle is for Tillie's loyalty, and it is her conversion to loving the hero that is the center of the story. Gang-raped, knifed, and left for dead as a teenager, she becomes the Capellans' translator and mascot:

> She was different these days—her eyes shone and she had a kind of tense, exalted smile. . . .
> "Tillie, it's dangerous. You don't know them."
> . . . She gave me the bare-faced stare.
> "They're dangerous?" (p. 59)

As the hero remarks, it was "permanent guerilla war inside," with "a six-inch layer of ice between her and everybody who shaved" (p. 59). The story sees this both as an "irrational sex phobia" (p. 72) and as something else; at one point the hero says:

> "You think your big playmates are just like yourself, only gloriously immune from rape. I wouldn't be surprised if you were thinking of going home with them. But you don't know them. . . . *Did you ever meet any American blacks who moved to Kenya?*" (p. 63; italics added)

Elsewhere his reasoning is explicitly political: "The American black who goes to Kenya often discovers he is an American first and an African second, no matter what they did to him in Newark" (p. 70).

Only after the news about the new ice age does the hero see "mad dreams dying in her [Tillie's] eyes" (p. 70). He concludes, with immense relief, "we had Tillie" (p. 71). The heroine's decision to throw in her lot with the male-dominant society that has raped her—a decision partly dependent on the hero's having also been raped—results in a symbolic re-living of her own rape (she pretends to be a raped Capellan in the faked film, which scares away the Capellans). She is then able to touch the hero and comment, "It's all relative, isn't it?"; and finally he says, "My mama came home with me" (p. 78).

If the story treats the Sex War scenario oddly, both inverting some of its elements and commenting critically on others, the reason is not far to seek. As the SF community now knows, "James Tiptree, Jr." is the pseudonym of Alice Sheldon. A woman does not, obviously, have the same stake in the myth as male authors may have. Eight years after this story, Tiptree published another story, "Houston, Houston, Do You Read?" in which present-day men who expect to take over a future, all-female world (a utopia, in fact) are competently and dispassionately killed. As one character says, "We simply have no facilities for people with your emotional problems."[4]

When women fight men, the battle is won by men because women are loyal to men. This piece of doublethink is made possible by splitting the female enemy into two: thus there are Capellan women and Earth women; as in "Yukks" there are sexy young women who are sympathetic, and unsexy old ones; as in *Gender Genocide* there are men-hating Lesbians and real women; as in "The Feminine Metamorphosis" there are good wives and mothers and unnatural businesswomen; as in "Ecce Femina!" there are women who shoot up Big E and women who don't. The real conflict is evaded. Moreover, solidarity among women either does not exist or is ruled out from the beginning; for example, Tillie is presented as without family, without friends, indeed without a social context of any kind. Thus her choice is—as it is in all these stories, for all the heroines—between evil (or in some cases decaying and sterile) female tyranny and some version of the hero, i.e., men. As Michael Korda says: "We need women . . . and hope that we can somehow ensnare, entrap, charm, hold one of them, as if by making our peace (on our terms) with one woman we can hold her captive in our camp, a prisoner of our side."[5] However, neither in marriage nor in the myths of the Rule of Women will this strategy work. Transferring the Sacred Object to one's own person and calling upon biology (or nature) to guard it only shifts the area of precariousness and consequent terror from the realm of artifacts to that of fantasy. Without such a shift (a very old ploy in Western history) phrases like "penis envy," "castrating bitch," and "emasculated male" would be meaningless as metaphors; "screw you" would not be an insult; and medieval "witches" could not have caused their "victims'" genitals to disappear. The centuries of coercion that lie behind the stories described here are not funny—heteroinstitutionality (as against freely chosen heterosensuality, which does not appear in these stories) is quite as dreadful as Ti-Grace Atkinson says it is.

Yet how unintentionally funny these stories are! Bruce McAllister's motorcycle gang member, "Queen Elizabeth," using "soda pop for strange purposes" (never specified [p. 127]); Edmund Cooper's determinedly charging into his favorite formula ("It was X. It was Y. It was Z. It was Q"); or Nelson Bond's teenage heroine who sobs, sticks out her chin, recognizes George Washington's essential maleness, and flings herself at the hero. The male ignorance betrayed by such fictions is appalling; the male wishes embodied in them are little short of soul-killing. But consider the title I almost used for this paper (and a very good one it is, too): *The Triumph of the Flasher.*

Not all SF concerned with role reversals, all-female worlds, or male domination, is, of course, of the Flasher variety. Some of the material mentioned in Moskowitz's introduction to the book cited appears to be pro-feminist in intention, as is Frederik Pohl's *Search the Sky* (which contains a brief satiric sketch of a role-reversal society), Theodore Sturgeon's *Venus Plus X* (a human, hermaphroditic society), and Mack Reynolds's *Amazon Planet,* in which the author sets up a role-reversal façade very like Berger's—armed female warriors and simpering men—only to reveal beneath it a peaceful and substantially egalitarian world. And the all-female world of John Wyndham's "Consider Her Ways" is a pro-feminist discussion of romantic love and the feminine mystique (although Wyndham creates another of those beehive-like societies structured by biological engineering). More doubtful is Poul Anderson's *Virgin Planet,* an all-female world in which the women span the whole range of human temperaments and activities. However, what will happen when men return to the planet (the women wished to be worthy of their vanished men, who died of a plague, and so became warriors, ship captains, etc.) is unclear. John Boyd's *Sex and the High Command* is a Sex War story of the cheerful-inane school in which the women win, having found a drug that produces both orgasm and pregnancy, i.e., a substitute for the Sacred Object.[6]

However, the above stories pale before an extraordinary phenomenon of the last few years—a number of feminist utopias, all but one written by women and all in every way the opposite of the Flasher books.[7] The feminist utopias, to the degree that they are concerned with the "battle of the sexes" (and most are) see it as a long, one-sided massacre whose cause (not cure) is male supremacy. They are explicit about economics and politics, fairly sexually permissive, demystifying about biology, emphatic about the necessity for female bonding, concerned with children (who hardly exist in the Flasher books), non-urban, classless, communal, relatively peaceful while allowing room for female rage and female self-defense, and serious about the emotional and physical consequences of violence. The Flasher books perceive conflict between the sexes as private and opt for a magical solution *via* a mystified biology. The feminist utopias see such conflict as a public class conflict, so the solutions advocated are economic, social, and political. Strikingly, no Flasher book I was able to find envisioned a womanless world (or dared to say so); about half the feminist utopias matter-of-factly excluded men.

NOTES

This essay first appeared in *Science-Fiction Studies,* Volume 7 (1980).

1. Parley J. Cooper, *The Feminists* (New York: Pinnacle Books, 1971); Joan Bamberger, "The Myth of Matriarchy: Why Men Rule in Primitive Society," in Michelle Zimbalist Rosaldo and Louise Lamphere, eds., *Woman, Culture, and Society* (Stanford, 1974).

2. Michael Korda, *Male Chauvinism! How It Works* (New York, 1973) p. 232.

3. Ti-Grace Atkinson, *Amazon Odyssey* (New York, 1974), pp. 13–24; Philip E. Slater, "Sexual Adequacy in America," *Intellectual Digest* (Nov. 1973):17–20.

4. James Tiptree, Jr. [pseud. of Alice Sheldon], "Houston, Houston, Do You Read?" in Tiptree, *Star Songs of an Old Primate* (New York: Ballantine, 1978).

5. Korda, p. 222.

6. Frederik Pohl and C. M. Kornbluth, *Search the Sky* (New York: Ballantine, 1954); Theodore Sturgeon, *Venus Plus X* (London: Gollancz, 1969); Mack Reynolds, *Amazon Planet* (New York: Ace, 1975); John Wyndham, "Consider Her Ways," in *Sometime, Never* (New York: Ballantine, 1956); John Boyd, *Sex and the High Command* (New York: Weybright & Talley, 1971); Poul Anderson, *Virgin Planet* (New York: Avalon Books, 1959).

7. I have treated a group of these works in a paper entitled "Recent Feminist Utopias," presented at the MLA panel on women and SF in Chicago, 1977. The paper has been accepted for publication in an anthology edited by Marleen Barr of the State University of New York at Buffalo, to be published by the Bowling Green State University Popular Press, Bowling Green, Ohio. The works are: Monique Wittig, *Les Guérillères* (New York: Viking Press, 1971); Ursula Le Guin, *The Dispossessed* (New York: Harper & Row, 1974); Joanna Russ, *The Female Man* (New York: Bantam Books, 1975); Suzy McKee Charnas, *Motherlines* (New York: Berkeley, 1978); Samuel Delany, *Triton* (New York: Bantam Books, 1976); Marge Piercy, *Woman on the Edge of Time* (New York: Knopf, 1976); Marion Zimmer Bradley, *The Shattered Chain* (New York: Daw Books, 1976); Catherine Madsden, "Commodore Bork and the Compost," *The Witch and the Chameleon*, no. 5–6 (1976); James Tiptree, Jr. [pseud. of Alice Sheldon], "Houston, Houston, Do You Read?" and Raccoona Sheldon [also a pseud. of Alice Sheldon], "Your Faces, O My Sisters!" both in *Aurora: Beyond Equality*, ed. Susan Janice Anderson and Vonda McIntyre (New York: Fawcett World Library, 1976); and Sally Gearhart, *The Wanderground* (Watertown, Mass.: Persephone Press, 1978).

This paper is much indebted to Sam Moskowitz's collection *When Women Rule*, which does a considerable service to SF not only by the stories he reprints but also by those discussed and listed in the introduction. The author is personally indebted to David Hartwell for calling her attention to and making available a copy of *When Women Rule*.

5

On the Fascination of Horror Stories, Including Lovecraft's

I n a perfect world I would not have to be a feminist and gay activist and I could spend my life discussing H. P. Lovecraft. I am a horror-story freak and a Lovecraft freak. By "horror story" I don't mean the modern kind in which people do gory and nasty things to each other but the older kind in which the source of fear is (usually) some alteration in reality. Fantasy, in short. The supernatural. Ghost stories. A great many science-fiction writers and readers enjoy both s.f. and "horror," as do I. In a perfect world, there would be unlimited used-book stores of fantasy and wonderful libraries of it and a Lovecraft Café where folks could hang out from time to time and discuss H[oward] P[hillips] L[ovecraft]'s work when the mood struck them. And he would've lived twice as long and written much more. What writers do with fantasy in general is to me much more fascinating than most depictions of life-as-it-is (well, as it's spozed to be, anyway). It's more obviously what literature is in the last analysis. I do think, also, that literary criticism is stuck in psychoanalytic explanations of such work, explanations that sometimes work (on, say, Bram Stoker) but which really do not cover the preoccupations of writers like Lovecraft or Poe (whose obsessions with obsession may have had something to do with the addictions he in fact lived through). It's a fascinating subject.

"What do they see in H. P. Lovecraft?" you (Darko Suvin) asked me several months ago, and as I once drove Damon Knight almost to tears by announcing that I had not only read *At the Mountains of Madness* straight through but also enjoyed it (this was years ago), I feel it incumbent upon me to answer.

I think I now know.

At an SF fan gathering last week there was much reminiscing about horror stories. Not only did everyone have a favorite (if one can use that word about fiction which in fact scared the bejeezus out of people between ages six and sixteen), but people talked of their remembered "favorite" as an expression of something real about the world, a description of life the reader truly believed in, or at least suspected was true. Thus:

> "There was this story about a man who got caught between Tuesday and Wednesday and everyone had the Wednesday script except him so he kept making mistakes. For years I really thought everyone knew this big secret about life except me and I had missed it."
>
> "Vampires? I married one."
>
> "Of course the house is haunted by an evil presence. I can feel it the moment I walk in the door. But it's not the house: it's _____. I keep telling my other roommates we have to get rid of him."
>
> "When I was little, I thought the whole world was made of fungus. I used to go through the woods, shuddering and looking for something not made of fungus. I used to wonder if *I* was made of fungus."

There's nothing new in interpreting horror stories and horror films as crude descriptive psychology, but I believe that most work in this area has been done from an intrapersonal, Freudian point of view, and so concentrates on issues of sexuality and guilt, which is fine for some work (especially nineteenth-century fiction, e.g., Arthur Machen's *Black Crusade*) but which leaves out issues like the relation of self to other or the ontological status of the self, in short, the characteristic issues of much modern horror fiction.

The party-goers, sophisticated people, were saying as much: I thought everyone had the secret of living but me; I thought the world was made of "bad stuff" (Laing's phrase in *The Divided Self*); vampires are metaphors for emotional parasitism; and so on. They didn't go on to say (but I will) that these images of basic human concerns are, as one would expect, very concrete, very bodily, very "extreme," and although grotesque and frightening, in some sense also reassuring. They validate perceptions that need validating, especially in adolescence—i.e., under the bland, forced optimism of American life terrible forces are at work, things are not what they seem, and if you feel lonely, persecuted, a misfit, and in terror, you aren't crazy. You're right.

Horror fiction is *a fiction of extreme states* (Adrienne Rich uses the phrase "poetry of extreme states" to describe some of Emily Dickinson's work) and the message is (as Rich notes): *Someone has been here before.*

You're not alone. That is a comforting and important message to receive in a culture that is bent on denying the destructive, the irrevocable, the terrifying, and the demonic. When I was fifteen, Lovecraft's "The Color Out of Space," with its malevolent, parasitic, alien life inhabiting everything around the characters, scared me (for months I was afraid to look up at tree branches at night: I expected to see them moving by themselves) but I kept reading the story. It was infinitely preferable to the repressions of the 1950s and the suburban future I was supposedly headed for. Looking back, I suspect *it was the 1950s and that imaginary future, in fictional form.*

Such social criticism as is contained in even the best horror fiction is usually implicit. Even in such a fine novel as Shirley Jackson's *The Haunting of Hill House* (a modern Gothic with the values reversed and a criticism of patriarchy: Jackson has other fiction of this sort) the movement is toward individual tragedy, not politics.* Stories like Charlotte Perkins Gilman's "The Yellow Wallpaper" are rare, though nothing in the genre precludes them.

About Lovecraft and his fans:

Schizophrenia as diseased ontology. Laing's patient (in *The Divided Self*) convinced that his body was stinking and rotting, though no one else could smell or see this. Lovecraft's imagery of the rotting, walking corpse, once (in the tragic "The Outsider") the victim-teller of the tale, or the shapeless, horrid, usually fetid monster, sometimes a threat from the outside ("The Haunter of the Dark"), sometimes one's own blood kin (there's one story, the name of which I forget, in which the unclean spirit is a sort of collective family ghost which is vanquished by the narrator's uncle), sometimes one's blood kin and oneself ("The Weird Shadow Over Innsmouth"). I don't mean, of course, to say that Lovecraft was schizophrenic, but that he was able to fashion artistic images that express certain basic issues in human experience, issues that matter to all of us, though they trouble some of us more and others of us less.

To mention other writers' work: "The Yellow Wallpaper" deals with issues of autonomy, separation, and individuation by creating a powerful horror-story image (the other self coming out from behind the wallpaper). The story is political protest. It is also a horror story and has been anthologized as "pure" horror. I read it at fifteen and it scared me; when I re-read it at thirty-five I was amazed that I had so completely missed the feminist message. I then gave it to my women's studies class, and it scared *them.*

Another example: what is the monster under the ancestral moat, who demands human sacrifices once a year but is generally harmless to all not of the family line? I believe it to be a metaphor for the kind of unspoken family command or "script" of which modern psychology so often speaks, injunctions like Be a failure, Never have enough, Live without love, and so on.

The monster that assures the family's prosperity at the cost of lives *outside* the family line is another matter: like deals with the devil (if seriously treated), this is a poetic, personal, felt version of Brecht's "What keeps a man alive? He lives off others."

I think we tend to be aware of veiled sexuality and aggression in horror fiction (e.g., *Dracula*) or guilt (much of LeFanu's work), but I don't think much has been done with other psychology.

At its best, horror fiction does attempt to give the subjective, undiluted, raw, absolute, global experience-in-itself of these basic human issues. Hence the primitiveness, the crudity, the coarseness of texture of even the best of such stories, like Poe's, although such coarseness is not a defect. It is a consequence of the material, which is a common psychology of experience, not an individual psychology of particular characters. In treating phenomena and not people, horror fiction very much resembles SF; perhaps this resemblance is one reason for the overlap of readers and authors. The resemblance may also illuminate the silly-simple metaphysics readers seem to find irresistible in SF. (Are we really aliens and not humans? How can we tell?) Such supposedly epistemological and ontological questions may function like the images in horror stories, as metaphors for other, much more basic, issues.

Perhaps the very nature of fiction militates against the use of horror-story material as narrative fiction. Although the horror-story image feels true (at least at the time one feels like that), it's not the whole truth of anybody's situation and so a moment's reflection will qualify the impact of the image. To my mind, even the best examples of pure horror story (like Poe's) are badly weakened by the necessity of keeping the reader from that moment of reflection. Avoiding thought is not a good recipe for art. I suspect that the most aesthetically successful examples of the genre move toward tragedy or social protest or something besides horror-story *per se*. Probably the ideal place for the raw, undiluted experience-treated-as-the-whole-truth is in lyric poetry, which is not under an obligation to add to the question *What does it feel like?* the further question *Yes, but what is it, really?* Sylvia Plath's "The Muses" is a piece of this sort. And Shirley Jackson's best work (*The Haunting of Hill House*, "The Lovely House," etc.) is, for me, rescued by the implicitly social dimension. In fact a good case can be made for Jackson as a proto-feminist writer.*

You might be interested to know that at the party one very bright young woman described her adolescent reading of SF as a genuinely subversive force in her life, a real alternative to the fundamentalist community into which she had been born. This alternative had nothing to do with the cardboard heroes and heroines or the imperial American/engineering values which she had skipped right over. What got to her were the alien landscapes and the alien creatures. We scholars perhaps tend to forget how much subversive potential both SF and fantasy have, even at their crudest. Orwell to the contrary, there really is a certain subversive force to statements like *Big Brother is ungood*. Of course if people stay at this level without analysis and without remedies, nothing happens except a constant desire for repetition of the original, elementary validation. That is, you have addiction, a phenomenon well exemplified by the Lovecraft fans, who seem to constitute a perpetual audience for more HPL, more posthumous collaborations with HPL, more biographies of HPL, more imitation HPL, and so on.

Does any of this illuminate Lovecraft's popularity?

N O T E S

This essay first appeared in *Science-Fiction Studies*, Volume 7 (1980).

*I am indebted for this view of Jackson's work to a student of mine at the State University of New York at Binghamton, Barbara Nichols.

6

A Boy and His Dog: The Final Solution

What to do with majority/oppressor culture is a continuing problem for minority/oppressed groups. Most of us settle for crumbs—the allusion, the implication, the single line, the "good scene," the dominant-group character whom one can "identify with" without having to face the nastiness of the minority ones (who are two-dimensional or defamatory). The following review was published in 1975. After seeing the film discussed below, I found that crumbs were not enough and that I would no longer settle for the kind of cultural product that blithely blamed me for the ills of its far more loathsome male characters. I still think that Harlan Ellison's story of the same name is a very different matter from the film (for which Ellison wasn't responsible); in the story everyone is loathsome, and Quilla June has a solid beef against her ghastly father, i.e. when escaping "Topeka," she stuns him by confronting him with what she knows to be his own secret desires: incest with her. (That is, after all, a fairly good reason to be angry at your father.) Luckily, I am an artist and can make good the extraordinary deficit of any representation in popular culture of people like me and feelings like mine by writing them into stories; people who feel the lack but aren't artists must have a harder time of it. All minority/oppressed art has a wonderful freshness about it (when it is honest) and one of the most heartening things about the last forty-odd years in the United States is the emergence of so many artists who find their grounding in lesbian experience, gay experience, female experience, the experience of being a woman or man of color, being disabled, any combination of the above, and many more. Langston Hughes's, Cheryl Wade's and Chrystos's poems, Toni Morrison's and Red Jordan Arobateau's fiction—these are only a few of the marvelous things that exist outside the pale of the dominators, as Québecoise historian Lise Noël calls them.
It all starts when you say no.

The Denver area is full of male feminists. Two of them, both science-fiction writers, urged me to see *A Boy and His Dog*, the feature-length film made from Harlan Ellison's science-fiction story of the same name. Both men are friends of mine, and Harlan Ellison is a friend of mine also; yet must I proclaim publicly right here that sending a woman to see *A Boy and His Dog* is like sending a Jew to a movie that glorifies Dachau; you need not be a feminist to loathe this film. I don't know whether Ellison supervised the making of the film or whether he approves of it, so this review will deal entirely with the film and not with Ellison's story.[1] Kate Millett called Norman Mailer's *An American Dream* a novel about how to kill your wife and live happily ever after; *A Boy and His Dog* is about how to feed your girl friend to your dog and live happily ever after. This film is in the direct line of descent of hundreds of Hollywood movies in which a designing and dangerous woman tries to part loyal male buddies; *Boy* has essentially the same ending as *Casablanca*, although in the latter film getting rid of the woman is romantically glossed over— i.e., she is renounced, not made into dog food. Samuel Delany, an excellent science-fiction writer and critic, has invented the word "homo-sexist" to describe films like *Butch Cassidy and the Sundance Kid*, in which the woman is a dim tag-along, brought in to placate the audience, which might be expected to grow uneasy at a film in which the main emotional entanglements between men and women are either secondary or rejected.[2]

In this sense, *Boy* is a homosexist film. It is not a homosexual film— I want to make that clear. If there are constant jokes made about the "fuzzy butt" of the telepathic dog, Blood, and if the dog is pictured as immensely appealing, this is not because the dog rouses erotic feelings in either Vic (the hero) or anybody else; it is because he doesn't, and it is therefore safe to love him. *Boy* is affectionate toward the dog, who is asexual; it is the girl, Quilla June, corrupt, dangerous, but powerfully attractive, that the film finds evil and menacing. Stories in which the world's evil is attributed to women or women's sexual attractiveness are hardly new in Western culture, and there are times you'd swear *Boy* was a remake of *Samson Agonistes* or even the story of the Garden of Eden, although the garden here (a world devastated by World War Three) is a pretty bleak and minimal one.

Stories that portray a noble, talented, or sympathetic man done in by an evil temptress depend heavily on the plausibility of the temptress, and it's here that *Boy* falls down—it's a good film until the utter impossibility of Quilla June, Vic's girl friend, destroys it. Among other good things, the movie has a splendid performance by the dog—pieced together by the director, one assumes, but at times one wonders; the dog's a better actor than many human ones. And the film has that rare science-fiction virtue one might call Not Shoving Your Nose In It. Remember those films in which somebody says, "My God, Sheila! Don't you realize what this means? Those unknown monsters that devoured a little girl and killed old Grandpa Perkins are the mutated ants caused by radiation from the bomb tests held three years ago in the Arizona desert!" Well, nobody in *Boy* ever talks like this. The film does not painfully belabor the obvious, but gives you the science-fiction background and detail you need quickly, dramatically, and above all, obliquely. But you buy the considerable virtues of the movie by having to endure (once again) a story whose main point is that women are no damned good and men are better off without us, even when it means killing us.

Vic, the boy, survives (with the help of his telepathic dog, Blood) in a ruined, sterile, war-devastated America in which rape and murder are commonplace. He attempts to rape Quilla June, the girl, only to be unexpectedly trapped by love; she tempts him down to the underground world of "Topeka,"³ a 1950-ish midwestern small-town world like a Ray Bradbury story gone totalitarian, and he finds himself a prisoner. Quilla sets him free, wishing him to kill the leaders of this ghastly place, but the leaders' robot executioner is all but unkillable (although Vic manages to short out one of them, there are plenty more in the warehouse), and the lovers flee aboveground. A wounded, weakened Blood, waiting aboveground for Vic, has waited too long: Vic is forced to choose between Blood's life and Quilla June's, and he chooses his real friend, the dog.

From the above synopsis (if you hadn't seen the film) you might guess that both societies are intolerable, that both characters are driven, and that any course of action taken by anybody will, of necessity, be tragic. This is not the case. For example, the film presents the judicial executions in "Topeka" as horrifying, while casual murders aboveground are a grim sort of fun—Vic's and Quilla's reactions giving the audience its cue in both cases. The murders are also paced differently and shown differently. A key line in the film—Vic shouts that he wants to go back to the dirt aboveground so that he can feel clean—characterizes her form of Hell as infinitely worse than his. He is a loser below-

ground and a winner aboveground, but the film translates this difference into a moral difference between the two societies. (I might add that
the line itself is television-ghastly; Vic has been carefully created as
someone who would not give a damn about feeling morally clean and to
whom such a self-conscious fatuity as the line would be impossible.)
Above all, Vic and Blood are lovable and good, and Quilla June is
manipulative and bad, so Vic's final choice is a foregone conclusion.
Unfortunately, the foregoneness of the conclusion destroys its drama;
since feeding your girlfriend to your dog is neither suspenseful nor
tragic—it's necessary and she deserves nothing better—the end dwin-
dles to a sour joke, exactly as the audience took it. It isn't hard to see in
this film another repetition of the common American idea that if only
men could get away from civilization (i.e., women) and civilization's
troublesome insistence that one actually interact with others, life (men's
lives) would be much better. Even though Vic's life, after Quilla, will be
lived in a bleak and ruined world, he will be free; *Boy* is surprisingly like
Huckleberry Finn, with Blood as the undemanding and loving companion who isn't quite human, like Nigger Jim. The movie, however, goes
farther than Twain did; civilization ("Topeka") is totally corrupt and
woman is not simply avoided but wiped out, a necessity if man (who has
now seen through her bitchery and is no longer a slave to his gonads) is
to go off with his real friend, the dog.

   Boy presents its woman as corrupt and produced by a corrupt society;
only by murdering her can man avoid her dangerous fascinations. A
sexless relationship is better, "love" is rotten, and Vic's becoming disillu-
sioned with "love" and returned to his old friend (the dog) is the plot of
the film. Quilla June is therefore an important character, and the film's
judgment of her is the linch-pin of the plot.

   Quilla June at first looks like a brave woman. By coming aboveground
she risks death, not to mention rape. She is also surprisingly competent;
she knows how to shoot. However, we soon find that her escapade is
neither patriotic nor curious, but fueled by greedy ambition, for the
elders of "Topeka" have sent her up with the promise of reward. Later
she braves the rulers of "Topeka" (including her own father) by freeing
Vic, but this action is not undertaken because she likes him or repents of
having trapped him; instead, she wishes him to kill—for her—the
"Committee," which rules this underground society. Why she can't do
this herself is something of a puzzle, for she apparently knows how to
shoot and guns are available, but perhaps the film wants to characterize

her as simultaneously dangerous and helpless. She has persuaded other teenagers to rebel against the rulers of "Topeka," an accomplishment which you might think would show her as something of a political mastermind, but no, they are all boys—there are no girls in Quilla's rebellion—so it is probable that she has seduced them into submission, as she did Vic. She is no Joan of Arc (or even Evita Peron), but only Mata Hari. The government of "Topeka" is viciously conformist, but no credit accrues to Quilla for wanting to destroy such a setup; for what she really wants, as she makes plain to Vic, is to replace those currently in power with herself. The film simultaneously presents her as enormously dangerous and powerful (because of her sexuality) and totally helpless (although she must know about the robot executioner, all she does is scream for Vic to protect her, though earlier she was daring enough to bash in heads). Back on the surface (in her wedding dress, a good touch) she reveals that she is not only helpless but stupid; she whines unpleasantly and "manages" Vic badly—and this is fatal, because he is now her only protector.

According to Samuel Delany,[4] literary characterization proceeds by means of three kinds of actions: gratuitous, purposeful, and habitual, and well-written characters perform all three. (This classification certainly applies to realistic fiction, and I suspect it applies to all fiction, however stylized.) Sexist literature produces two kinds of female characters, both imperfect: the Heroine, whose actions are all gratuitous, and the Villainess, whose actions are all purposeful. Neither performs habitual actions.[5]

Now Quilla June perfectly fits this formula for a Villainess—she is all calculation. She has no habits and what a difference it would make if she did—bite her fingernails, for example, or wince uncontrollably whenever her dreadful Daddy comes too close! But aside from a few clumsy betrayals of hatred, Quilla never does anything spontaneously (that is, gratuitously) any more than she does anything out of habit; she is all outside, all mask, and the few revelations of her feelings are simply revelations that Quilla is *hateful*. The inner life that makes Blood and Vic so lovable is withheld from Quilla June; she is a grotesque enormity, a totally manipulative Bitch. We are shown that she is "ambitious," but it's hard to know what ambition is supposed to mean here (it seems to be only another word for hate) since what she wants is neither flattery, glory, nor self-importance, but only revenge.

In addition to repeating the theme of Love Between Buddies, the film strongly resembles those 1950s films in which the Good Girl is bait, used to bind the Bad Boy to the Conformist System—except that the 1950s films I'm thinking of are on the side of the System (of which the Good Girl is an artifact), and this film most emphatically is not. Clearly, *Boy* intends to attack the Conformist System (a remarkably nasty one in this film); judgment is pronounced upon it by Vic, and its representative, Quilla June, is destroyed by him.

What is odd is that Quilla June, far from representing "Topeka," is in fact trying to destroy it, and that "Topeka," far from being hurt by Quilla June's death, is protected by it. One might begin to suspect that "Topeka" has an interest in having Quilla destroyed, and that, far from being its representative, she is its scapegoat—expendable, unnecessary, but useful at times for containing the rage of punks like Vic.

That is, thinking you are attacking society when you condemn or ravage the hypocritical Nice Girl Next Door is the exact equivalent of thinking that stealing from the local supermarket makes you a Communist.

The Nice Girl Next Door, although she is often perceived as the most protected and most valuable citizen in a sexist society, is neither. She isn't even really in the society at all. She's a figurine, a possession, a commercial product, something the film recognizes at one point when it shows a long line of girls in bridal dresses (same uniform, different faces) waiting in a hospital corridor to be led in and "married" to Vic. ("Topeka" is taking semen samples from him as he lies wired to a machine that stimulates his brain in order to induce orgasm; each girl in turn stands under a horseshoe of flowers in her white gown, a minister solemnly reads the marriage service, the machine is turned on, and the resulting semen is neatly labeled, presumably with the name of the "wife.") The Nice Girl is socially powerless, useful at best for the minor policing of teenage boys, useful as a reward or a "responsibility" but hardly a citizen in her own right—after all, the major policing in a sexist society is done by others, overwhelmingly by adult males. When Vic destroys Quilla he is destroying a victim, a quasi-slave, a piece of useful property. He is certainly not harming "Topeka." And the film does not present Quilla's destruction as Quilla's tragedy; on the contrary, it is she who is the real menace; it is she who must be punished.

This is scapegoating.

The movie hates "Topeka," but it executes Quilla June. Are the two identical? To think they are is comparable to the theories that maintained that the only flaw in antebellum southern slavery was the wretched character and corrupting influence of the slaves themselves. This logic is a form of Philip Wylie's Momism, in which women are "society" and a man escapes from "society" and its obligations by avoiding women; the usual American form of this illusion is the concept of marriage as a trap into which men are tricked by women. But if society is really constituted by *other men* (as "Topeka" certainly seems to be), then no escape is possible; avoiding women leaves a man just as open to intimidation by other men, i.e., by "society." *Boy* avoids the problem of society-as-other-men by splitting the world in two: in underground "Topeka" there are relatively free women (that is, young people and members of the lower classes are oppressed regardless of sex), while aboveground women are prostitutes, drudges, or rape victims, and hence powerless. The real ruler of "Topeka" is clearly Quilla's Daddy, but the fight with him is never joined at all. Indeed, the film doesn't even seem interested in him. This is especially odd since the role (a very brief one) is played by Jason Robards, Jr., and you'd think that out of sheer dramatic expediency the movie would give him more to do. I might add that the rulers of the underground society are presented as quite straightforwardly cynical and callous, which seems to me a bad mistake; "Topeka," in its enforced imitation of Kansas 1905 (or a daydream thereof) is a mind-bendingly surreal place. I don't believe the leaders would be exempt from the general craziness, quite the contrary (*1984*, q.v.). This aspect of "Topeka" is well conveyed in the film, for example by the white face-makeup and the misty, purplish sky—so close that it gives you instant claustrophobia.

It is nonsense to insist that the real danger in a tyrannical, self-hating, hypocritical, piously horrible society is pretty, scheming, little girls. The Nice Girl looks like the most sacred and the most privileged citizen of this ghastly commonalty, but in reality her rights (as opposed to the rights of her owners) are nonexistent. In D. W. Griffith's *Orphans of the Storm*, for example, to lay a finger on Lillian Gish looks like a desecration, but she is far from being society or even a citizen of it; she has been invented, constructed, meant, *put there* in the film either to be raped or saved-from-rape—what other purpose can there possibly be for her unhuman helplessness and childishness? The Victorian gentlemen who so assiduously protected their daughters' maiden purity were not hypocrites when they visited whorehouses stocked with twelve-year-old girls; they were simply acting on the identical assumption about the high value of maiden purity. In such a setup, pretty girls are about as much privileged citizens as a diamond ring is a privileged citizen. Like money or jewels, women are counters for use in business or warfare between men. Punk loners (who are much more part of "society" than Vic is part of "Topeka" in *Boy*) can go on terrifying or killing waitresses or cheerleaders forever under the impression that they're heroically attacking society; this is what happens in both *Boy* and *The Wild Ones,* a movie whose anger (and evasions) thrilled a whole generation.

Confusing Nelson Rockefeller with his car is a useful delusion to inculcate in punks; this way they attack the car instead of the man. After all, if the punks ever found out the car was only a possession, there might be real trouble. But as long as movies assume that the use of women to bind men to respectability is an instinct or a scheme by women (who must act through men in order to attain any power or safety), and not a circumstance set up by powerful men, rebels can expend their emotion on reincarnations of the Bitch Goddess forever.

The war between fathers and sons is as chronic a conflict in patriarchy as the war between classes (that is, between upper-class and lower-class men), though not nearly as revolutionary in its potential. In both conflicts women are useful scapegoats, blamable and punishable for everything. After all, Son will eventually make it to the state of Father and will have his own Daughter/Wife he can own ("protect") from other Fathers, a Daughter he can give to another Son as payment for continuing the status quo. Son can even be counted on to punish Daughter if Daughter gets out of hand. Thus a real alliance between Daughter and Son is made eternally impossible, and luckily so, for such an alliance would be almost as dangerous for patriarchy as one between Daughter and Mother. Between classes, scapegoats are even more useful: Lower-class Man is not going to make it at all, i.e., he will never replace Upper-class Man; so using Lower/Upper-class Woman as scapegoat both distracts him from the real situation and bribes him to endure it.

The evils of female sexuality and the obligatory punishment of its carriers is the grand, eternally useful scapegoat of Western patriarchy. It is the one topic on which Fathers and Sons, Upper-class Men and Lower-class Men can heartily agree. And they can agree (and collude) while enjoying the comforting illusion that they are engaged in dangerous, revolutionary activities. I believe the makers of *Boy* really thought they were violating a sacred taboo when they fed Quilla June to Blood, but there is certainly no such taboo extant now in fiction or film. In fact,

I doubt there ever was one. For quite a while twentieth-century literature and films have specialized in exploitation, self-aggrandizement, and violence directed against women; writers who use such devices can congratulate themselves on being daring while taking almost no risks. This violence didn't start with *Frenzy,* either; Griffith could show Lillian Gish in various threatening situations time after time, Gloria Swanson could be carried half-naked out of the surf (this in 1919), and De Mille could elevate orgy to a shlock art. How much freedom had any of them to violate real taboos—for example, to attack free enterprise? The sacredness of the Nice Girl is important only when it gives one group of Sons or Fathers a reason to wallop another; otherwise nobody cares. The one taboo is highly ambivalent and strongly titillating (the treatment of Mom in American movies, with its mingling of exploitation, adulation, and venom, is an even plainer case) but the second taboo is absolute.

Naked ladies in bathtubs or rape (a subject surprisingly present in late-nineteenth-century European theater) don't get you into trouble with the censors, certainly not persistently. If you are Mae West and you try to demystify sex, removing both pruriency and sentimentality from the subject, you get into trouble with the Hays Office. If you are Charlie Chaplin, you end up in much worse trouble, and not with the Hays Office, either.

If you look carefully at the structural (though not sexual) position of Blood in the triangle dog-boy-girl, you find that he is really Vic's other woman, in fact, Vic's wife. Blood, presented as a better person than Quilla June, nonetheless controls his relationship with Vic through identical manipulativeness of the traditional feminine sort: he is by far the more dependent, he is smaller, he cannot handle firearms, and he depends on Vic for food. Suavely dignified as the dog is, his pretensions are always at (very comic) odds with his behavior. He's a mooch, a coaxer, a charmer, a wheedler, a jealous sulk, a self-dramatizer who gets his way by ostentatiously parading his wounded feelings. He even fulfills the common American wifely function (remember Maggie and Jiggs?) of trying to make Vic cultured. In short, he acts very like a wife, even to the traditional parallel that when Blood wants something, like going Over the Hill, and Vic doesn't, Blood has to do without. It might be objected that Blood works for his keep as a sort of assistant to Vic, but then so do wives; child care, shopping, cooking, and cleaning are hardly female hobbies. One example of the film's virulent misogyny is the presentation of Quilla June as strictly a luxury article. Another evidence of loading the deck (very striking, too) is the scene in which Quilla calls Blood "cute"—the audience roars with scorn, but of course the talking dog *is* cute, and this cuteness is precisely what the audience has been relishing all evening. Moreover, Blood's will and Vic's will usually run in the same channels; pets (which is what the dog is, even if he can speak) are less demanding and more loyal than human friends. I suspect the reason the film does not present a friendship between two men as the alternative to the relationship between Vic and Quilla is not only that throwing over your girl friend for a boy would suggest homosexuality, but that a friendship between two men could not possibly be as harmonious as one between a boy and a dog.

If Quilla June is seen as evil by the film, I suspect the main reason is that she's not Vic's dog. The horrid surprise waiting for the lover of this silky, pettable creature is that she has her own will, that it is not at all like his, and that sex gives her power over him. Her dependency is a parody of the dog's; it ought to render her loyal and unthreatening, and yet it only makes her scheming and deceptive. (That dependency makes women devious is a state of affairs patriarchy has been complaining about for centuries.)

There are extraordinarily good moments in this film, like Vic's stupidsly grin when he's told that he's about to act out the ultimate punk sexual fantasy, or the echo of fairytale in Vic's staying underground "too long" because of the wicked enchantress, just as if "Topeka" were Elf Hill. But I can no longer buy fine moments at the price of colluding in my own murder.

A reader might object at this point that Quilla June is not all women but only one, and that a film which presents her as a bitch who deserves to be killed is not attacking all women but only one. My answer to this is threefold: first, the film replicates a pattern that is very common in Western culture, if not elsewhere; second, the film shows nothing of Quilla except her sexual power and her bitchiness; third, the film doesn't present any alternative to Quilla. Who else is there? The dirty, worn-out drudges we see topside? The faceless prostitute glimpsed in one scene? Miss Ms. (what a name!), that older Quilla? The sad, obedient schoolgirls of "Topeka," totally controlled by their parents? Many Hollywood films used to present us with two alternatives: a woman could be a Bitch or she could be the June Allysonian Nice Girl. I suppose it's an advance of sorts to stop holding out the June Allyson type as an ideal, but all *Boy* does is combine the two and insist that the Nice Girl *is* the Bitch.

Early in *Boy,* Vic finds a woman raped and murdered by a rover-pack and comments on what a waste the murder was; she might've been good for a few more times. But by the end of the film the only logical attitude he (or we) can adopt—the whole film has been devoted to proving this point—is that Vic was wrong: the only good woman is a dead woman and the only way a man can have sex with a woman safely is to kill her afterward. This morality is the morality of King Shahriyar, and while *The Thousand and One Nights* presents this morality as insane, *Boy* presents it as exemplary, perhaps even heroic.[6]

Here is a conversation a friend of mine had recently with a twelve-year-old, omnivorous reader:

He asked her what books she liked to read.

"Oh, you know, books about people," was the not very clear answer.
He asked her if she read any books with women as the central characters.
"Oh," she said with scorn, "I don't read books about *women*."[7]

At twelve she has already made the equation: women = nonpeople. And no wonder. Perhaps someday she'll stop reading books, as I may stop going to the movies.

I'm going to pull a flip-flop on the makers of *A Boy and His Dog*. I'm going to send them to see a marvelously entertaining, absolutely profound, great science-fiction film that's just come out. I am especially going to recommend it to Harlan Ellison, the author of the story on which *A Boy and His Dog* is based (he is a Jew, as I am), and the director of *A Boy and His Dog* (who is, I believe, Black).

The movie is called *The Triumph of the Will,* and it's about this great hero and chucklesome charmer called Adolf Hitler who had the perfect solution to all the ills of society.

He murdered *you,* boys.

N O T E S

This essay first appeared in *Frontiers*, Volume 1, no. 1 (Fall 1975).

1. The story is, to my mind, somewhat different from the film; no one in the story is totally sympathetic or totally evil, and in particular the events surrounding the two main characters' escape from the story's underground society—he's an intruder and she's a native, but both are misfits—are such as to preclude

choosing one character as morally better than the other. The story's point seems to be that both the societies, aboveground and underground, are rotten. Furthermore, the story is told from the male character's point of view, a technique that admits both his relative ignorance of the other people in the tale and his natural bias in favor of himself. Films do not have a narrator, and what is seen through the subjective point of view in the story becomes the objective truth of the film.

2. Samuel Delany, in correspondence, April 20, 1975.

3. Named so by the inhabitants. It appears to be located somewhere under the Pacific slope, which is now desert.

4. In *Women and Science Fiction: A Symposium,* to appear in *Khatru,* nos. 3 and 4 (Spring 1975). The symposium will be published as a booklet by Mirage Press sometime in 1976.

5. A good example of the gratuitous Heroine is the help and comfort accorded the two male characters by the lady of *Butch Cassidy;* Pauline Kael has made sufficient comment on her supposed motivations: spinsterhood, boredom, and being "at the bottom of the heap" as a pioneer schoolteacher out West (of all things!).

6. Shahriyar's attitude is possessive, due to the wound given his sense of property (adultery); Vic's attitude is self-defense. This may represent some kind of progress, but hardly the conscious kind.

7. Samuel Delany again, in *Women and Science Fiction: A Symposium.* He is one of the few male feminists I know who truly deserves the name, and he is a first-rate theoretical critic. His forthcoming novel, *Triton* (New York: Bantam, 1976), deals with male sexism, women as an oppressed class, and a genuinely nonsexist society.

Part Two

7

What Can a Heroine Do?
or Why Women Can't Write

*T*he following essay was written in 1971 and published in 1972 in Susan Koppelman's Images of Women in Fiction: Feminist Perspectives, *one of the earliest pioneering anthologies in a field that was later to blossom as the rose. Although the jargon common today in so much feminist literary criticism and even in queer literary criticism did not exist then (cheers! say I), we were aware of the same issues, and we wrote about them. I do not think that now I would conclude a manifesto like this one with praise of science fiction (it can be just as good or bad as anything and just as timid, clichéd, and dull), but at the time I was, I think, getting ready to write my own science fiction and was—without being explicitly aware of it—looking for a way out of the cultural deprivation described in the essay. That so many women like myself could actually read and enjoy (or watch and enjoy) the kind of white boy's fiction (Susan Koppelman's phrase) that all of us had spent our life reading, explicating, analyzing, and assuming to be Fiction itself is, I think, a tribute to the unselfishness and empathy of the human imagination. But how much more fun it is (not to mention enlightening) to see through the assumption . . . and change it. The essay was written in the years immediately following a three-day symposium on women, hosted by the (then) School of Home Econom-ics during the 1969–1970 intersession. No other college in Cornell University would touch the subject. The result was a ferment of talk (reflected in the attributions listed in the notes) that lasted for years. I went home feeling that the sky had fallen. One of the most immediate results was my understanding that "English literature" had been badly rigged, and out of that insight came this essay.*

1. Two strong women battle for supremacy in the early West.

2. A young girl in Minnesota finds her womanhood by killing a bear.

3. An English noblewoman, vacationing in Arcadia, falls in love with a beautiful, modest young shepherd. But duty calls, she must return to the court of Elizabeth I to wage war on Spain. Just in time the shepherd lad is revealed as the long-lost son of the Queen of a neighboring country; the lovers are united and our heroine carries off her husband-to-be lad-in-waiting to the King of England.

4. A phosphorescently doomed poetess sponges off her husband and drinks herself to death, thus alienating the community of Philistines and businesswomen who would have continued to give her lecture dates.

5. A handsome young man, quite virginal, is seduced by an older woman who has made a pact with the Devil to give her back her youth. When the woman becomes pregnant, she proudly announces the paternity of her child; this revelation so shames the young man that he goes quite insane, steals into the house where the baby is kept, murders it, and is taken to prison where—repentant and surrounded by angel voices—he dies.

6. Alexandra the Great.

7. A young man who unwisely puts success in business before his personal fulfillment loses his masculinity and ends up as a neurotic, lonely eunuch.

8. A beautiful, seductive boy whose narcissism and instinctive cunning hide the fact that he has no mind (and in fact, hardly any sentient consciousness) drives a succession of successful actresses, movie produceresses, cowgirls, and film directresses wild with desire. They rape him.

Authors do not make their plots up out of thin air, nor are the above pure inventions; every one of them is a story familiar to all of us.[1] What makes them look so odd—and so funny—is that in each case the sex of the protagonist has been changed (and, correspondingly, the sex of the other characters). The result is that these very familiar plots simply will not work. They are tales for heroes, not heroines, and one of the things that handicaps women writers in our—and every other—culture is that there are so very few stories in which women can figure as protagonists.

Culture is male.[2] This does not mean that every man in Western (or Eastern) society can do exactly as he pleases, or that every man creates the culture *solus,* or that every man is luckier or more privileged than every woman. What it does mean (among other things) is that the society we live in is a patriarchy. And patriarchies imagine or picture themselves from the male point of view. There is a female culture, but it is an underground, unofficial, minor culture, occupying a small corner of what we think of officially as possible human experience. Both men *and women* in our culture conceive the culture from a single point of view—the male.

Now, writers, as I have said, do not make up their stories out of whole cloth; they are pretty much restricted to the attitudes, the beliefs, the expectations, and, above all, the plots that are "in the air"—"plot" being what Aristotle called *mythos;* and in fact it is probably most accurate to call these plot-patterns *myths.* They are dramatic embodiments of what a culture believes to be true—or what it would like to be true—or what it is mortally afraid may be true. Novels, especially, depend upon what central action can be imagined as being performed by the protagonist (or protagonists)—i.e., what can a central character *do* in a book? An examination of English literature or Western literature reveals that of all the possible actions people can do in this fiction, very few can be done by women.

Our literature is not about women. It is not about women and men equally. It is by and about men.

But (you might object) aren't our books and our movies full of women? Isn't there a "love interest" or at least a sexual interest in every movie? What about Cleopatra? What about Juliet? What about Sophia Western, Clarissa Harlowe, Faye Greener, Greta Garbo, Pip's Estella, and the succession of love goddesses without whom film history would hardly exist? Our literature is full of women: bad women, good women, motherly women, bitchy women, faithful women, promiscuous women, beautiful women? Plain women?

Women who have no relations with men (as so many male characters in American literature have no relations with women)?

Oddly enough, no. If you look at the plots summarized at the beginning of this article, and turn them back to their original forms, you will find not women but images of women: modest maidens, wicked temptresses, pretty schoolmarms, beautiful bitches, faithful wives, and so on. They exist only in relation to the protagonist (who is male). Moreover, look at them carefully and you will see that they do not really exist at all—at their best they are depictions of the social roles women are supposed to play and often do play, but they are the public roles and not the private women;[3] at their worst they are gorgeous, Cloud-cuckooland fantasies about what men want, or hate, or fear.

How can women writers possibly use such myths?

In twentieth-century American literature there is a particularly fine example of these impossible "women," a figure who is beautiful, irresistible, ruthless but fascinating, fascinating because she is somehow cheap or contemptible, who (in her more passive form) destroys men by her indifference and who (when the male author is more afraid of her) destroys men actively, sometimes by shooting them. She is Jean Harlow, Daisy Faye, Faye Greener, Mrs. Macomber, and Deborah Rojack. She is the Bitch Goddess.

Now it is just as useless to ask why the Bitch Goddess is so bitchy as it is to ask why the Noble Savage is so noble. Neither "person" really exists. In existential terms they are both The Other and The Other does not have the kind of inner life or consciousness that you and I have. In fact, The Other has no mind at all. No man in his senses ever says to himself to *himself*: I acted nobly because I am a Noble Savage. His reasons are far more prosaic: I did what I did because I was afraid, or because I was ambitious, or because I wanted to provoke my father, or because I felt lonely, or because I needed money, and so on. Look for reasons like that to explain the conduct of the Bitch Goddess and you will not find them; there is no explanation in terms of human motivation or the woman's own inner life; she simply behaves the way she does because she is a bitch. Q.E.D. No Other ever has the motives that you and I have; the Other contains a mysterious *essence*, which causes it to behave as it does; in fact "it" is not a person at all, but a projected wish or fear.

The Bitch Goddess is not a person.

Virgin-victim Gretchen (see number five, above) is not a person. The faithful wife, the beautiful temptress, the seductive destroyer, the devouring momma, the healing Madonna—none of these are persons in the sense that a novel's protagonist must be a person, and none is of the slightest use as myth to the woman writer who wishes to write about a female protagonist.

Try, for example, to change the Bitch Goddess/Male Victim story into a woman's story—are we to simply change the sex of the characters and write about a male "bitch" and a female victim? The myth still works in male homosexual terms—Man and Cruel Youth—but the female equivalent is something quite different. Changing the sex of the protagonist completely alters the meaning of the tale. The story of Woman/Cruel Lover is the story of so many English ballads—you have the "false true lover" and the pregnant girl left either to mourn or to die, but you do not have—to indicate only some elements of the story—the Cruel Lover as the materially sumptuous but spiritually bankrupt spirit of our civilization, the essence of sex, the "soul" of our corrupt culture, a dramatization of the split between the degrading necessities of the flesh and the transcendence of world-cleaving Will. What you have instead, if the story is told about or by the woman, is a cautionary tale warning you not to break social rules—in short, a much more realistic story of social error or transgression leading to ostracism, poverty, or death. Moral: Get Married First.

No career woman, at least in literature, keeps in the back of her mind the glamorous figure of Daisy Faye, the beautiful, rich, indifferent boy she loved back in Cleveland when she was fighting for a career as a bootlegger. Reversing sexual roles in fiction may make good burlesque or good fantasy, but it is ludicrous in terms of serious literature. Culture is male. Our literary myths are for heroes, not heroines.

What can a heroine do?

What myths, what plots, what actions are available to a female protagonist?

Very few.

For example, it is impossible to write a conventional success story with a heroine, for success in male terms is failure for a woman, a "fact" movies, books, and television plays have been earnestly proving to us for decades. Nor is the hard-drinking, hard-fighting hero imagined as female, except as an amusing fluke—e.g., Bob Hope and Jane Russell in *The Paleface*. Nor can our heroine be the Romantic Poet Glamorously Doomed, nor the Oversensitive Artist Who Cannot Fulfill His Worldly Responsibilities (Emily Dickinson seems to fit the latter pattern pretty well, but she is always treated as The Spinster, an exclusively female— *and sexual*—role). Nor can a heroine be the Intellectual Born into a Philistine Small Town Who Escapes to the Big City—a female intellectual cannot escape her problems by fleeing to the big city; she is still a woman and Woman as Intellectual is not one of our success myths.

With one or two exceptions (which I will deal with later) all sub-literary genres are closed to the heroine; she cannot be a Mickey Spillane private eye, for example, nor can she be one of H. Rider Haggard's adventure-story Englishmen who discovers a Lost Princess in some imaginary corner of Africa. (She can be the Lost Princess, but a story written with the Princess herself as protagonist would resemble the chronicle of any other monarch and would hardly fit the female figure of Haggard's romances, who is—again—the Other.) The hero

whose success in business alienates him from his family is not at all in
the position of the heroine who "loses her femininity" by competing
with men—*he* is not desexed, but *she* is. The Crass Businessman genre
(minor, anyway) is predicated on the assumption that success is masculine and a good thing as long as you don't spend all your time at it; one
needs to spend the smaller part of one's life recognizing the claims of
personal relations and relaxation. For the heroine the conflict between
success and sexuality is itself the issue, and the duality is absolute. The
woman who becomes hard and unfeminine, who competes with men,
finally becomes—have we seen this figure before?—a Bitch. Again.

Women in twentieth-century American literature seem pretty much
limited to either Devourer/Bitches or Maiden/Victims. Perhaps male
authors have bad consciences.

So we come at last to the question of utmost importance to novelists—What will my protagonist(s) do? What central action can be the
core of the novel? I know of only one plot or myth that is genderless, and
in which heroines can figure equally with heroes; this is the Abused
Child story (I mean of the Dickensian variety) and indeed many
heroines do begin life as Sensitive, Mistreated Waifs. But such a pattern
can be used only while the heroine is still a child (as in the first part of
Jane Eyre). Patient Griselda, who also suffered and endured, was not a
Mistreated Child but the adult heroine of a peculiar kind of love story.
And here, of course, we come to the one occupation of a female
protagonist in literature, the one thing she can do, and by God she does
it and does it and does it, over and over and over again.

She is the protagonist of a Love Story.

The tone may range from grave to gay, from the tragedy of *Anna
Karenina* to the comedy of *Emma*, but the myth is always the same:
innumerable variants on Falling In Love, on courtship, on marriage, on
the failure of courtship and marriage. How She Got Married. How She
Did Not Get Married (always tragic). How She Fell In Love and Commit-
ted Adultery. How She Saved Her Marriage But Just Barely. How She
Loved a Vile Seducer And Eloped. How She Loved a Vile Seducer,
Eloped, And Died In Childbirth. As far as literature is concerned,
heroines are still restricted to one vice, one virtue, and one occupation.
In novels of Doris Lessing, an authoress concerned with a great many
other things besides love, the heroines still spend most of their energy
and time maintaining relations with their lovers (or marrying, or
divorcing, or failing to achieve orgasm, or achieving it, or worrying
about their sexuality, their men, their loves, and their love lives).

For female protagonists the Love Story includes not only personal relations as such, but *bildungsroman,* worldly success or worldly failure, career, the exposition of character, crucial learning experiences, the transition to adulthood, rebellion (usually adultery) and everything else. Only in the work of a few iconoclasts like George Bernard Shaw do you find protagonists like Vivie Warren, whose work means more to her than marriage, or Saint Joan, who has no "love life" at all. It is interesting that Martha Graham's dance version of Saint Joan's life turns the tale back into a Love Story, with Saint Michael (at one point, in the version I saw) inspiring Joan by walking astride her from head to foot, dragging his robe over her several times as she lies on her back on the stage floor.

How she lost him, how she got him, how she kept him, how she died for/with him. What else is there? A new pattern seems to have been developing in the last few years: authoresses who do not wish to write Love Stories may instead write about heroines whose main action is to go mad—but How She Went Crazy will also lose its charm in time. One cannot write *The Bell Jar,* or *Jane Eyre,* good as it is, forever.

A woman writer may, if she wishes, abandon female protagonists altogether and stick to male myths with male protagonists, but in so doing she falsifies herself and much of her own experience. Part of life is obviously common to both sexes—we all eat, we all get stomach-aches, and we all grow old and die—but a great deal of life is not shared by men and women. A woman who refuses to write about women ignores the whole experience of the female culture (a very different one from the official, male culture), all her specifically erotic experiences, and a good deal of her own history. She falsifies her position both artistically and humanly: she is an artist creating a world in which persons of her kind cannot be artists, a consciousness central to itself creating a world in which women have no consciousness, a successful person creating a world in which persons like herself cannot be successes. She is a Self trying to pretend that she is a different Self, one for whom her own self is Other.

If a female writer does not use the two, possibly three, myths available to a she-writer, she must drop the culture's myths altogether. Is this in itself a bad thing? Perhaps what we need here is a digression on the artistic advantages of working with myths, i.e., material that has passed through other hands, that is not raw-brand-new.

The insistence that authors make up their own plots is a recent development in literature; Milton certainly did not do it. Even today, with novelty at such a premium in all the arts, very little is written that is not—at bottom—common property. It's a commonplace that bad writers imitate and great writers steal. Even an iconoclast like Shaw "stole" his plots wholesale, sometimes from melodrama, sometimes from history, sometimes from his friends.[4] Ibsen owes a debt to Scribe, Dickens to theatre melodrama, James to other fiction of his own time— nothing flowers without a history. Something that has been worked on by others in the same culture, something that is "in the air" provides a writer with material that has been distilled, dramatized, stylized, and above all, clarified. A developed myth has its own form, its own structure, its own expectations and values, its own cues-to-nudge-the-reader. When so much of the basic work has already been done, the artist may either give the myth its final realization or stand it on its head, but in any case what he or she does will be neither tentative nor crude and it will not take forever; it can simply be done well. For example, the very pattern of dramatic construction that we take as natural, the idea that a story ought to have a beginning, a middle, and an end, that one ought to be led to something called a "climax" by something called "suspense" or "dramatic tension," is in itself an Occidental myth— Western artists, therefore, do not have to invent this pattern for themselves.

Hemingway, whom we call a realist, spent his whole working life capitalizing on the dramatic lucidity possible to an artist who works with developed myths. The Bitch Goddess did not appear full-blown in "The Short and Happy Life of Francis Macomber"—one can find her in Fitzgerald—or Hawthorne, to name an earlier writer—or Max Beerbohm, whose *Zuleika Dobson* is certainly a Bitch Goddess, though a less serious one than her American cousins. "Macomber" is the ultimate fictional refinement out of the mess and bother of real life. Beyond it lies only nightmare (Faye Greener in West's *Day of the Locust*) or the half-mad, satiric fantastications Mailer uses to get a little more mileage out of an almost exhausted pattern.

"Macomber" is perfectly clear, as is most of Hemingway's work. Nobody can fail to understand that Mrs. Macomber is a Bitch, that the White Hunter is a Real Man, and that Macomber is a Failed Man. The dramatic conflict is extremely clear, very vehement, and completely expectable. The characters are simple, emotionally charged, and larger-than-life. *Therefore* the fine details of the story can be polished to that point of high gloss where everything—weather, gestures, laconic conversation, terrain, equipment, clothing—is all of meaning. (Compare "Macomber" with *Robinson Crusoe,* for example; Defoe is much less sure from moment to moment of what he wants to say or what it means.) One cannot stop to ask why Mrs. Macomber is so bitchy—she's just a Bitch, that's all—or why killing a large animal will restore Macomber's manhood—everybody knows it will—or why the Bitch cannot tolerate a Real Man—these things are already explained by the myth.

But this kind of larger-than-life simplicity and clarity is not accessible to the woman writer unless she remains within the limits of the Love Story. Again: what can a heroine do?

There seem to me to be two alternatives open to the woman author who no longer cares about How She Fell in Love or How She Went Mad. These are (1) lyricism, and (2) life.

By "lyricism" I do not mean purple passages or baroque raptures; I mean a particular principle of structure.

If *the narrative mode* (what Aristotle called "epic") concerns itself with *events* connected by the *chronological order* in which they occur, and *the dramatic mode* with *voluntary human actions* which are connected both by *chronology and causation,* then the principle of construction I wish to call *lyric* consists of *the organization of discrete elements* (images, events, scenes, passages, words, what-have-you) *around an unspoken thematic or emotional center.* The lyric mode exists without chronology or causation; its principle of connection is *associative.* Of course, no piece of writing can exist purely in any one mode, but we can certainly talk of the predominance of one element, perhaps two.) In this sense of "lyric" Virginia Woolf is a lyric novelist—in fact she has been criticized in just those terms, i.e., "nothing happens" in her books. A writer who employs the lyric structure is setting various images, events, scenes, or memories to circling round an unspoken, invisible center. The invisible center is what the novel or poem is about; it is also unsayable in available dramatic or narrative terms. That is, there is no action possible to the central character and no series of events that will embody in clear, unequivocal, immediately graspable terms what the artist means. Or perhaps there is no action or series of events that will embody this "center" at all. Unable to use the myths of male culture (and apparently unwilling to spend her life writing love stories), Woolf uses a structure that is basically non-narrative. Hence the lack of "plot," the repetitiousness, the gathering-up of the novels into moments of epiphany, the denseness of the writing, the indirection. There is nothing the female characters can *do*—except exist, except think, except feel. And critics (mostly male) employ the usual vocabulary of denigration: these novels lack important events; they are hermetically sealed; they are too full of sensibility; they are trivial; they lack action; they are feminine.[5]

Not every female author is equipped with the kind of command of language that allows (or insists upon) lyric construction; nor does every woman writer want to employ this mode. The alternative is to take as one's model (and structural principle) not male myth but the structure of one's own experience. So we have George Eliot's (or Doris Lessing's) "lack of structure," the obviously tacked-on ending of *Mill on the Floss*; we have Brontë's spasmodic, jerky world of *Villette,* with a structure modeled on the heroine's (and probably author's) real situation. How to write a novel about a person to whom nothing happens? A person to whom nothing but a love story is *supposed* to happen? A person inhabiting a world in which the only reality is frustration or endurance—or these plus an unbearably mystifying confusion? The movement of *Villette* is not the perfect curve of *Jane Eyre* (a classic version of the female Love Story)—it is a blocked jabbing, a constant thwarting; it is the protagonist's constantly frustrated will to action, and her alternately losing and regaining her perception of her own situation.[6] There are vestiges of Gothic mystery and there is a Love Story, but the Gothic mysteries turn out to be fakery, and the Love Story (which occupies only the last quarter of the book) vanishes strangely and abruptly on the last page but one. In cases like these the usual epithet is "formless," sometimes qualified by "inexperienced"—obviously life is not like *that,* life is not messy and indecisive; we know what life (and novels) are from Aristotle—who wrote about plays—and male novelists who employ male myths created by a culture that imagines itself from the male point of view. The task of art—we know—is to give form to life, i.e., the very forms that women writers cannot use. So it's clear that women can't write, that they swing wildly from lyricism to messiness once they abandon the cozy realms of the Love Story. And successes within the Love Story (which is itself imagined out of genuine female experience) are not important because the Love Story is not important. It is a commonplace of criticism that only the male myths are valid or interesting; a book as fine (and well-structured) as *Jane Eyre* fails *even to be seen* by many critics because it grows out of experiences—events, fantasies, wishes, fears, daydreams, images of self—entirely foreign to their own. As critics are usually unwilling to believe their lack of understanding to be their own fault, it becomes the fault of the book. Of the author. Of all women writers.

Western European (and North American) culture is not only male in its point of view; it is also Western European. For example, it is not Russian. Nineteenth-century Russian fiction can be criticized in much the same terms as women's fiction: "pointless" or "plotless" narratives stuffed with strange minutiae, and not obeying the accepted laws of dramatic development, lyrical in the wrong places, condensed in the wrong places, overly emotional, obsessed with things we do not understand, perhaps even grotesque. Here we have other outsiders who are trying, in less than a century, to assimilate European myths, producing strange Russian hybrids (*A King Lear of the Steppe, Lady Macbeth of Mtensk*), trying to work with literary patterns that do not suit their experiences and were not developed with them in mind. What do we get? Oddly digressive Pushkin. "Formless" Dostoevsky. (Colin Wilson has called Dostoevsky's novels "sofa pillows stuffed with lumps of concrete.") Sprawling, glacial, all-inclusive Tolstoy. And of course "lyrical" Chekhov, whose magnificent plays are called plotless to this very day.

There is an even more vivid—and tragic—example: what is an American Black writer to make of our accepted myths? For example, what is she or he to make of the still-current myth (so prominent in *King Lear*) that Suffering Brings Wisdom? This is an old, still-used plot. Does suffering bring wisdom to *The Invisible Man?* When critics do not find what they expect, they cannot imagine that the fault may lie in their expectations. I know of a case in which the critics (white and female) decided after long, nervous discussion that Baldwin was "not really a novelist" but that Orwell was.

Critical bias aside, all artists are going to be in the soup pretty soon, if they aren't already. As a culture, we are coasting on the tag-ends of our assumptions about a lot of things (including the difference between fiction and "propaganda"). As novelists we are working with myths that have been so repeated, so triply-distilled, that they are almost exhausted. Outside of commercial genres—which can remain petrified and profitable indefinitely—how many more incarnations of the Bitch Goddess can anybody stand? How many more shoot-'em-ups on Main Street? How many more young men with identity problems?

The lack of workable myths in literature, of acceptable dramatizations of what our experience means, harms much more than art itself. We do not only choose or reject works of art on the basis of these myths;

we interpret our own experience in terms of them. Worse still, we actually perceive what happens to us in the mythic terms our culture provides.

The problem of "outsider" artists is the whole problem of what to do with unlabeled, disallowed, disavowed, not-even-consciously-perceived experience, experience which cannot be spoken about because it has no embodiment in existing art. Is one to create new forms wholesale— which is practically impossible? Or turn to old ones, like Blake's Elizabethan lyrics and Yeats's Noh plays? Or "trivial," trashy genres, like Austen's ladies' fiction?

Make something unspeakable and you make it unthinkable.

Hence the lyric structure, which can deal with the unspeakable and unembodiable as its thematic center, or the realistic piling up of detail which may (if you are lucky) eventually *add up to* the unspeakable, undramatizable, unembodiable action-one-cannot-name.

Outsiders' writing is always in critical jeopardy. Insiders know perfectly well that art ought to match their ideas of it. Thus insiders notice instantly that the material of *Jane Eyre* is trivial and the emotionality untenable, even though the structure is perfect. George Eliot, whose point of view is neither peccable nor ridiculously romantic, does not know what fate to award her heroines and thus falsifies her endings.[7] Genet, whose lyrical mode of construction goes unnoticed, is meaningless and disgusting. Kafka, who can "translate" (in his short stories only) certain common myths into fantastic or extreme versions of themselves, does not have Tolstoy's wide grasp of life. (That Tolstoy lacks Kafka's understanding of alienation is sometimes commented upon, but that does not count, of course.) Ellison is passionate but shapeless and crude. Austen, whose sense of form cannot be impugned, is not passionate enough. Blake is inexplicable. Baldwin lacks Shakespeare's gift of reconciliation. And so on and so on.

But outsiders' problems are real enough, and we will all be facing them quite soon, as the nature of human experience on this planet changes radically—unless, of course, we all end up in the Second Paleolithic, in which case we will have to set about re-creating the myths of the First Paleolithic.

Perhaps one place to look for myths that escape from the equation Culture = Male is in those genres that already employ plots not limited to one sex—i.e., myths that have nothing to do with our accepted gender roles. There seem to me to be three places one can look:

(1) Detective stories, as long as these are limited to genuine intellectual puzzles ("crime fiction" is a different genre). Women write these; women read them; women even figure in them as protagonists. The slang name, "whodunit," neatly describes the myth: Finding Out Who Did It (whatever "It" is).

(2) Supernatural fiction, often written by women (Englishwomen, at least) during the nineteenth and the first part of the twentieth centuries. These are about the intrusion of something strange, dangerous, *and not natural* into one's familiar world. What to do? In the face of the supernatural, knowledge and character become crucial; the accepted gender roles are often irrelevant. After all, potting a twelve-foot-tall batrachian with a kerosene lamp is an act that can be accomplished by either sex, and both heroes and heroines can be expected to feel sufficient horror to make the story interesting. (My example is from a short story by H. P. Lovecraft and August Derleth.) However, much of this genre is as severely limited as the detective story—they both seem to have reached the point of decadence where writers are restricted to the re-enactment of ritual gestures. Moreover, supernatural fiction often relies on very threadbare social/sexual roles, e.g., aristocratic Hungarian counts drinking the blood of beautiful, innocent Englishwomen. (Vampire stories use the myths of an old-fashioned eroticism; other tales trade on the fear of certain animals like snakes or spiders, disgust at "mold" or "slime," human aggression taking the form of literal bestiality (lycanthropy), guilt without intention, the *lex talionis*, severe retribution for venial faults, supernatural "contamination"—in short, what a psychoanalyst would call the "archaic" contents of the mind.)

(3) Science fiction, which seems to me to provide a broad pattern for human myths, even if the specifically futuristic or fantastic elements are subtracted. (I except the kind of male adventure story called Space Opera, which may be part of science fiction as a genre, but is not innate in science fiction as a mode.) The myths of science fiction run along the lines of exploring a new world conceptually (not necessarily physically), creating needed physical or social machinery, assessing the consequences of technological or other changes, and so on. These are not stories about men *qua* Man and women *qua* Woman; they are myths of human intelligence and human adaptability. They not only ignore gender roles but—at least theoretically—are not culture-bound. Some of the most fascinating characters in science fiction are not human. True, the attempt to break through culture-binding may mean only that we

transform old myths like Black Is Bad/ White Is Good (or the Heart of Darkness myth) into new asininities like Giant Ants Are Bad/People Are Good. At least the latter can be subscribed to by all human races and sexes. (Giant ants might feel differently.)

Darko Suvin of the University of Montreal has suggested that science fiction patterns often resemble those of medieval literature.[8] I think the resemblance lies in that medieval literature so often dramatizes not people's social roles but the life of the soul; hence we find the following patterns in both science fiction and medieval tales:

I find myself in a new world, not knowing who I am or where I came from. I must find these out, and also find out the rules of the world I inhabit. (the journey of the soul from birth to death)

Society needs something. I/we must find it. (the quest)

We are miserable because our way of life is out of whack. We must find out what is wrong and change it. (the drama of sin and salvation)

Science fiction, political fiction, parable, allegory, exemplum—all carry a heavier intellectual freight (and self-consciously so) than we are used to. All are didactic. All imply that human problems are collective, as well as individual, and take these problems to be spiritual, social, perceptive, or cognitive—not the fictionally sex-linked problems of success, competition, "castration," education, love, or even personal identity, with which we are all so very familiar. I would go even farther and say that science fiction, political fiction (when successful), and the modes (if not the content) of much medieval fiction all provide myths for dealing with the kinds of experiences we are actually having now, instead of the literary myths we have inherited, which only tell us about the kinds of experiences we think we ought to be having.

This may sound like the old cliché about the Soviet plot of Girl Meets Boy Meets Tractor. And why not? Our current fictional myths leave vast areas of human experience unexplored: work for one, genuine religious experience for another, and above all the lives of the traditionally voiceless, the majority of whom are women. (When I speak of the "traditionally voiceless" I am not pleading for descriptions of their lives—we have had plenty of that by very vocal writers—what I am talking about are fictional myths *growing out of their lives* and told by themselves for themselves.)

Forty years ago those Americans who read books at all read a good deal of fiction. Nowadays such persons read popularized anthropology, psychology, history, and philosophy. Perhaps current fictional myths no longer tell the truth about any of us.

When things are changing, those who know least about them—in the usual terms—may make the best job of them. There is so much to be written about, and here we are with nothing but the rags and tatters of what used to mean something. One thing I think we must know—that our traditional gender roles will not be part of the future, as long as the future is not a second Stone Age. Our traditions, our books, our morals, our manners, our films, our speech, our economic organization, everything we have inherited, tell us that to be a Man one must bend Nature to one's will—or other men. This means ecological catastrophe in the first instance and war in the second. To be a Woman, one must be first and foremost a mother and after that a server of Men; this means overpopulation and the perpetuation of the first two disasters. The roles are deadly. The myths that serve them are fatal.

Women cannot write—using the old myths.

But using new ones—?

NOTES

1. Number three is a version of *The Winter's Tale;* number four, the life of Dylan Thomas, as popularly believed; number five, the story of Faust and Marguerite; and number eight, a lightly modified version of part of *The Day of the Locust.* The others need no explanation.

2. I am indebted to Linda Finlay of the Philosophy Department of Ithaca College for this formulation and the short discussion that follows it.

3. I am indebted to Mary Uhl for the observation that Dickens's women are accurately portrayed as long as they are in public (where Dickens himself had many opportunities to observe real women) but entirely unconvincing when they are alone or with other women only.

4. An overstatement. The plot of *Widowers' Houses* was a gift.

5. Mary Ellmann, *Thinking about Women* (New York: Harcourt, Brace & World, 1968). See the chapter on "Phallic Criticism."

6. Kate Millett, *Sexual Politics* (New York: Doubleday and Company, 1970), pp. 140–47.

7. In comparison with the organic integrity of Dickens's, I suppose.

8. In conversation and in a paper unpublished as of this writing.

Somebody's Trying to Kill Me and I Think It's My Husband: The Modern Gothic

ow do essays get written? Well, there we were in the early 1970s and this weird feminist writer was buy-ing groceries. And she noticed that there were books *in the supermarket—new thing. So she picked one up and read the back cover and said to herself, "My God, it's* Jane Eyre *all over again." So she called an editor friend (the late Terry Carr, who was then working for Ace Books in New York) and said, "Hey, what are these things?" and he told her and sent her a bunch of them. Then I (yeah) went through and underlined everything, saying "Well!" and wrote the essay. And later got a letter from one Edna Stumpf, who wrote a very good article on Gothics, which was published in* Colloquy *(1974), and another in the* Philadelphia Metropolitan *(1974) and we wrote each other about it (one of the great pleasures of the 1970s was finding so many other women doing such fine work on so many things), and then they took the Modern Gothics off the market, and something called Bodice Busters took their place. As Stumpf wrote, "you can never just write off a genre," and much that was sold under the "Gothic" label was reprints of writers like Shirley Jackson. I have found many copies of Isak Dinesen's wartime romance,* The Angelic Avengers, *sold among the Gothics and once—I vow—*Jane Eyre *promoted as "in the tradition of* Rebecca. *" (I am not sure but it's too good a story to leave out.) Stumpf credits editor Jerry Gross at Ace Books with the decision to promote the Gothic Romances in the United States—"all the excitement promised by marriage and career and seldom provided by either." Exactly. "A chance at the loot," says Stumpf. Carr agreed and provided the title.*

What fiction do American women read? God knows.

When pressed, She mumbles about ladies' slicks, fashion magazines, best-sellers, *et al.*, but if you pray earnestly and add that you want to know about fiction read exclusively by women, She finally relents and hands you three genres: confession magazines, nurse novels—and the Modern Gothic.

Anywhere paperback books are sold you will find volumes whose covers seem to have evolved from the same clone: the color scheme is predominantly blue or green, there is a frightened young woman in the foreground, in the background is a mansion, castle, or large house with one window lit, there is usually a moon, a storm, or both, and whatever is occurring is occurring at night.

These are the Modern Gothics. If you look inside the covers, you will find that the stories bear no resemblance to the literary definition of "Gothic." They are not related to the works of Monk Lewis or Mrs. Radcliffe, whose real descendants are known today as Horror Stories. The Modern Gothics resemble, instead, a crossbreed of *Jane Eyre* and Daphne du Maurier's *Rebecca*, and most of them advertise themselves as "in the du Maurier tradition," "in the Gothic tradition of *Rebecca*," and so on. According to Terry Carr, an ex-editor of Ace Books, their history in this country:

> . . . began in the early '60s. . . . But books like this have always been written, especially in England, where they were called romances . . . from about 1950 on; they were never big things over there, just a steady small market. It started at Ace . . . [which] bought some novels by Victoria Holt and Phyllis A. Whitney. They sold like anything. . . . [Ace] continued and expanded the Gothic list here, including especially buying rights to early novels by Dorothy Eden and Anne Maybury . . . both now big-selling writers.[1]

Modern Gothics, unlike nurse novels and the confession magazines, are read by middle-class women or women with middle-class aspirations, and for some reason the books written by Englishwomen have remained the most popular, at least at Ace. In 1970 I asked Terry Carr to provide me with some of their longest-selling and best-selling books; according to Mr. Carr they are "representative of the higher ranges of the field" and all seem to be reprints of earlier works (one as early as 1953).[2]

Also according to Mr. Carr:

> The basic appeal . . . is to women who marry guys and then begin to discover that their husbands are strangers . . . so there's a simultaneous

attraction/repulsion, love/fear going on. Most of the "pure" Gothics tend
to have a handsome, magnetic suitor or husband who may or may not be
a lunatic and/or murderer. . . . it remained for U.S. women to discover
they were frightened of their husbands.[3]

Here are the elements:

To a large, lonely, usually brooding, *House* (always named) comes a
Heroine who is young, orphaned, unloved, and lonely. She is shy and
inexperienced. She is attractive, sometimes even beautiful, but she does
not know it. Sometimes she has spent ten years nursing a dying mother;
sometimes she has (or has had) a wicked stepmother, a bad aunt, a
demanding and selfish mother (usually deceased by the time the story
opens) or an ineffectual, absent, or (usually) long-dead father, whom
she loves. The House is set in exotic, vivid and/or isolated *Country.* The
Heroine, whose reaction to people and places tends toward emotional
extremes, either loves or hates the House, usually both.

After a short prologue, this latter-day Jane Eyre forms a personal or
professional connection with an older man, a dark, magnetic, powerful
brooding, sardonic *Super-Male,* who treats her brusquely, derogates her,
scolds her, and otherwise shows anger or contempt for her. The Heroine
is vehemently attracted to him and usually just as vehemently repelled
or frightened—she is not sure of her feelings for him, his feelings for her,
and whether he (1) loves her, (2) hates her, (3) is using her, or (4) is
trying to kill her.

The Super-Male is not the Heroine's only worry. In the emotionally
tangled and darkly mysterious "family" set up in our House are hints of
the presence of *The Other Woman* who is at the same time the Heroine's
double and her opposite—very often the Other Woman is the Super-
Male's present wife or dead first wife; sometimes she is the Heroine's
missing cousin, or the woman the Super-Male appears to prefer to the
Heroine. The Other Woman is (or was) beautiful, worldly, glamorous,
immoral, flirtatious, irresponsible, and openly sexual. She may even
have been (especially if she is dead) adulterous, promiscuous, hard-
hearted, immoral, criminal, or even insane. If the Other Woman is dead,
the Heroine believes she cannot possibly measure up to the Super-
Male's memories. Her only consolation is to be kind, womanly, and
good, both to the Super-Male and (sometimes) to a *Young Girl,* often the
daughter of the Super-Male and his first wife. The Young Girl (if she
exists) is often being corrupted or neglected by the Other Woman (if
alive); in one case there is a Young Man (son of the Super-Male) who is

being neglected by his father. One Heroine has a younger sister, one a missing younger cousin (who is combined, in this case, with the Other Woman). The Heroine's task, in all cases, is to win the confidence of this young person, and convince her/him of her/his personal worth. If the person is a girl, this is done by buying her clothes.

In addition to the Heroine's other troubles, she gradually becomes aware that somewhere in the tangle of oppressive family relationships going on in the House exists a *Buried Ominous Secret,* always connected with the Other Woman and the Super-Male (whatever relation they happen to bear to one another in the novel). The Super-Male is at the center of the Secret; when she unravels the mystery about him (does he love her or is he a threat to her?) she will simultaneously get to the bottom of the Secret. Then the plot thickens.

Her happiness with the Super-Male is threatened.

Her life is threatened (sometimes several times).

Minor characters are killed.

Storms take place.

There is much ad-libbing of *Ominous Dialogue.*

And so on.

At some point—either because of other people's detective work or by chance—the *Secret Is Revealed.* It turns out to be immoral and usually criminal activity on somebody's part, centering around money and/or the Other Woman's ghastly (usually sexual) misbehavior. The six Gothics considered here employ the following Secrets: jewel smuggling, theft, and murder (*Columbella*); murder, impersonation, drug addiction, and intended blackmail (*I Am Gabriella!*); an insane mass murderer (*The Least of All Evils*); another insane mass murderer with a clothing fetish (*The Brooding Lake*); diamond theft and murder (*Nightingale at Noon*); murder and illegitimacy (*The Dark Shore*).

Coincidental with the revelation of the secret is the untangling of the Heroine's emotions—she is enabled to "sort out" the Super-Male (who is invariably guiltless, although he may have appeared otherwise) from everyone else, especially from a character I call the *Shadow-Male,* a man invariably represented as gentle, protective, responsible, quiet, humorous, tender, and calm. The Shadow-Male either wants to marry the Heroine or has—in one case—actually married her. This personage is revealed as a murderer and (twice) as an insane mass murderer of a whole string of previous wives. There are variations; sometimes two roles may be combined in one character, although in general it is astonishing how constant the elements remain. In one novel the Other Woman is a vanished cousin, in another an old school-friend; her villainy may range from crime to mere irresponsible flirting (which is, however, regarded very seriously by the novel). Sometimes the Other Woman is a minor character (*Nightingale*) but in every case the Other Woman is more worldly than the Heroine, more beautiful, and more openly sexual. The Other Woman is *immoral*. The Heroine is *good*. The Super-Male's competence ranges from judo (*I Am Gabriella!*) through a sardonic cynicism that always puts the heroine in the wrong (*Brooding Lake*) to the less tangible attributes of being a Canadian and a millionaire (*Dark Shore*). Although scenery ranges from exotic New Zealand to exotic northern Ontario (the novelist is English in this case), the House, the Heroine, the Super-Male, the Other Woman, the Ominous Dialogue, the Secret, and the Untangling are the staples of every one of these books.

Certainly the Gothic is worth some study as a genre written for women and by women; even the paperback editors who choose manuscripts are women, although their employers are men. In some ways these stories resemble the tales in the true-confession magazines. In a recent issue of the *Journal of Popular Culture*,[4] David Sonenschein has analyzed seventy-three such tales and drawn the following conclusions:

> The main "other" was usually a male . . . older . . . either the narrator's spouse or a previously unmarried single male. (p. 404)
> . . . the feeling of uneasiness underlying each story. (p. 405)
> . . . we also get a sense of some of the risks that simply being a woman may entail . . . (p. 402)
> Relationships are volatile, hostile, and even dangerous; in contrast to male-oriented erotica, it is *trauma, rather than sex, which is "just around the corner."* (p. 405; italics mine)

It is tempting to view the Gothics, with their perpetual Houses (in which, typically, the Heroine has a large emotional investment), their families or quasi-families, their triangles of young girl, older man, and older man's first wife, as a family romance. But the books are not love stories *per se*, nor are they usually concerned (except peripherally) with erotica; the culminations of the books' plots almost always involve attempted murder—the Heroine's being chased along a cliff by someone who wants to kill her (*Shore*), being locked into a room by a madman who earlier almost drowned her (*Lake*), being pushed over a cliff and later shut in a wall to suffocate (*Evils*), or being sexually attacked after

having been exposed to diamond thieves, believing that literally everyone in her family is trying to kill her and her younger sister, *and* finding
out that her adored blind father is a criminal *and* has pretended
blindness for years, *and* believing that the man she loves is a murderer
(*Nightingale*). As the Heroine of this one says, with some justification, all
is "a swirling vortex of confusion." (p. 136) Other Heroines are trapped
alive in caves, almost murdered, and flung against a wall by a "tall figure
enveloped in a hooded robe" (*Columbella,* p. 204), and almost run over
by a car. The commonest emotion in these novels is fear—but they are
not horror stories; the plot always involves murder (but they are not
stories of detection), and, while the heroine is rewarded with love
(without having caused it, deserved it, revealed it, or even asked for it),
there is no tracing of the growing bond between the lovers. The Modern
Gothic is episodic; the heroine does nothing except worry; any necessary detective work is done by other persons, often the Super-Male.
Whenever the Heroine acts (as in *Lake*), she bungles things badly. There
is a period of terror, repeated sinister incidents, ominous dialogue
spoken by various characters, and then the sudden revelation of who's
who and what's what. In terms of ordinary pulp technique, these novels
are formless. Even so, they obey extraordinarily rigid rules. There must
be a reason for these rules.

I would propose that the Modern Gothics are a direct expression of
the traditional feminine situation (at least a middle-class feminine
situation) and that they provide precisely the kind of escape reading a
middle-class believer in the feminine mystique needs, without involving elements that either go beyond the feminine mystique or would be
considered immoral in its terms.

For example, the Heroines are either on vacation, on a honeymoon,
or too young to do housework. If they spend ten years caring for an
invalid mother, the book begins just after the mother's death; if they
have married (and they marry wealthy men), the book begins with the
honeymoon; if they are poor, they are too young to cook and clean, and
the poverty is only temporary, anyway. They always find themselves in
exotic locales (the Virgin Islands, the French wine country, New Zealand, the Camargue, etc.). They are essentially idle women. *Nonetheless,*
whenever the occasion arises—and it is always an interpersonal occasion, never a housewife's vocational one—they have a keen eye for
food, clothes, interior decor, and middle-class hobbies (e.g., collecting
seashells, weaving, or collecting china). The novels contain some ex-

traordinarily impersonal descriptions of meals, rooms, and dresses, e.g., in *Columbella*, "crisp native pastry filled with cocoanut" (p. 84), "the cool sharp tang of lime" (p. 57), and "coffee that had been perfectly brewed" (p. 37). In *Evils* the Heroine is treated to "airy little shells bursting with a delectable and spicy hot mixture" and later "golden wheat cakes and amber syrup, the crisp bacon and plump sausages, the chilled melon with gobbets of fat, whiskery raspberries clinging to it" (pp. 30, 56). In *Nightingale* the Heroine's family is too poor to buy good food (tea is "four pieces of bread and butter on a plate and one plain biscuit," p. 24). When the family can afford steak, strawberries, and whiskey, however, it is not the Heroine who does the cooking. Even *Lake*, in which the Heroine hardly eats from arrival to attempted murder, contains the following housewifely diagnosis: "a plate of thick porridge, some toast which had already absorbed its butter and gone cold, and a cup of weak tea. Dundas had said that his daughter was a good housekeeper . . . did he really always have this kind of fare?" (pp. 98–99). If the above sound like ladies'-magazine articles, that is because they are; the vacationing protagonists of *Gabriella* subsist on hotel food, which allows the author to produce the following:

> *fricasée de poulet* with puffed out, golden potatoes and apples crystallized whole in sugar (p. 23) . . . jellied eggs with mushroom mayonnaise, *canard à l'Orange* . . . with a few drops of orange curaçao liqueur sprinkled on the slim slices of duck (p. 61) . . . river trout and then . . . purple grapes folded into a kind of *crepe suzette* (p. 137) . . . a long, crusty French loaf, some cheese, half a pound of wild strawberries, some cream, and a bottle of wine. (p. 160)

The oddity of such technical expertise in the midst of terror, romance, and murder is not that of the great detective's playing the violin; it is merely off-key. Consider:

> I played with a beautiful *omelette fines herbes* and managed a *soufflé*. But all the time I was conscious of the slow approaching shadow of menace and our unrealized part in it. (*Gabriella*, p. 107)

Even more relentless is the author's eye for female dress. For example, in *Columbella* no female character ever appears without careful note being taken of her clothes:

> . . . a long-legged, graceful teenager in blue Bermudas and a nautical white middy with a blue tie that matched her shorts (p. 37) . . . She wore pale green capris that stretched tightly over her girlishly flat stomach,

rounded hips, and hugged her thighs neatly with scarcely a wrinkle. A bit
of sleeveless white piqué tied in a bow between her breasts. (p. 40) . . . I
was dressed suitably enough for town in a blue denim skirt with deep side
pockets that I found handy, and a blue cotton overblouse. (p. 130) . . . The
princess lines of the linen dress were subtle and set off the rounding of her
slim young figure. From a circular neckline the dress curved gently at the
waist and flared to wider gores at the hemline. (p. 134)

Dark, given more to the mystification possible with a mosaic of
different points of view, still notes the various amenities of dressing,
bathing, and noting what other women look like:

> She wore a plain linen dress, narrow and simple, without sleeves. (p.
> 117) . . . She didn't dare stop to re-apply her lipstick. There was just time
> to brush her hair lightly into position. (p. 73) . . . "Dinner will be in about
> half an hour and the water's hot if you should want a bath." (p. 71) Her
> mouth was slim beneath pale lipstick, the lashes of her beautiful eyes too
> long and dark to be entirely natural, her fair hair swept upwards simply
> in a soft, full curve. (p. 42) . . . there was even more of a rush to have a
> bath, change, and start cooking for a dinner-party . . . she had just finished
> changing . . . (p. 16)

Clothes in *Lake* play too much part as clues (a pair of shoes, a red
nightgown, an old wedding dress) to be considered inorganic to the plot,
but here, as in *Columbella*—the Heroine shows her goodness of heart by
helping a young girl uncertain of her looks to dress up for a party;
moreover, an evening memorable mostly for ghostly voices and a
tropical storm includes "the pale blue satin nightdress . . . spread on the
bed for her." The young lady of the house then enters in "a turquoise-
colored velvet dressing-gown, her hair brushed down on her shoulders"
(pp. 80–81). Later another girl chooses a green coat, "lingering over it
longingly because it was the one she wanted most, but its price was too
high" (pp. 146–47).

Despite the poverty of the family in *Nightingale,* we still have one
character's brief scarlet shorts and snow-white sun top (p. 45), and a
dress the Heroine borrows for a party, "an inch too short and a couple of
inches too wide, but the color, a muted aquamarine, and its straight,
deceptively simple cut, had overcome my scruples" (p. 80). She too
dresses up the Younger Girl (her half-sister) for the same party (p. 81).
If nothing else, she can reflect that she has "put on Lucille's blue dress,
brushed my hair, and piled it high" (p. 102). Let a well-dressed stranger
appear and the author immediately reverts to type:

The shoes came first, black sandals with stiletto heels . . . slender legs, then an oyster[5] skirt, tight about slim thighs. . . . Indigo-black, bouffant hair caressed her cheeks and forehead. (p. 84)

In *Gabriella* we have:

A crocodile handbag, chocolate-brown gloves (p. 5) . . . an expensive suit of dark green raw silk, with a clip made of crimson stones shaped like an eagle, in her lapel (p. 18) . . . a pleated cream nylon dress and gold slippers (p. 82) . . . a jewel case with a soft zip top (p. 112) . . . a white silk dressing gown I had bought in Paris (p. 154) . . . a blouse . . . of hand blocked silk with green stars and moss roses . . . tan gloves (p. 118) . . . a tomato silk housecoat (p. 216)

When the Heroines of Gothics are not noticing other people's clothes (or their own) or being thrown off cliffs, or losing the men they love, they often spend their time thus:

I unpacked quickly, showered, and put on a cool dress of black linen with touches of lime green. I slid my feet into high heeled black sandals and fixed gold star earrings in my ears. (*Gabriella*, p. 14)

Or they note interior décor:

It was a room of austere beauty, comfortably but sparsely furnished to effect that cool, uncluttered look so necessary in the tropics. The ceiling was lofty, giving one a sense of space and grandeur. From the center of an elaborate plaster rosette hung a crystal chandelier, while carved plaster cornices decorated the far reaches of the ceiling. . . . Most of the furniture had that simplicity of design which belongs to the countries of Scandinavia, fluid of line and built of smooth, light woods . . . near the foot of the curving stairs in one corner of the room hung a Chagall print of red poppies and green leaves in a tall vase. . . . (*Columbella*, p. 28)

We went through regal double doors and into a beautifully furnished room. Soft blues and greens in brocade and silk glowed in the single light from a standard lamp near the dressing table. In the fine old four-poster . . . (*Gabriella*, p. 197)

I gasped involuntarily, barely noting the wide floor-boards, the sparsely utilitarian nature of the ancient furniture. My eyes went up the walls, from the simple panelled dado, about five feet in height, to plain plastered walls penetrated by stone mullioned windows that rose to a magnificent hammerbeam roof, enriched with elaborately scrolled Renaissance detail. (*Evils*, p. 14)[6]

. . . the big brick fireplace with the dead remnants of a fire, the low chairs and the large low settee covered with bright cushions, the pictures on the walls strategically placed to hide the discolored spots in the wallpaper, the large white rug in front of the fireplace, the gilt-framed mirror that gave back a dusky lamplit reflection of the room. The illusion of luxury . . . (*Lake*, p. 9)

These novels are written for women who cook, who decorate their own houses, who shop for clothing for themselves and their children—in short, for housewives. But the Heroines—who toil not, neither do they spin—know and utilize (sometimes bizarrely) the occupation of their readers. "Occupation: Housewife" is simultaneously avoided, glamorized, and vindicated.

Modern Gothics are surprisingly conservative about sexuality, yet the sexuality that does appear in them is of a very prurient kind. Heroines are impeccably virginal (until married) and can even criticize a friend for being "mercenary" for accepting an expensive gift from a man she didn't intend to marry (*Lake*, p. 65). The Heroine who does so (this is in 1953) does not get beyond the "intense charm" (presumably erotic) of the moment when she buries her face against the Super-Male's tweed jacket, only a few pages from the endpapers. The eighteen-year-old Heroine of *Nightingale*, whose family relationships are so complicated that it takes the reader ninety-four pages to unravel them, nonetheless feels "a leap of nausea that left me sick and shivering" at a stranger's mention of her father's mistress, although "[t]he discovery of Hugo's relationship with Dodie was years old" (p. 40). The mad villainess of *Columbella*, eventually revealed to be a jewel thief and smuggler, is criticized in the strongest terms possible; she has not only stolen a bracelet as a school-girl, but:

> "I'm afraid she's merely graduated into taking more important property. Such as other women's husbands. And she's wildly extravagant."
> (p. 17)

When the villainess of this book actually threatens to run the Heroine over with her (the villainess's) car, it is clear that she has passed beyond the pale not only of good manners or decency but of simple sanity. It would be interesting to compare criminal acts in Modern Gothics with criminal acts in modern crime stories and weigh the relative horribleness of the acts themselves in the two genres. The Heroine of *Shore* (1965) explains how she met the Super-Male:

> ". . . the next day he phoned and asked to take me out to a concert. I went. I shouldn't have because of Frank" [her escort] "but then . . . well, Frank and I weren't engaged, and I—I wanted to see Jon again." (p. 127)

Jon does not, however, as a Super-Male and an older, once-married man, impose such a stringent moral code upon himself:

> ... he ... would have despised himself for having a woman within days of his coming marriage. It would have meant nothing, of course, but he would still have felt ashamed afterwards, full of guilt because he had done something which would hurt Sarah if she knew ... (p. 41)

This is as far as the Gothic seems to go in spotting even a Super-Male's purity. But for the married Heroine, sex becomes an entirely different matter. No longer bodiless and yet within the code of romance—the result is a very strange fusion of prurience and exaltation, i.e., the confusion of values described by Firestone (sex = personal worth) combines with the "religious" eroticism Greer notes in romance stories.[7] Thus the Super-Male's erection becomes the criterion of the Heroine's self-approval—and yet the whole business must somehow take place within the limits of the romantically sexless. As long as everything is kept vague, we are all right; thus in *Shore* the Heroine's wedding night (blissful, by convention) is rendered thus:

> ... when he stooped his head to kiss her on the mouth at last, she was conscious first and foremost of the peace in her heart before her world whirled into the fire. (p. 66)
>
> When he bent over her a moment later,* and she felt the love in every line of his frame flow into hers, she knew he would never again belong to anyone else except her. (p. 159)

We are one stage away from the non-kiss at the end of *Lake*. Still romantic, though perhaps a little dithery about what turns out to be only necking, is this passage in *Nightingale:*

> His free hand was on my throat, his lips pressed on mine, hunger and passion in them. That was all I wanted. It was mine, and I took it greedily. ... When he pushed me from him, it was to demand in a voice that was harsh and breathless: "Melly ... do you know what you're doing?" "Yes," I said. (p. 115)

What she is doing is not clear, but the married are under no such constraint. The Heroine of *Evils*, who gasps, "horrified," when she thinks her young cousin may have been rolling in the hay with a boyfriend (p. 100), nonetheless describes her own romantic interludes thus:

> And seeing Mark, wide-shouldered and narrow-hipped, standing back turned to me, I knew the past didn't matter. ... Only the present and the joyful future ahead of us, were real. ... he turned, our eyes met, and then

---

*The Super-Male is *never* short.

he came to me swiftly, catching my hands up in his until finally we were close, one body, as our lips met. . . . "You're cold, darling," Mark whispered. "I know how to warm you." (p. 34)

He caught my shoulders, "Don't you know there have been lots of people killed in the tub?" he cried. But *his stern manner faded as his hands slipped.* A trio on my nearby portable radio sang of love and passion while my dripping arms held Mark close. . . . (p. 49; italics mine)

The more sexuality gets into these scenes, the more discordant becomes the insisted-upon romantic aura. Quintessentially:

He shoved his cup into my unoccupied hand . . . and solemnly untied my other shoulder strap. I sat giggling like a school girl, each hand burdened with a teacup, my nightgown rumpled about my waist. . . . I didn't care about the unexpected trip. Not any more. *Only the moment mattered and the moment became increasingly beautiful and memorable.* (*Evils,* p. 56; italics mine)

Of course the Heroine's husband in *Evils* is not a Super-Male but a Shadow-Male; perhaps something is wrong with his technique. The Heroine of *Gabriella* is married to a genuine Super-Male, a lean, dark, tigerish judo expert who snaps at her in brusque, masculine fashion throughout the book. He is as romantic as any, sometimes:

Then he lay, his arms around me, his body against mine. "Karen! Oh, Karen!" Above us, at last, a bird broke into song. (p. 161)

Nick pulled me to my feet and drew me close. I could feel the hard beat of his heart as he kissed me; the strength that seemed to pour from his body into me. My blood raced, quivering, as he held me more tightly . . . it was the immediate passion of his love for me. . . . There was [*sic*] just Nick and I caught up in our lovely desire for each other. . . . (p. 136)

But there is always the possibility that desire is only desire:

I lay close against Nick, strengthened by contact with that hard body. He put an arm under my shoulder and turned to me. But the problem Maxine had set us still lay heavily on my mind. "Tomorrow," I began, "we must—" "Let's leave tomorrow." I lifted my head and saw his eyes in the semi-moonlight. They were alight and alive. . . . Nick had raced through France for this—for *me!* (*Gabriella,* p. 41)

The birds had better sing like mad, or even a Gothic Heroine might wonder whether "this" and "me" are always identical.

Most striking about these novels is the combination of intrigue, crime, and danger with the Heroine's complete passivity. Unconscious foci of intrigue, passion, and crime, these young women (none of whom is over thirty) wander through all sorts of threatening forces of which they are intuitively, but never intellectually, aware. Most of all, *they are of extraordinary interest to everyone*—even though they are ill-educated, ordinary, characterless and usually very hazily delineated, being (as one might suspect) a stand-in for the reader. Sometimes Heroines are very beautiful (although they don't know it) or heiresses (which they don't know, either) or possess some piece of information about the Secret (which they are incapable of interpreting). Their connection with the action of the novel is always passive; they are focal points for tremendous emotion, and sometimes tremendous struggle, simply because they exist. At her most enterprising, a Heroine may (like the Heroine of *Lake,* whose relation to the Super-Male is the nearest to equality of any shown in the books) recklessly toss about pieces of information that expose her to being drowned or pushed off a glacier. Alice (the Heroine) tries to solve the mystery of her school-friend's disappearance and does, in fact, unearth certain clues (which she misinterprets). But the Super-Male is the real detective of the piece. Even when faced with a miserably unhappy young girl, a Byronic Super-Male, and a mad, greedy, criminal Other Woman, the Heroine of *Columbella* can only display her womanly goodness and try to win the young girl's confidence by appreciating her drawings and buying clothes for her. As the Super-Male declares to her:

> "Perhaps now I've found a new source of sanity—and honesty and decency. Things I thought I'd lost for good during the last few years. A source that isn't a place but a person—you!" (p. 125)

Here too the Heroine finds clues to a murder—after the important persons in the book have already done so. In the midst of family relationships that would baffle Oedipus, the Heroine of *Nightingale* does—nothing at all. The Heroine of *Evils* has amnesia—she also bungles about looking for clues that the Super-Male already knows. The detective in *Gabriella* is the Heroine's husband, whom she trails perpetually—again, there are several attempts of hers which either come to nothing or land both of them in trouble (which he fixes).

In the face of this really extraordinary passivity—for if the protagonist of a novel is not active in some way, what on earth is the novel about?—it is tempting to see these books as genuine family romances, with the Heroine as the child who is trying desperately to understand what the grown-ups are up to, a description that fits *Nightingale* perfectly. At their best Heroines merely stand (passively) for love, goodness, redemption, and innocence. They are special and precious because they are Heroines. And that is that.

I have called the Gothics episodic, but that does not mean that the books have no central theme. The emotional center is that "handsome, magnetic suitor or husband who may or may not be a lunatic or murderer"[8]—i.e., it is the Heroine's ambivalence toward the Super-Male that provides the internal dramatic action of the book. The Heroine of *Lake*, for example, does not know if her former sweetheart is the murderer of her friend or not (two other men may be, one of whom—the Shadow-Male—starts out by being dependable and gentle and ends up with "tiger's" eyes and a collection of the clothing of the women he has killed). The Heroines of the Gothics are constantly reading men's expressions—in *Lake*, the Heroine's eyes meet the Shadow-Male's and:

> They gave an illusion of warmth because his mouth was tender. But really they were empty windows, waiting for that dark person to get out. (p. 130)

Another Heroine reacts to the Super-Male she will eventually love in this way:

> I didn't like the man. He seemed to cast off vibrations that put the entire room in a subtle turmoil. And seeing how Priss looked at him, I was afraid for her. . . . He looked as though he was gluttonous. . . . He would ruthlessly take what he wanted. . . . (*Evils*, p. 4)

Similarly the Heroine of *Dark* begins by mistrusting her husband-to-be (things get worse):

> . . . she felt the other familiar feeling of nervousness. . . . She loved Jon and knew perfectly well that she wanted to marry him, but he remained an enigma to her at times and it was this strange unknown quality which made her nervous. She called it the Distant Mood. (p. 58)

Even when the Super-Male is not a physical danger, sexuality itself provides enough threat (or that and the possibility of being disliked or harshly judged). The Heroine of *Columbella* notes the hero's "straight, rather harsh mouth," his "grim" smile, while his "cold, judicial" comments about her outrage her. Even worse is his "disturbing presence" and "alarming gentleness." As she finally decides:

> I knew why I was uncomfortable with this man. It was because a current seemed to spring into being between us when we were together—a strangely disturbing current composed of a mixture of antagonism and attraction, perhaps in equal parts, so that I did not truly know which force was the stronger. (p. 75)

We know, of course. But when the man the Heroine loves is trying to pin a murder rap on her father, the conflict becomes much worse; almost all of *Nightingale* is composed of tremendous emotional oscillations undergone by the Heroine, at one moment believing that the Super-Male loves her, at the next that he is only using her as a source of information, at one moment that her father (another Super-Male) is not a murderer, at the next moment that he is:

> I couldn't be sure. I wasn't sure of anything: whether Charles Lewis was a sane man who, for four years, had been driven by a trigger-hot passion for revenge, or whether he was a madman obsessed with a phantom nightmare. (p. 49)
> For a few seconds I was caught in a rush of hope that seemed as if it would bring me to the surface of the dark waters in which I'd been drowning. . . . I felt the smile break on my face, and then I saw his eyes watching me, narrowed and fiercely intent. And suddenly the offer he'd made seemed machine-tooled in treachery. I felt as sick as if I'd just escaped from stepping off a precipice. (p. 152)

It is no wonder that, after ten chapters of such ups and downs, the Heroine remarks, "I had the eerie sense that I'd lost the power to evaluate the simplest emotion" (p. 100). When the most important person in your life is your man, when you can't trust him (and can't trust anyone else), it becomes exceedingly important to "read" other people's faces and feelings. This is what most real women spend their time doing; therefore the novels not only portray them doing it, but glamorize and justify what in real life is usually necessary, but boring. In one way the Gothics are a kind of justified paranoia: people *are* planning awful things about you; you *can't* trust your husband (lover, fiancé); everybody's motives *are* devious and complex, only the *most* severe vigilance will enable you to snatch any happiness from the jaws of destruction. In addition to hurricanes, madness, attempted murder, skeletons falling out of cupboards, diamond smuggling, theft, drug addiction, impersonation, and voodoo, the Modern Gothics make extensive use of what I would like to call Over-Subtle Emotions, a "denseness" of interpersonal texture that is, at its most complex, simply baffling, and at its simplest, bathetic. For example:

> It was a long, slow glance, guarded, half-apprehensive, half-exultant, that passed between Ariadne and Jager. In a way I couldn't understand, much less explain, it possessed an element of familiarity, as if they were not strangers . . . but in some way allies. Vague, unresolved suspicions coursed through my mind and got nowhere. (*Nightingale,* p. 88)

Suddenly my mind cleared and I knew. Something fell sharply and shockingly into place. "Last night, up by the château, Johnnie threatened me. . . . From—from a distance it could have seemed that he and I—" "Were in the throes of a love affair? Well?" "And Goliath saw us. He can't have heard what we said. . . . But don't you see?—if he thought I was having an affair with Johnnie and you had found out—?" "Sweet heaven. You mean Johnnie was killed because he probably knew the truth behind Maxine's impersonation? And we were sent down here to find the body—?" "And be implicated! If Goliath told the police what you had seen, you could be regarded as the jealous husband." "Yes," he said slowly. "I see what you mean." (*Gabriella*, p. 142)

For some reason his seemingly idle discussion made me as uncomfortable as did the shell. It was as if his talk of good and evil, his reference to flaws of beauty . . . the man spoke in symbols that carried a deeper significance—perhaps as a hint of warning, meant for me? Or was I being fanciful again? . . . Again I had that uneasy sense of a deeper meaning and knew that he watched me intently with his pale, luminous eyes. (*Columbella*, p. 49)

Where was Ada now? If she was downstairs . . . I would ask her. Plump and plain, I would ask her about Mrs. Engleford. Ask her about the skeleton in the garden. Ask her what *really* happened to Mark's mother. Because somehow I knew Ada had the answers, if only she would divulge them. (*Evils*, p. 125)*

It was curious how the pupils of his eyes expanded as she watched. Like a startled cat's, like a tiger's. Why should Katharine think his eyes were like a tiger's when the rest of his face was so bland and genial? (*Lake*, p. 114)

He was near Rivers now, but he could not see him properly. The man had not moved at all, and the odd half-light was such that Jon could not see the expression in his eyes. He was aware of a sharp pang of uneasiness, a violent twist of memory, which was so vivid that it hurt, and then an inexplicable wave of compassion. (*Dark*, p. 35)**

The Heroine is such a virtuosa at this sacred version of everyday gossip that she knows even more than the mere fact that danger exists; she knows it *has all happened before.* The eeriest plot element in these books is the constant "doubling" of the Heroine—she is always in some fashion a "stand-in" for someone else, usually someone who has been killed. This someone is often the Other Woman (who is or was wicked), but it may be (as in *Columbella*) the Other Woman's daughter, who is being destroyed by her mother just as the Heroine's confidence has been

---

*There is no reason for the Heroine to believe this at this time. She turns out to be correct, however.

**This is not explained for almost 100 pages.

undermined by *her* selfish, vain, attractive, irresponsible mother. In *Gabriella,* the Heroine's cousin is the double—she vanishes and in her turn impersonates a girl who has been killed. In *Evils* the Heroine has several predecessors, including her kind aunt, who was better to her than her own (bad) mother.[9] The Heroine of *Nightingale* has a younger half-sister, who suffers with her, and for whom she is very concerned, and a "mother" in the person of her father's mistress, irritable, aging, selfish, and vain, whom she starts out hating and learns—gradually—to pity. In two of the books, *The Dark Shore* and *The Brooding Lake,* the doubling is so explicit that the characters themselves comment on it. Sarah, the Heroine of *Dark,* has married a man whose first wife was murdered; not only does Sarah constantly compare her inadequate self to the dead Sophia (even their names are similar), but several characters remark that the two women look alike. Eventually the doubling goes so far that Sarah is warned:

> "It's all happening again, can't you realize that? It's all happening again—we're all here at Clougy . . . and you've been assigned Sophia's role." (p. 132)

In *Lake,* in order to resolve the mystery of a friend's disappearance, the Heroine begins to "impersonate" her friend, Camilla. She dresses like her, wears her "mantle—of trouble or danger, or whatever other complicated atmosphere it carried" (p. 46). She writes to the absent Camilla (who has in reality been murdered):

> Why were things getting dangerous? Seriously, you must tell me because it looks as if your mantle (and a troubled one) has fallen on me and I shall have to cope with these three indignant swains. (p. 48)

So far does the doubling go that Alice is proposed to by the man who was going to marry Camilla. Alice accepts:

> The queer thing was that she didn't know whether she was being herself or Camilla as she answered, "You're so kind. How can one refuse you?" She was almost sure she would never have answered a proposal of marriage in those words. It was as if Camilla had spoken them. (pp. 117–18)

The doubling goes even farther; the fiancé (a Shadow-Male) almost drowns Alice as he drowned Camilla; then the theme escalates into the grotesque as Alice is trapped in a room containing two wax dummies dressed in wedding gowns belonging to the madman's earlier-murdered brides, while a minor character in wig and Camilla's squirrel coat impersonates the dead woman outside in order to terrify the madman into a confession.

What does this doubling mean? Is it that every woman fears the same man and undergoes the same fate? Is it an echo of the family romance in which Heroine plays daughter, the Super-Male is father, and the Other Woman/First Wife plays mother? Are the two identical?

The Super-Male may indeed be a disguised version of the Heroine's (wished-for) father. He is older than the Heroine, more intelligent, taller, stronger, cooler-headed, richer, and of higher social position. And the Heroine is certainly presented as a kind of child; she is precious to the Super-Male simply because she exists (like a child) and she is never independent. She has no profession in any of the books except for *Lake*, where there is some unconvincing background about her having been part of a traveling acting company. This particular Heroine is a bit snippy about her "independence," which soon collapses into an engagement with a madman and rescue by the Super-Male, who remarks:

> "Little Alice! . . . Silly little lamb! You see, it took the sheep in wolf's clothing to rescue you." (p. 186)

The Gothics obviously envision the relation between Super-Male and Heroine as neither abnormal nor unusual, but as the standard, even ideal, relation between men and women.

Independent women or women who have professions occur as follows:

> *Lake.* An (ugly) young girl who will be a doctor and a sympathetic but stereotyped spinster teacher (a minor character).
> *Gabriella.* A middle-aged woman, owner of a château in the French wine country, who is a drug addict and dependent on her manager. She commits suicide.
> *Evils.* A deaf, ugly, deformed, middle-aged woman who makes an elaborate hobby of weaving. She finds happiness with a deaf, ugly, deformed, middle-aged man.
> *Dark.* The Super-Male's beautiful, brilliant, illegitimate half-sister, who loves music and plays the piano. She is in telepathic communion with the Super-Male, but unfortunately she depends on him (in this strange, telepathic way) while he can get along without her. She becomes promiscuous, then frigid, and goes into retreat in a convent, after taking upon herself the blame for the death of the Super-Male's first wife.

The Modern Gothics are neither love stories nor stories of women-as-victims. *They are adventure stories with passive protagonists.*

After all, what can a Heroine do?

1. She can be attached to a man.
2. She can be unknowingly involved in some family/criminal secret.
3. She can be threatened by murder.
4. She can be saved.
5. She can be uncertain of her man's real intentions toward her.
6. She can guess at his and other people's intentions or emotions.

And she can do all this within the confines of the feminine mystique.[10]

Since the Gothics are escape reading, they leave out women's real, tedious, everyday work—childbearing, child-rearing, and housekeeping. These have no place in the Gothics; only the prelude to them (the capture of, or relations with a man) is allowed, and that is very much glamorized.

The problem of the female protagonist in literature is still with us. If we assume that everything outside the domestic affections and the capture of a husband is masculine, we have a protagonist who cannot:

1. Solve an intellectual puzzle (whodunit or science fiction)
2. Build a career (the success story of the bright boy from the provinces)
3. Travel and have adventures (the adventurer has adventures; the adventuress has sexual adventures only)
4. Carry out a political conspiracy
5. Head a religious movement
6. Grow up and form her character (the *bildungsroman* matters only if the protagonist is going to be someone in particular or do something; the Heroine's destiny is always the same—marriage. No matter what sort of character she has, she will not become a philosopher, artist, general, or politician).

The Love Story is—for women—*bildungsroman,* success, failure, education, and the only adventure possible, all in one.[11]

As I said before, the Modern Gothic is an accurate reflection of the feminine mystique and a glamorized version of the lives many women do live. The apparent sado-masochism of the genre is partly an artifact of the narrative premise—that the Heroine must remain passive (or incompetent) in situations that call overwhelmingly for activity and decision; therefore any connection the Heroine has with the situation must be that of Victim. Part may be "feminine masochism" but even where the sado-masochistic overtones are strongest (as in *Nightingale*) the Heroine's suffering is the principal action of the story *because it is the only action she can perform.* The Modern Gothic, as a genre, is a means of enabling a conventionally feminine Heroine to have adventures at all. It may also be a way that conventionally feminine readers can see their own situation—dependent and limited as it is—validated, justified, and glamorized up to the hilt, without turning Heroines either into active persons or into sexually adventurous persons, both of whom violate the morality of conventional femininity.

1. Housework, etc. is banned. I'm on holiday.

2. I'm upper-middle-class, not lower-middle-class.

3. My upward mobility is achieved through marriage.

4. I'm a good girl—modest, not too pretty but quite pretty, not too rich but rich enough, womanly, loving, dependent, and somehow "average" (even though I am uniquely precious).

5. The Super-Male *really exists* (all evidence to the contrary).

6. *He really loves me,* even though I am not strikingly beautiful, brilliant, talented, famous, or rich. I do not see why he loves me, but he does. He may appear to treat me badly or brusquely; still, he loves me.

7. I do nothing. I do not have to do anything. Merely because I exist, violent emotions and acts spring into being.

8. I am rewarded for being good. Aggressively sexual, beautiful, worldly women are wicked and are punished accordingly. Men don't *really* like them.

9. I have intense emotional relations with places—houses, weather, nature. (Scenery-painting is often the best-written part of these books.)

10. I have pretty, romantic clothes (but not sexy or flamboyant ones). Clothes really are very important.

11. *My sexual value is my personal value and is respected by all except villains and villainesses.* Men's desire is a testimony to my personal, individual worth. I have no character, interests, or achievements, but those who do come to a bad end (if female).

12. I am a virtuosa at interpreting faces and feelings. This ability is not "wasted" on the everyday drudgery of infants' needs or husbands' grumpiness—it is vital in saving my life and the happiness of all about me. (Even if I come to the wrong conclusions, my intense over-reading of everyone else's emotions is still justified.)

13. If I don't know what's happening, that's all right; my man does.

14. I can't save myself, but my man will do it for me.

15. Life with the Super-Male is *really satisfying.*

TRANSLATION

1. If I must be passive, I might as well make the most of it.

2. If I must suffer, I will do so spectacularly and luxuriously.

3. I really want to get in on those jewel-smugglings and murders and exciting stuff.

4. If my man treats me badly, that's because he's masculine, not because he's bad. There are bad men and good men; the problem is simply telling which is which. There are bad women and good women; I'm not a bad (read: sexual, aggressive) woman.

5. Conventionally masculine men are good men (even if they treat me badly) and conventionally feminine women are good women. This makes behavior very easy to judge. It also validates conventional sex roles.

6. I am bored and therefore make much of trifles.

7. *Something* is trying to hurt me and tear me down—but I don't know what it is. I suspect it's my man, or men in general, but that's an unthinkable thought.

8. Nobody respects me except when they're sexually attracted to me or benefiting from my selflessness (read: treating me as a convenience). CONCLUSION: I will go read another Gothic novel.

APPENDIX (VERBATIM)

SUPER-MALES

Lake. . . . his peculiar, mocking merriment (p. 12) . . . his tilted eyes narrowed with laughter (p. 20) . . . brows drawn down in one of their storms of impatience. . . . Suddenly she knew what the three men were like: the squat, alert-eyed keas; and they, trembling Katharine, Margaretta in her hot childish dress, and herself, foolish and impulsive, and not very brave, were the defenseless lambs.

Gabriella. Nick could move swiftly as a tiger when he chose. (p. 39) . . . all my explanations did not check Nick's anger with me. (p. 106) . . . he had that whippy look of a healthy, disciplined man. His hair was very dark and his mouth long and mobile. . . . (pp. 6–7) I knew that light of determination on Nick's face only too well. . . . (p. 47) . . . Nick was a master of judo. . . . (p. 71)

Columbella. . . . in his late thirties, forceful, tall, rather overwhelming. The sort of man who used to alarm me at first glance. (p. 20) He was a ruggedly built man and I had to look up at him, for all that I am fairly tall. His eyes were a very dark brown, with heavy brows slashed above, emphasizing the angular, marked bone structure of his face. His hair was as dark as his eyes . . . there were deep creases running down each cheek. . . . (p. 21)

Evils. . . . a great hulking fellow . . . stood there facing us belligerently (p. 39) . . . almost sneered now, looking down at his own huge feet in their dirty sneakers . . . he flexed a wicked looking hand. . . . He looked as though he was gluttonous in all his appetites. He would ruthlessly take what he wanted. . . . (p. 41) . . . his blatant masculine appeal . . . (p. 85) Here was a man who could juggle women with bravado. . . . (p. 96) . . . brazen effrontery . . . (p. 97) I could feel it. The sheer, unrestrained animal vitality . . . this brutal, stalking, almost savage man . . . this turbulent avalanche of raw sexuality. (p. 98)

Dark. Those eyes. You looked at those eyes and suddenly you forgot . . . tiresome things which might be bothering you . . . as soon as he touched those piano keys you had to listen. He moved or laughed or made some trivial gesture with his hands and you had to watch him. (pp. 17–18) Jon always got what he wanted. . . . He wanted a woman and he had only to crook his little finger; he wanted money and it flowed gently into his bank account; he wanted you to be a friend for some reason and you became a friend. . . . (p. 22) Jon ordered the meal, chose the wines, and tossed both menu and wine-list on one side. (p. 61) . . . Jon spent two hours making involved transatlantic telephone calls and dealing with urgent business commitments. . . . (p. 66)

Nightingale. . . . arrogance, an aura of dark metaled pride . . . (p. 12) . . . tall, dominating . . . (p. 13) The same face, lean and dark under a high proud brow, from which near black hair rose in a thick crest. Grey eyes, cooly assured under vigorous brows. (p. 34) Like lightning fury struck his face. His voice had the cutting quality of fine-honed steel. (p. 39)

HEROINES

Columbella. Often enough my mother had told me that I was born to spinsterhood and the service of others. (p. 9) . . . all my natural instincts to aid, to support, to defend . . . (p. 27) . . . an enveloping loneliness crept upon me . . . (p. 34) His cheek was against my hair and I could hear without astonishment the words he was whispering. Soft endearments they were—words like "dearest" and "beloved.". . . (p. 124)

Gabriella. I wear glasses. . . . Heaven knew, when I first had to wear them I was plunged in gloom. . . . I have the large family mouth and short nose, like Maxine's, only hers has beautiful, flaring nostrils that give her face a defiant, dramatic look. (p. 13) ". . . they and their ancestors were born in captivity. Karen, dear, some things are better that way. *You* are!" (p. 185) He suffered the same reaction as a mother who, fearful for her child's safety, slaps him when he comes home unharmed. (p. 106)

Evils. I was twenty-four. Until Mark came into my life, I'd never—not ever, not even once—had a date with anyone. "It's not that you're unattractive," . . . my only close friend said to me once. "You've got a lovely, calm face and those nice neat features. Why, you've even got a goshdarn good figure, if you'd ever wear anything decent . . . you're so quiet and withdrawn no one ever gets a chance to know the real you. . . ." (p. 7) . . . when I was twelve, Mother sent me . . . to a summer camp (mostly, I realized even then, to get rid of me) . . . (p. 8) "Yes, Tracy, you were bound to a selfish, bad-tempered woman. . . . She'd sent you to the basement for a bottle of wine. . . . You . . . dropped the bottle, and . . . your mother struck you, turned on her heel, and left you to stumble and fall backwards down the basement steps." (p. 87) ". . . I knew from the first minute I saw you that I'd never let anything happen to you, hurt you, ever. You're the sweetest little thing, so serious, so . . ." (p. 118)

Lake. ". . . my father would have to sandwich me somewhere between the wing structure and the undercarriage of his new plane and I'd simply be an embarrassment to my mother . . ." (p. 14) Obedience to his direction . . . had become a habit. (p. 15) Alice felt immeasurably forlorn. . . . (p. 65) She felt so alone, so unwanted. (p. 82) . . . his eyes had grown hard and contemptuous. (p. 109) If one hadn't known him so well . . . one would not have been conscious of the subtle undertones of contempt. . . . (p. 123) "Oh, my darling! My poor little Alice! My wonderful crazy brave little fool!" (p. 189)

Nightingale. . . . my appalling innocence . . . (p. 12) I'd outlived the stage of being embarrassed by our hermit life. (p. 17) I was as lonely as Emma. She begged money from strangers. I begged love! (p. 44) I tried to imagine what it was like to be on a holiday, with gay outlandish clothes and money in your pocket. I couldn't. (p. 104) "Melly, don't you believe in your own beauty? Aren't you used to men appreciating it?" I shook my head. . . . (p. 107)

Dark. . . . her clear, unsophisticated view of life and the naive trust which he loved so much. (p. 40) Sarah's voice, very clear and gentle . . . (p. 45) Sarah, beneath her gay smile and excited eyes, felt very small and lost and nervous . . . she was caught in a violent wave of homesickness and the tears refused to be checked. (p. 65) She felt ashamed, inadequate, tongue-tied. (p. 72) . . . unwanted tears pricking at the back of her eyes . . . everything became blurred and she could no longer see. (p. 73) "I love you," he said . . . and his voice was unsteady . . . "I love love love you and you're never never going to have to go through anything like this again." (p. 158)

SHADOW-MALES (all murderers)

Evils. . . . gentleness . . . tender consideration of everything I did and said, the quiet humor . . . a composite of all the elegant English stars I've seen on the late night movies . . . the mild blue eyes were crinkled, the long lashes tangled, the handsome narrow face alight with amusement. (p. 13) . . . the gently sensual mouth . . . (p. 35)

Lake. . . . a round, fresh-colored, surprisingly young face beneath gray hair. The man's eyes were light-colored and smiling. He looked very pleasant . . . his solid figure and firm handshake . . . (p. 19) He gave an impression of kindness and common sense and utter dependability. (p. 35) . . . his mild, old-fashioned way. (p. 37) He smelled pleasantly of shaving soap. (p. 102)

Dark. . . . a tall man, unobtrusively good-looking, with quiet eyes and a strong mouth . . . as she echoed the greeting, the lawyer's cautious scrutiny faded into a more formal appraisal and there was warmth in his eyes and kindness in the set of his mouth. (p. 112) He could cope with the situation. . . . He's spent his life dealing with other people's problems. (p. 126) He didn't hurry . . . calmly, with a slight air of irritability. (p. 134) . . . forced to fight back in self-defense. (p. 135)

THE OTHER WOMAN

Columbella. I had never seen anyone so arrestingly alive. . . . (p. 25) . . . she was a figure of such loveliness in her red and gold . . . (p. 62) She was a dangerous woman . . . and evil—evil! (p. 82) She could move like a panther . . . a spoiled child . . . dangerous . . . with the ready cruelty of a child. . . . (p. 94) . . . her strange warped nature . . . (p. 119) . . . the only man she had never owned . . . she would never stop until she destroyed him completely. (p. 138)

Nightingale. . . . a sophisticated young woman who wore her model clothes as if she'd been born to them . . . her gestures were free and graceful like those of a princess in undisputed possession of every horizon in sight. (p. 84)

Lake. Camilla had thrived on emotional complications. To her they were the spice of life. (p. 15) ". . . she has the whole male population at her feet. . . . How does she do it?" (p. 13) She was a scamp. . . . One always ended by reluctantly forgiving her for her outrageous behavior.

... (p. 117) Camilla's eyes had that sleepy adoring expression whenever she wished. (p. 24) ... the flighty little witch ... (p. 26) She was attractive ... but silly, easily flattered, unreliable, and ... extraordinarily deceitful. (p. 32)

Gabriella. ... rich russet hair swathed round a small, imperious head; greenish-bronze eyes that even in a "still" photograph seemed restless; a wayward mouth, full and a little pouting, and a figure so slim it fooled you into thinking she was fragile. (p. 8) She had been brought up to believe that what money could buy would always be hers. She was not trained for work and had an innate dislike for discipline. ... But her assets were enormous. Not only was she beautiful, but she had that female magnetism that is the strongest weapon any woman can have in life. ... (p. 11) ... always headstrong and impulsive ... (p. 198)

Dark. ... the voluptuous indolence, the languid movements, the dreadful stifled boredom never far below the lush surface ... (p. 23) ... how much she loved life, even if life merely consisted of living ... far from the glamor of London. (p. 63) She behaved like a spoiled child. ... She flirted at her weekend parties and made Jon go through hell ... with her tantrums and whims. ... She flaunted her infidelity. ... (p. 103) She wore skintight black slacks and ... a halter—some kind of flimsy arrangement which left her midriff bare and exposed an indecent amount of cleavage. (p. 104)

NOTES

This essay first appeared in the *Journal of Popular Culture*

1. In correspondence, November 18, 1970.

2. I was attracted to the field by happening to pick up Fawcett's *Columbella,* by Phyllis Whitney, 1966. The books provided by Ace are: *Nightingale at Noon,* by Margaret Summerton, 1962; *The Least of All Evils,* by Helen Arvonen, 1970; *The Dark Shore,* by Susan Howatch, 1965; *I Am Gabriella!* by Anne Maybury, 1962; *The Brooding Lake,* by Dorothy Eden, 1953 (by Macdonald & Co., Ltd.).

3. In correspondence, November 18, 1970.

4. *Journal of Popular Culture,* Fall 1970, IV, 2, "Love and Sex in the Romance Magazines," by David Sonenschein, Department of Anthropology, University of Texas, Austin, Texas.

5. Typically the word "oyster" here is a fashion-magazine word, not that of an artist or observer. The entire vocabulary is similar—"tomato silk," "chocolate-brown," "lime green," "that cool, uncluttered look," and so on. The descriptions are magazine-ish set pieces, not part of the story. Typically, the "Chagall print" (above) does not lead to a discussion of art or the owner's taste or anything else.

6. How ancient any of this can really be is in question, since the house—Engleford Court—is situated in Northern Ontario. The heroine asks no questions, however. Picturesqueness—not authenticity—is what counts.

7. Shulamith Firestone, *The Dialectic of Sex*, Morrow, 1970, pp. 167–70; Germaine Greer, *The Female Eunuch*, McGraw-Hill, 1970, pp. 167–85.

8. Terry Carr, q.v.

9. She keeps having *déjà vu* experiences—recollections via her aunt's letters that seem to be intended to warn her of her aunt's fate—in fact, she remembers the letters only in time to avoid being murdered by the same man (her own husband).

10. Carol Carr, science-fiction writer, calls the helplessness of the Gothic Heroines "the feminine version of conquering the environment." In conversation, December 1970.

11. Consider the recent film about Isadora Duncan, which concentrated on her sex life, not on her dancing or her Bolshevism, which the film managed to make merely silly. Even so, *Isadora* had to be re-titled, and became *The Loves of Isadora*.

9

On Mary Wollstonecraft Shelley

Science fiction editors and writers are often polymaths, with odd kinds of erudition. I am thinking, for example, of Anne McCaffrey's opera training, Samuel Delany's mathematics and French symbolist poetry, and James Blish's knowledge of James Joyce and James Branch Cabell, to name only a few. David Hartwell, a science fiction editor who once earned a Ph.D. in medieval studies, has both edited a literary magazine, The Little Magazine, and indulged the hobby of reprinting science-fiction classics in hard-cover for libraries. In 1973 or 1974 (I'm afraid I don't remember which) he asked me to provide an introduction for a hard-cover reprint of a late-nineteenth-century edition of Mary Shelley's Tales and Stories. I protested that I didn't know anything about her. He persisted. He sent me her biography (Walling's), the text of the proposed collection and Mathilda (a fascinating short novel not in print then or now—somebody should bring it out) and said, "Do it." I did. With women writers, especially those labeled "minor," criticism as it is usually practiced may be less than helpful. I don't think that Wollstonecraft Shelley is a great writer (I would not hesitate to describe some other supposedly minor nineteenth-century writers, like Sara Orne Jewett and Elizabeth Stuart Phelps that way) but I think there is much to be said about her from a feminist perspective. Ellen Moers, whose work on Shelley proved helpful, published the fine Literary Women in 1977. I think we (I mean feminist literary critics in English) are just beginning to be able to make the actual tradition of women's literature in English remotely intelligible. It has suffered not only wholesale suppression but also misrepresentation, with writers let into the canon (as in this case) although their work is less good than that of writers judged inferior (like Jewett), with non-major writers (like Wollstonecraft Shelley) presented as evidence that women's writing is inferior (when others, who are better, have been omitted completely) and

*with both kinds misrepresented. I think I understand Wollstonecraft
Shelley's "retreat" into fantasy and science fiction in such works as*
Frankenstein *and* The Last Man—*like Baudelaire, like Poe, like
Woolf, she picked up the novel-as-it-was, thought "I can't use this,"
and created a new field. In the 1950s, when I was taught English
literature, dissatisfaction with reality was supposed to be A Very Bad
Thing. It was only in the 1960s that the power of dissatisfaction and
desire exploded into radical utopianism (as it did in Wollstonecraft
Shelley's early years) and students in Paris spray-painted on walls
such slogans as* "Soyons raisonnables. Demandons l'impossible." *[Let's be reasonable/right. Let's ask the impossible.] Wollstonecraft Shelley's use of fantasy is an instance of this and her work
draws strongly on very female experience, from the terror of isolation
in* The Last Man *to what Moers calls the myth of birth in* Frankenstein. *So science fiction had a mother. Well!*

Is Mary Shelley a bad writer? Damon Knight, in his *In Search of
Wonder,* defines a certain category of fiction as follows:

> The hypothetical reader who, looking up from one of the books dealt
> with in this chapter, should remark, "This isn't half bad," would be
> wrong. These books are half bad. They are the work of an infuriating
> small group of highly talented writers who operate . . . in the innocent
> conviction that their every word is golden.
>
> A totally bad book is a kind of joy in itself, like a completely ugly dog;
> but these in-betweens, in which the author seems on alternate pages a
> genius and an idiot, are almost unbearable.[1]

I would propose that Mary Shelley—both in her novels and in her
short stories—is exactly this sort of writer, not because of the "innocent
conviction" described above (in fact, she rewrote meticulously, as
Elizabeth Nitchie points out in her introduction to *Mathilda*),[2] but for
complex reasons. And since the forces that make her short stories such
uneven reading may well be the ones that also made her—as the author
of *Frankenstein*—the first modern science-fiction novelist and the originator (according to Brian Aldiss)[3] of the greatest single myth of the
industrial age, these (admittedly hypothetical) forces bear some looking
into, as do the short stories, her other novels, and her extremely
interesting *Mathilda,* a work of some 45,000 words, unpublished in her
lifetime, which finally saw print in 1959.[4]

It is hardly surprising to find that Mary Shelley avoids realism à la Zola, but she avoids far more than that; Richard Garnett (whose introduction to the first collection of her tales and stories was reproduced in *Tales and Stories*) says simply, "No writer felt less call to reproduce the society around her. . . . The bent of her soul was entirely towards the ideal."[5] Muriel Spark cites Shelley's predilection for "vast events" and "general ideas . . . [these] are what Mary manipulates with ease."[6] And although William Walling's conclusion that Shelley "required, even at her best, a good deal of space"[7] is certainly a just assessment, the reasoning leading to it is surely somewhat flawed. An addiction to the general and abstract does not in itself insist upon lengthy treatment; quite the contrary, the fewer specific details there are in a work of fiction, the shorter that work had better be. The abstract can be tolerated a good deal more easily if there is (quite simply) less of it. Nor does Shelley, in fact, avoid historical or what one might call anthropological-picturesque detail, as in "The Evil Eye," "A Tale of the Passions," "The Sisters of Albano," or "The Dream." Her novel *Valperga* was, in Percy Shelley's words, "raked out of fifty old books."[8] Yet these works are all marred by the "overwriting and sentimentality" that Walling finds in all her writing.[9] Mary Shelley is not avoiding realism as much as she is avoiding reality itself.

What she might have done with realistic social observation is strikingly illustrated by a few pages of "The Elder Son" in which the author traces, with an accuracy and tone surprisingly reminiscent of Jane Austen, the process by which an inexperienced young woman can be led into an engagement with a man she not only does not love, but positively dislikes. The story, however, ends melodramatically, fully indulging what Garnett calls the author's "taste for exalted sentiment."[10] A taste for exalted sentiment, a style derived from the eighteenth century, a passionate longing for high-toned heroines, idealized heroes (in these stories "chestnut" hair becomes a detail one learns to anticipate with trepidation), picturesque settings, extremely emotional suffering (she seems to particularly enjoy those which involve divided loyalties in women, e.g., "The Dream," "The Mourner," "The Swiss Peasant," "The Brother and Sister," and "The Sisters of Albano")—these are not technical errors in Mary Shelley's stories, but her own deliberate choices. She prefers the ideal to the real.

What can such a writer write about?

Certainly not heroes and heroines. Ellen of "The Mourner," with "her angel expression of face, her nymph-like figure, her voice whose tones were music," is the least effusively described of Shelley's young women (p. 95). Here is one of the most effusively described, Idalie of "The Pole":

> Her hair, of a golden and burnished brown (the color of the autumnal foliage illuminated by the setting sun) fell in gauzy wavings round her face, throat, and shoulders. Her small, clear forehead, gleaming with gentle thought; her curved, soft and rosy lips; the delicate moulding of the lower part of the face, expressing purity and integrity of nature, were all perfectly Grecian. Her hazel eyes, with their arched lids and dark arrowy lashes, pierced the soul with their full and thrilling softness. She was clad in long and graceful drapery, white as snow; but, pure as this garment was, it seemed a rude disguise to the resplendent softness of the limbs it enfolded. . . . And not alone for Ladislas was this hour the dawn of passionate love. The same spell was felt in the heart of Idalie. One moment their eyes met and glanced upon each other, the look of exalted, eternal love—mute, blessed, and inexpressible. . . . Rapture thrilled their breasts. . . . (p. 283)

Nor are gentlemen exempt; Idalie's lover, Ladislas, is

> . . . scarcely two-and-twenty. In stature he was tall, and his form was moulded in such perfect proportions, that it presented a rare combination of youthful lightness and manly strength. His countenance, had you taken from it its deep thoughtfulness and its expression of calm, intrepid bravery, might have belonged to the most lovely woman, so transparently blooming was his complexion, so regular his features, so blond and luxuriant his hair. (pp. 274–75)

And here is the chief of a band of Greek patriots in "Euphrasia":

> He was known as the bravest among the brave; yet gentle as a woman. He was young and singularly handsome; his countenance was stamped with traces of intellectual refinement, while his person was tall, muscular, and strong, but so gracefully formed that every attitude reminded you of some Praxitelean shape of his own native land. Once . . . the thoughts, which presided in his brow, had been as clear and soft and gladsome as the godlike brow itself. (p. 312)

One is not surprised to learn (in the same story) that the chieftain's sister, Euphrasia, "while a child . . . improvised passionate songs of liberty" (p. 320). Nor does Euphrasia die when she should; she lingers (and talks) for two whole pages after what ought to have been a genuinely poignant scene. But Mary Shelley does not know where to stop—or, more accurately, she does not want to. When confronted with the picturesque details of Italian or Greek customs, she is exact ("The

Evil Eye," "The Pole"); when dealing with comic peasants, who need not be ideal, she is likewise historically and dramatically accurate (even amusing, as in the character of old Monna Gegia in "A Tale of Passions"). The ideal and the realistic coexist in the same stories, even in the same family; Idalie, of "The Pole," lives in a family descibed by her protectress as:

> . . . wild and strange. There is a brother who they say is a complete ruffian; brave as a Pole and as unprincipled as an Italian: a villain quite varnished in picturesque, like one of your Lord Byron's corsairs and giaours . . . a younger sister; the most uncontrollable little creature, who chose to pretend my house was insupportable and ran away into Calabria or Campagna, and set up as a *prima donna*. But these, to be sure, are the children of a second wife, an Italian. . . . (p. 284)

Ladislas, who has been imagined on the ideal plane, finds this talk "heartless"; yet in a few pages the younger sister (a very nice rattlebrain) is complaining that "out starts our blessed brother Giorgio . . . and began one of his most terrific bothers" (p. 286)—that is, he disapproves of her singing, which leads him to sit Svengali-like in the theatres in which she performs, with his arms folded, "fixing his horrible looks upon me as I sing!" She continues:

> [H]ow many times have I rushed out of the theatre, and spent the nights in the great wide Maremma, beset by robbers, buffaloes and wild boars. . . . But I cannot stay any longer. I am wanted at the rehearsal; so, farewell, dearest Idalie. (p. 288)

Such characters are spear-carriers and are never allowed to dominate the stories; nor does Shelley's interest in picturesque historical detail (almost all the stories are set in medieval Italy, medieval France or Germany, or present-day—but picturesque—Italy, Greece, and so on) extend to psychological verisimilitude or dialogue that is not overinflated (the stories rank much lower than the novels in this respect). Walling locates "the curious lack of reality in the social background of much of her fiction"[11] in an innate conservatism unconsciously at war with her husband's ideas—a conflict she could never clarify because of her melancholy (and possibly guilty) dedication to his memory.[12] (One might add that the same situation existed with Mary Shelley's lifelong idealization of her dead mother. Mary Wollstonecraft was a feminist but her daughter was not, despite Brian Aldiss's confusion of feminism with intellectuality in his novel *Frankenstein Unbound*, which uses the group at the Villa Diodati as characters.)[13] Mary Shelley was the mother of four children (three of whom she lost before she was twenty-two), a wife who lost her husband at the age of twenty-four, right after a nearly fatal miscarriage, and the daughter of a mother who died at her birth and a cold and unsympathetic father who inflicted a detested stepmother on his four-year-old child. She was a woman always prone to depression, often in ill health, who could write seventeen years after Percy Shelley's death, while editing his poems, "I am torn to pieces by memory"[14] and that, later, "Illness did ensue . . . driving me to the verge of insanity,"[15] a woman who—in short—was not only constitutionally melancholy but had good reason to be.

Such a writer might well shun the here-and-now and court a world of idealized heroes and heroines, picturesque peasants, noble struggles for freedom (Greece, of course, provided a living model, as did Poland), medieval history, and considerable melodrama, including much roman-ticized suffering. At their best, the family reunions in the following stories are a painful reminder of the author's own lifelong loneliness; at their worst, they degenerate completely into bathos, as in the "The Pilgrims," in which separation, reunion, and final forgiveness provoke an epidemic of fainting unmatched outside Jane Austen's *Love and Freindship* [*sic*].[16] Elizabeth Barrett Browning, subjected involuntarily to the same isolation from the real that Mary Shelley actively sought, was capable of "The Dead Pan." The author of these *Tales and Stories* has a character in *Valperga* called Euthanasia. The same retrospective demon seems to have been at work in both cases. Yet Elizabeth Browning was not an idiot but a journalist manquée.[17] And Mary Shelley is neither a fool nor a hack.

She is a refugee.

When the here-and-now of un-idealized human relations is intoler-able, one can find refuge in nature, as do many of Shelley's protagonists. Indeed, her descriptions of nature are—again and again—the best writing she does, whether minutely or rhapsodically and broadly:

> The Coliseum falls and the Pantheon decays,—the very hills of Rome are perishing—but the Tiber lives for ever, flows for ever, and for ever feeds the land-encircled Mediterranean with fresh waters. (p. 2)
> The road leading to the inn is rocky and narrow; on one side is an orange grove extending to the sea; on the other, an old Roman wall, overgrown by blossoming shrubs, enormous aloes, floating tangles of vines, and a thou-sand species of parasite plants peculiar to the South. (p. 274)

Of a boat gliding on the Bay of Baia, she can write, "In all that plane of blue light it was the only moving thing," and the first paragraph of

Mathilda is exact both in detail and in mood, free from either hyperbole or sentimentality. Yet one cannot make a story out of scenery alone; and even moments of excellence (for example, Mathilda's eerie walk through the wet fields to find her drowned father, which she thinks will go on "for ever and ever,"[18] or her vengeful, consciously tragic proposal to drink poison with Woodville[19]) give way the next moment to hair-tearings à la Ophelia[20] or encomiums on Woodville that must be read to be disbelieved.[21]

There is one other outlet for a sensibility that cannot or will not grapple with the here-and-now, and it is indeed for this kind of fiction that Mary Shelley is remembered. The author of *Frankenstein* and *The Last Man* could—at times—move into the speculative and the future, into what we now call science fiction.

Science fiction *per se* does not, of course, proceed from the motive of avoiding reality; such attempts produce the same bad effects there as in any other fiction; and Mary Shelley is not a first-rate science-fiction writer. Her two novels in this mode (and what might be called science fiction or the fantastic in "The Mortal Immortal" and "Transformation") are uneven and (in *The Last Man*) slow and badly constructed. Other hands have taken up the themes she used and done better with them; it is no accident, for example, that in 1931 Universal Pictures moved Shelley's thunderstorm, with its massive electrical energy, from Victor Frankenstein's grief-stricken walk in the mountains (where Shelley had placed it) to the scene of creation itself—where it obviously belongs, an immensely enriched metaphor for the artificial power of giving life to the magnificent figure created by Boris Karloff and twenty-odd pounds of makeup. The same lightning, reminiscent of Sinai, sends Elsa Lanchester's hair frilling straight up in *Bride of Frankenstein*. Not that the films are altogether an improvement; they too are very uneven, and (for example) the entire symbolic complex of creature/creator, Adam/God (with the references to *Paradise Lost*) is badly underemphasized, despite the homunculi of the second film. There has been no single, definitive version of the story to date. Yet, despite the flaws of *Frankenstein* and *The Last Man*, Shelley seized on the two great myths of the industrial age, and, at least in the case of *Frankenstein: A Modern Prometheus*, created the first definite, unmistakable, science-fiction novel.

Every robot, every android, every sentient computer (whether benevolent or malevolent), every non-biological person, down to the minuscule, artificially created society in Stanislaw Lem's *Cyberiad* ("The Seventh Sally"—it's small enough to fit into a small box)[22]—is a descendent of that "mighty figure" Shelley dreamed one rainy night in the summer of 1816 and gave to the world two years later. In her own introduction to the 1831 edition of *Frankenstein*, the author describes the dream that provided the germ of the novel: ". . . the hideous phantasm of a man stretched out, and then, on the workings of some powerful engine, show[s] signs of life, and stir[s] with an uneasy, half-vital motion."[23] In his *Billion Year Spree*, Brian Aldiss (himself a writer of science fiction) quotes the above passage and adds, "It was science fiction itself that stirred."[24]

In such works Shelley could follow her bent for what Nitchie calls "the wonderful and the strange."[25] Declaring her intention of writing what was to become *The Last Man*, in a letter to Leigh Hunt in 1824, Shelley speaks of her projected work as "wild & imaginative."[26] As the preface to the 1831 edition of *Frankenstein* puts it:

> The event on which this fiction is founded . . . [is] not of impossible occurrence. I shall not be supposed as acccording the remotest degree of serious faith in such an imagination; yet . . . I have not considered myself as merely weaving a series of supernatural terrors . . . the story . . . is exempt from the disadvantages of a mere tale of spectres or enchantment. It . . . [can] afford a point of view to the imagination for the delineating of human passions more comprehensive and commanding than any which the ordinary relations of existing events can yield.[27]

The above is a very good definition of science fiction.

Mary Shelley, avoiding the here-and-now, took one path into the past (illustrated by most of the stories in this volume) and one into the future (shown here, if feebly, by "The Mortal Immortal"). It was the second that made her famous. (One might object that *Mathilda*, a work of considerable interest and merit, is set in the present; yet only in Thomas Love Peacock's affectionately parodic *Crochet Castle* do we find the complete unrealism of the-society-lady-living-in-the-wilderness—and Peacock's Susannah Touchandgo at least lives with a Welsh farm family. Mathilda's seclusion is total—and totally operatic. The real descendents of this unpublished novella, or rather its first cousins *via* a common ancestor, are Daphne du Maurier's *Rebecca* and the publishing category known today as the Modern Gothic. These are as much about incestuous, Byronic father-figures as is Mathilda—only none of them dares say so out loud.[28]

The Last Man, although it may be based on what Walling calls "a fashionable theme of early nineteenth-century literature,"[29] and thus not original with the author, is nonetheless another of modern industrialism's most pervasive myths: the end of the world imagined as natural—*not* supernatural—catastrophe. It is also one of the most stubbornly ubiquitous plots in science fiction. From *Earth Abides* to *The Day of the Triffids*, every novel in which humanity is done in by pollution, plague, overpopulation, alien invasion, or World War III echoes Mary Shelley's creation. Story after story has used the events of her novel: the global point of view (very like that of H. G. Wells's "The Star"), the quarrel over which countries will take in which refugees, the collapse of civilized life, with it consequent pillage and murder, bands of outlaws roaming a demoralized countryside, the contrast of fruitful nature and degenerate humanity, domestic animals turned wild, deserted cities, the last man's trying to find in art galleries and libraries some alleviation of loneliness, his rejoicing at finding an animal companion, and (sometimes) even the final vision of himself as forever alone under the imagined gaze of the sun, the moon, angels, the spirits of the dead, and (ultimately) God.[30] As Aldiss comments, "she chose to set her fiction far away in the future, as if feeling that a distance of over two and a half centuries in some way lent additional grandeur to her grand theme."[31]

It is only a small step from this to Percy Shelley's dictum that poets are "the mirrors of the gigantic shadows which futurity casts upon the present." (It is, by the way, a step Aldiss takes.) Every serious writer of science fiction ever since has aspired to be exactly this. But oddly enough, it is not the best who have succeeded; the beginnings, the inspiration, the actual creation of themes and ideas, may very well come from what Knight called the "half bad"—as indeed they did come from Mary Shelley.

In a music review published in December 1891, George Bernard Shaw briefly sketches a theory of art, one which has immediate application to music, but which seemed to him to apply as well to the other arts:

> . . . worshippers cannot bear to be told that their hero was not the founder of a dynasty. But in art the highest success is to be the last of your race, not the first . . . to make an end—to do what cannot be bettered.
> . . . if the beginner were to be ranked above the consummator, we should, in literary fiction, have to place Captain Mayne Reid . . . above Dickens, who simply took the novel as he found it, and achieved the feat of compelling his successor . . . either to create quite another sort of novel, or else to fall behind . . . as a superfluous imitator. . . . Praxiteles, Raphael and Co., have great men [*sic*] for their pioneers, and only fools for their followers.[32]

The most concise statement of this view appears six years later:

> ... when a great genius lays hands on a form of art ... he [*sic*] makes it
> say all that it can say, and leaves it exhausted. Bach has got the last word out
> of the fugue, Mozart out of the opera, Beethoven out of the symphony,
> Wagner out of the symphonic drama. ... It is only when we are dissatisfied
> with existing masterpieces that we create new ones; if we ... only try to
> repeat the exploit of their creator by picking out the tidbits and stringing
> them together [we end with] ... a "new and original" botching. ... [33]

In her historical set-pieces, Mary Shelley is in the position of what Shaw
describes as "bringing a reaping machine to glean a crop ... after the
harvest."[34] But her achievements as an originator are another matter
entirely, although (with the exception of *Frankenstein*, which was very
popular) neither she nor her audiences seem to have differentiated
between the two kinds of work. And indeed, the same sensibility, the
same flight from reality, the same craving for something above or
beyond the realistic, are at work in both. Shaw, although he posits a
theory of art that accounts for the "consummator," does not indicate
where to look for beginnings. Perhaps Shelley's work is one such place:
"gleanings" mixed with creation so that one cannot tell them apart *at the
time*. Only the passage of time eventually reveals what in her work is the
last of an exhausted old mode and what will lead to the creation of a
new. One may even speculate that beginnings always occur (or at least
become publicly visible) at the level of quality Damon Knight called
"half bad."

If Shelley's science fiction is better than her medieval romances,
better still are some of her informal, incidental writings—"The Mortal
Immortal" is a feebly comic work, but her remarks on Polidori's incomplete ghost story (in her introduction to the 1831 edition of *Frankenstein*)
are charming:

> Poor Polidori had some terrible idea about a skull-headed lady who
> was so punished for peeping through a key-hole—what to see, I forget—
> something very shocking and wrong, of course, but when she was
> reduced to a worse condition than the renowned Tom of Coventry, he did
> not know what to do with her, and was obliged to dispatch her to the
> tomb of the Capulets, the only place for which she was fitted.[35]

What Mary Shelley might have written under happier circumstances—during a less barren period in English literature, with a happier
childhood, without the deaths of children and husband which darkened

her life—must, of course, remain a matter of conjecture. One may attempt to divine flashes of it in this volume of stories, together with the traces of her unhappiness: the endless reconciliations, the emotional orgies, the insistence on elevated, unreal nobility. In *The Last Man*—in order to generalize and idealize her own widowhood—Shelley adopts a male *persona*, that of Lionel Verney; yet the last human group in the novel is clearly her own family: herself (Lionel), Percy (Adrian), and a little girl presented as the orphaned daughter of Lord Byron (Raymond) but called "Clara" (the name of the author's own dead child). A world that considered real dead babies to be equally important in literature as universal plague or the male creation of life in the laboratory (blasphemous not because it takes the privilege of creation away from mothers, who create naturally, but because it robs God, the ultimate Father) might have allowed Shelley to write very differently. Instead of "my hideous progeny," *Frankenstein*, as she calls it,[36] we might have had Mary Shelley dealing with the here-and-now—a better novelist perhaps, but then perhaps also a worse mythmaker. The question must remain forever open.

However, her journal entries describing her reaction to the death of her first child when she was seventeen (do dead babies lead to live Frankenstein's-monsters? Ellen Moers thinks so) can be seen as a memorial to the standard she might have attained, speculative though such possibilities must be:

> Monday, Mar. 6—Find my baby dead. Send for Hogg. Talk. A miserable day. . . .
>
> Thursday, Mar. 9—Read and talk. Still think about my little baby. . . .
>
> Monday, Mar. 13—Shelley and Clara go to town. Stay at home and think of my little dead baby. This is foolish, I suppose; yet . . . whenever I am left alone to my own thoughts, and do not read to divert them, they always come back to the same point—that I was a mother, and am so no longer. . . .
>
> Sunday, Mar. 19—Dream that my little baby came to life again; that it had been only cold, and that we rubbed it before the fire, and it lived. Awake, and find no baby. I think about the little thing all day. Not in good spirits.[37]

N O T E S

This essay first appeared in *Tales and Stories*, by Mary Wollstonecraft Shelley (Boston: Gregg Press, 1975).

1. Damon Knight, *In Search of Wonder*, 2d ed., rev. and enl. (Chicago: Advent, 1967), p. 61.

2. In *Studies in Philology*, Extra Series no. 3 (October 1959), pp. xiv–xv.

3. Brian Aldiss, *Billion Year Spree: The True History of Science Fiction* (Garden City, N.Y.: Doubleday, 1973), p. 23.

4. The text of *Mathilda*, edited with an extensive introduction by Elizabeth Nitchie, was published as a separate number in the "Extra Series" of *Studies in Philology*. See note 2 above.

5. Richard Garnett in Mary Wollstonecraft Shelley, *Tales and Stories*. Reprint of 1891 ed. (Boston: Gregg, 1975), p. x.

6. Quoted in William A. Walling, *Mary Shelley* (New York: Twayne Publishers, 1972), p. 109.

7. Ibid.

8. Ibid., p. 53.

9. Ibid., p. 73.

10. Garnett in Shelley, *Tales and Stories*, p. x.

11. Walling, p. 99.

12. Ibid., pp. 75ff, 88–94.

13. Brian Aldiss, *Frankenstein Unbound* (New York: Random House, 1973). The confusion may be attributed to the central character and, one hopes, not to the author.

14. Walling, p. 136.

15. Ibid.

16. The most ineffable line in this wildly comic parody of the sentimental novel is "We fainted alternately upon a sopha." The dying Sophia also advises the heroine, Laura, to "Run mad as often as you choose; but do not faint—." The entire text of this work may be obtained in Jane Austen, *Minor Works*, R. W. Chapman, ed. (London: Oxford University Press, 1972).

17. Virginia Woolf, *The Second Common Reader* (New York: Harvest Books, 1932), pp. 182–92. Woolf does not call Elizabeth Browning a journalist but stresses her love of politics, arguments, social life, and everything that could feed her "lively and secular and satirical" mind (p. 187). Woolf's list of Elizabeth Browning's talents—"brilliant descriptive powers, her shrewd and caustic humor"—makes a good case for what we would now be quite willing to accept as reportage (p. 192).

18. "Mathilda," *Studies in Philology*. Extra Series no. 3 (October 1959), p. 45.

19. Ibid., p. 67.

20. Ibid., p. 20.

21. Ibid., pp. 55ff.

22. Stanislaw Lem, *The Cyberiad: Fables for the Cybernetic Age* (New York: Seabury Press, 1974), pp. 161–72. One might consider this entire book a descendent of *Frankenstein*, since there are, strictly speaking, no human characters at all—*everyone* is mechanical.

23. *Three Gothic Novels*, Peter Fairclough, ed. (Harmondsworth: Penguin Books, 1973), p. 263.

24. Aldiss's chapter on Mary Shelley is entitled "The Origins of the Species." See Aldiss, *Billion Year Spree*, p. 24, for his admiring statement.

25. Walling, p. 72.

26. Ibid., p. 80.

27. *Three Gothic Novels*, p. 267. According to the introduction to the 1931 edition, Percy Shelley wrote the original preface.

28. According to Professor Judith Long Laws of Cornell University (in conversation, fall 1971), the intense emotionality of the Modern Gothics and the romance magazines is a form of pornography for women who read them. Many feminist writers, including Phyllis Chesler in *Women and Madness* and Germaine Greer in her chapter on "Romance" in *The Female Eunuch*, suggest that the quintessential form of sexually arousing experience/fantasy for women in a patriarchal culture is father-daughter incest. See Joanna Russ, "Somebody's Trying to Kill Me and I Think It's My Husband: The Modern Gothic," *Journal of Popular Culture*, 6 (Spring 1973), 666–91.

29. Walling, p. 82.

30. Abridged versions of *The Last Man* have appeared twice, to my knowledge: in *Strange Signposts*, Roger Elwood and Sam Moskowitz, eds. (New York: Holt, Rinehart and Winston, 1966), and in *Speculations: An Introduction to Literature through Fantasy and Science Fiction*, Thomas E. Sanders, ed. (New York: Glencoe Press, 1973). Nobody seems able to bear it at full length. One sometimes wishes that what James Blish calls the British writers of "one-lung" catastrophes would read it once and die.

31. Aldiss, *Billion Year Spree*, p. 34.

32. George Bernard Shaw, *Music in London*, vol. 1 (London: Constable and Co., 1956), p. 293.

33. George Bernard Shaw, *Our Theatres in the Nineties*, vol. 3 (London: Constable and Co., 1954), pp. 236, 318.

34. Ibid., vol. 2, p. 99.

35. *Three Gothic Novels*, p. 262.

36. Quoted by Ellen Moers in "Female Gothic: The Monster's Mother," *New York Review of Books*, March 21 and April 4, 1974. Moers's treatment of *Frankenstein* stresses its importance as a myth of birth. However, none of Moers's treatment of Gothic writing by women in the eighteenth and nineteenth centuries deals with the social conditions experienced by them, outside of a quasi-Freudian reference to the sexuality of the nursery. Moers sees childhood as determining (supposed) adulthood, but does not see who or what determines the conditions of child life or what children learn.

37. Walling, p. 17.

Recent Feminist Utopias

finished The Female Man *(one of the novels cited in the following essay) in 1971. It saw publication in 1975, some years after Monique Wittig's* Les Guérillères. *The women's movement that first flowered in the 1970s had its repercussions in science fiction as it had in so many other literary and extra-literary areas in the United States. The following is an attempt to sum up what had been happening in science fiction and the common themes and common terms all of us seemed to turn to when we wrote. I do not think most of this should be conceptualized as "influence" since I wrote* The Female Man *without having read* Les Guérillères, *Gearhart wrote at least some of the stories in* The Wanderground *before* The Female Man *came out, and all but one of the utopian stories or novels considered below resemble not only each other but also the nineteenth-century feminist utopias Carol Pearson talks of and Charlotte Perkins Gilman's* Herland. *What we have here is, I suspect, parallel evolution.*

In the last few years, science fiction in the United States has seen a mini-boom of feminist utopias, a phenomenon obviously contemporaneous with the women's movement itself. Of the books and short stories considered in this paper, the earliest—not actually American but possibly a catalyst for some of the others—was Monique Wittig's *Les Guérillères*,[1] brought out in English translation by Viking in 1971. The latest—Suzy McKee Charnas's *Motherlines*[2]—was published by Berkley-Putnam in 1978. Of the group of works I will be considering here, Ursula Le Guin's *The Dispossessed*[3] was published in 1974 and my own *The Female Man*[4] in 1975. The remaining seven works (two of which are by a single

author) appeared in 1976. These are Samuel Delany's *Triton*,[5] Marion
Zimmer Bradley's *The Shattered Chain*,[6] Marge Piercy's *Woman on the Edge
of Time*,[7] Sally Gearhart's *The Wanderground: Stories of the Hill Women*,[8]
Catherine Madsden's "Commodore Bork and the Compost,"[9] and two
stories by Alice Sheldon, "Your Faces, O My Sisters! Your Faces Filled of
Light!"[10] under the pseudonym of Raccoona Sheldon and "Houston,
Houston, Do You Read?" under the pseudonym of James Tiptree, Jr.[11]

Although "utopia" may be a misnomer for some of these works,
many of which (like *Triton* or *The Dispossessed*) present not perfect
societies but only ones better than our own, "feminist" is not. All these
fictions present societies (and in one case, a guild organization) that are
conceived by the author as better in explicitly feminist terms and for
explicitly feminist reasons. In only one work, *The Dispossessed*, is feminism *per se* not the author's primary concern; it is secondary to Le Guin's
communitarian anarchism. No doubt such a formulation does less than
justice to Le Guin's work, but oversimplifications are necessary in
dealing with so many works in so short a space. Even though *The
Dispossessed* is feminist and utopian (rather than a feminist utopia as
such) and though the society in *The Shattered Chain* is a group (the Guild
of Free Amazons) within the larger society of the planet Darkover, these
works form a remarkably coherent group in their presentation of
feminist concerns and the feminist analyses that are central to these
concerns.

Moreover, they imagine their better—and feminist—societies in strikingly similar terms. Science fiction is a small field and it's likely that
these writers have read one another (with the exception of Wittig, who
could not have read the others' works, although they have probably
read *Les Guérillères*); nonetheless it is significant exactly what these
writers choose to imitate. In Carol Pearson's recent "Women's Fantasies
and Feminist Utopias,"[12] an essay covering six modern works (five of
which I also examine in this paper) and two that "grow out of the
nineteenth-century women's movement," Charlotte Perkins Gilman's
Herland and Mary Bradley Lane's *Mizora*, Pearson finds "surprisingly
numerous areas of consensus among such seemingly divergent
works."[13] She does not, in fact, find it necessary to distinguish between
the two older novels and their modern cousins. It seems to me reason-
able to assume that, just as Gilman and Lane were responding to the
women's movement of their time, so the works I discuss here are not
only contemporaneous with the modern feminist movement but made

possible by it.* Both sets of books become even more interesting in the light of the twentieth-century tradition of American science fiction. I have argued elsewhere that American science fiction (until the 1970s) has in general ignored both woman's estate and the problems of social structure with which feminism deals.[14] Even such honorable exceptions as Theodore Sturgeon and Damon Knight, to name only two, could only indicate their distress at a state of affairs in which women were perceived as inferior and men were encouraged in machismo, without providing the political analysis that did not, at that time, exist, since earlier feminism had been buried and the new feminism of the late 1960s had yet to occur. For example, Sturgeon's *Venus Plus X*[15] presents no political analysis of sex class, and its solution—literal unisex—places the blame for oppressive social conditions on the biologically innate temperament of the sexes, a solution the authors I am considering here would certainly reject, because of either the assignment of blame to biology or the assignment of blame to both sexes equally. Aside from such atypical works, most American science fiction can be divided into three categories according to its attitude toward sex roles: the status quo (which will be carried into the future without change), role reversals (seen as evil), and fiction in which women (usually few) are shown working as equals alongside men; but the crucial questions about the rest of society (e.g., personal relations and who's doing the work women usually do) are not answered. When science fiction between 1965 and 1975 has dealt with feminist insights, it has usually been by the expansion of that last category, with the usual evasions: parenting and human nurturing take place offstage, as do the effects of such work on the personalities of those who do it. The work women do in acting out sexual and power fantasies for the emotional R & R of men is either not present or it is taken for granted as a natural part of the human scene. Work that is both sex- and class-limited (for example, the drudgery of maintenance and production as well as the drudgery of housework) is usually ignored altogether. When such work occurs, it is part of the natural world and is not examined; it is something the superior hero must escape from or something that is to be done away with (vaguely)

---

*Pearson covers some of the materials I focus on in this paper, notably the communal nature of the societies portrayed, the absence of crime, the relative lack of government, and the diffusion of the parental role to the whole society. She also treats the lack of dualistic thinking, the importance of mothering and the philosophical and religious attitudes of the societies portrayed.

by machinery, or something that, although boring and dehumanizing, is nonetheless better than the boredom presumed to follow (in the mass of ordinary people, not in the hero) from its absence.

In view of this general previous neglect, the works treated in this paper are remarkable not only for their explicit feminism but for the similar forms the feminism takes. They not only ask the same questions and point to the same abuses; they provide similar answers and remedies.

For one thing, the societies portrayed in these tales are, with one exception, *communal*, even *quasi-tribal*. Government does not exist or hardly exists, although there is sometimes a council dealing with work assignments (seen as the main problem of government). *Les Guérillères* is self-consciously "tribal" in its imagery. The Anarresti of *The Dispossessed* are anarchists; their communities recall in flavor the Israeli kibbutz. The core of social structure in *The Female Man* is families of thirty to thirty-five persons; children have free run of the planet past puberty, and "the kinship web is world-wide."[16] In "Your Faces, O My Sisters!" the society imagined by the mad, present-day protagonist practices common worship in the open, as do the characters in the Gearhart stories, who live in small groups in a setting so natural as to recall primatologists' descriptions of the nightly nests gorillas make in trees. In "Houston, Houston" government exists largely to shift people from job to job; families are groups of women cloned from the same stock, who refer to each other as "sisters" and keep a family book. The two Judys in the story (their names, Judy Dakar and Judy Paris, recall the feminist painter Judy Chicago) refer to "The Book of Judy." The society in "Commodore Bork and the Compost," a spoof of *Star Trek,* is a small, closed society in a spaceship, in which everyone is related, while in *Woman on the Edge of Time* the world consists of many such family-communities, in which everyone knows and is a relative of everyone else. *Motherlines* is literally tribal, with its horse-riding nomads who raid each other's camps for horses. Carol Pearson has suggested that women's visions of utopia use the family as a model for social structure, but the unowned, non-patriarchal family, headed by nobody.[17] Certainly the groupings in most of these tales go beyond small-town neighborliness into genuine family cohesion or at the least (in *The Dispossessed*) the cooperation and comradeship expressed by the Anarresti word "ammari." (Le Guin translates the word as "brothers.") Only in *Triton* is there an urban society in which one can meet real strangers, though even here we're told that Lux, the biggest city on Triton, numbers only ten thousand people.

Without exception the stories are ecology-minded. Such concern is common in science fiction nowadays. However, many of the stories go beyond the problems of living in the world without disturbing its ecological balance into presenting their characters as feeling a strong emotional connection to the natural world. The Gearhart stories are the most insistent about this, the characters on occasion talking to (and listening to) trees. A native of the Ark in "Commodore Bork" describes in lyrical terms the ship's compost room, in which "the eggshells, the cabbage leaves, the tampons softly moldering" make the visitor from the *Invictus* feel ill, and tells a defector from that ship (the only female officer on it), "If you get homesick for metal surfaces, I'll even take you up to the navigation rooms."[18] *Woman on the Edge of Time* is so suffused with the feeling of harmony with nature that one quotation would understate the importance of this in the novel, while in "Houston, Houston" the spaceship of the utopian society contains not only chickens but an enormous kudzu vine, and the women who run the ship talk excitedly about the possibility of getting a goat. The Anarresti spend much of their time out-of-doors (it would be interesting to do a line count of outdoor versus indoor scenes on Anarres), and the most lyrical parts of *The Dispossessed*, to my mind, take place outdoors, as do most of the While-awayan scenes in *The Female Man*. Only in *Triton* is there no connection with the out-of-doors, since in this case the "out of doors" is the surface of a moon of Neptune, an environment absolutely hostile to life.

Triton is also an exception to another rule that prevails in this group of fictions; except for it, all the societies presented are *classless*. Le Guin's book is a long discussion of this fact; the other stories simply take it for granted. Even Bradley's Guild of Free Amazons, which exists on a feudal world in which class is omnipresent and an absolutely assumed social constant, abolishes class distinctions within its own organization, i.e., it does not model its structure on the hierarchy of the world around it. Even "Commodore Bork," while it pokes fun at the *Invictus's* chain of command and casually mentions its own job-shifting, does not argue the point. So pervasive are the results of this classlessness—e.g., the informality of tone, the shifting of jobs from person to person, the free choice of jobs whenever possible—that the authors' not discussing their worlds' forms of government seems neither ignorance nor sloppiness. Rather, classlessness is an assumption so absolute that it need not be discussed. Similarly, few of these societies (except perhaps that of *The Dispossessed*) examine gender stereotypes to see if they are true, or argue against them. We merely see that they are not true and do not apply. For example, on the Ark one of the natives asks the woman officer from the *Invictus* (in mild bafflement), "Do they make you do that to your hair?"[19]

Triton, the only utopian society here that is class-stratified, is also the only society engaged in international (or rather, interplanetary) war. However, this war is very different from those usual in science fiction, for example, Joe Haldeman's *The Forever War* or Robert Heinlein's *Starship Troopers*, in which inter-species war resembles (respectively) the Korean War or the Pacific theater in World War II, with more advanced technology. Delany's war, science-fictionally ingenious, consists almost entirely of sabotage, the results of which are like natural disaster. In *Motherlines* there are occasional clashes between the border guards of the Riding Women and the Holdfasters (the gynocidal society of the Eastern seaboard) who accidentally stray into their territory. In *Woman on the Edge of Time* there is a war going on between the utopian society of the novel and a dehumanized, class-stratified, mechanical society, which holds the moon and a few remote bases on earth—and yet this war may be only a possibility in another continuum. Even the possibility is kept on the margins of the book. In *Les Guérillères* there is a war between the women and the men—presented, however, pretty much in metaphor (as is everything else in the book). The Anarresti of *The Dispossessed* constitute one, warless society, nor is there a war going on between them and their mother/sister planet, Urras. There are no wars in the other utopias, although in at least two cases ("Houston, Houston" and one society of the four in *The Female Man*) there were—or rather, may have been—wars in the past. Even these are not national, territorial wars, but, in one case, a sexual Cold War and, in the other, a general breakdown of society caused by biological, natural disaster.

In short, the violence that does occur in these stories (with the exception of *Triton*) is that of ideological skirmish, natural disaster, social collapse, and/or something that may have occurred in the past but is not happening in the present. (One might argue that women's usual experience of war is just that: social collapse and natural disaster. Certainly few women have experienced war as part of a military hierarchy and few expect to do so.) None are dramatically full-scale shooting wars and none are central to the plots of the stories. (The war in *Triton* is confined to its effect on helpless civilians; it occurs in two fairly brief episodes.) In general violence seldom occurs and is taken seriously when it does occur, *Triton* in particular focusing on the anguish of helpless people harmed or killed by the sabotaging of Triton's artificial gravity. Violence in these tales has emotional consequences and is certainly not presented as adventure or sport.

Classless, without government, ecologically minded, with a strong feeling for the natural world, quasi-tribal in feeling and quasi-familial in structure, the societies of these stories are *sexually permissive* in terms I suspect many contemporary male readers* might find both unspectacular and a little baffling, but which would be quite familiar to the radical wing of the feminist movement, since the point of the permissiveness is not to break taboos but to separate sexuality from questions of ownership, reproduction, and social structure. Monogamy, for example, is not an issue, since family structure is a matter of parenting or economics, not the availability of partners. *Woman on the Edge of Time* is reproductively the most inventive of the group, with bisexuality (they don't perceive it as a category and so don't name it) as the norm, exogenetic birth, triads of parents of both sexes caring for children, and all three parents nursing infants. Exclusive homosexuality (also not named) is an unremarkable idiosyncracy. *The Shattered Chain*, the most conservative in its sexual/reproductive arrangements (necessarily since its Guild is only an organization embedded in a larger feudal society), nonetheless presents two separate, legal forms of marriage—one more than we have!—and the Free Amazons are casual about male and female homosexuality. In *The Dispossessed*, monogamy (which has no legal status), casual promiscuity, homosexuality and heterosexuality are all acceptable, and adolescent bisexuality is the norm. I find that Le Guin's biases for monogamy and heterosexuality show (there seems to be only one male homosexual on Anarres and no female ones and the monogamous people we see are clearly nicer—at least in adulthood—than the promiscuous) but the auctorial intention is clear. "Commodore Bork" is cheerful about homosexuality, heterosexuality, promiscuity, and a reproductive technique that allows one woman to have a baby "with" another; everybody parents. The response to all of this by the Captain of the *Invictus* is to try to seduce all the young women he meets, telling them (in effect): What's a nice girl like you doing in a place like this?

---

*The matter is amply dealt with in the literature of the feminist movement. Briefly, these stories would be very much out of place in *Playboy* and its imitators, as well as in the underground press (e.g., underground comics).

Triton, always the exception, goes beyond the permissiveness of the other works into an area of argument I suspect the other authors might find both witty and unpleasantly mechanical, since Delany divorces sex from affection (as the other works do not) and both recognizes and, philosophically speaking, honors erotic specializations like sadism that the other authors ignore. That is, he considers no uncoerced form of sexuality privileged. *Triton's* is the only society in the group that provides for sex-change surgery, although the novel's detestable protagonist is the only character in the book who takes the change as seriously as do contemporary transsexuals. The other characters seem to see it as a form of cosmetic surgery. On Triton, transsexing as gender-role change is impossible, since Triton's is a society in which it is impossible to be "masculine" or "feminine." As in Piercy's book, parenting is shared by all the members of a family and men suckle infants.

There remain six works in which the only sexuality portrayed is matter-of-factly Lesbian, and necessarily so, since the societies described contain only women. Since Lesbianism is a charge routinely made against feminists (the recent sexual-preference resolution at the women's conference in Houston was passed in part to combat the disuniting of women that arises from such a charge), and since many men appear to believe that the real goal of all feminists is to get rid of men, it is important to investigate the reasons why these authors exclude men from their utopias. In the two-sexed utopian societies, Lesbianism is one among many forms of freedom, but a world without men raises two questions: that of Lesbianism and (lurking behind it) the question of separatism. I believe the separatism is primary, and that the authors are not subtle in their reasons for creating separatist utopias: if men are kept out of these societies, it is because men are dangerous. They also hog the good things of this world.

In "Houston, Houston" the intruders (men from our time) into an all-female world are given a disinhibiting drug. The results are megalomania, attempted rape, horrifying contempt, and senseless attempted murder. One of the women comments with obvious irony, "You have made history come alive for us." The men will be killed; "we simply have no facilities for people with your emotional problems."[20]

In "Your Faces, O My Sisters!" (by the same author) a madwoman who believes she is living in a future, all-female utopia, and is therefore safe anywhere at any time, is raped and murdered by a male gang in a city at night.

In *Motherlines* the heroine, a native of the society of the Holdfast, where all women are chattel slaves owned in common by all men, escapes only because she has been trained as a runner. She is pregnant with a child, the product of rape. She meets the Riding Women, strong, free, nomad Amazons who travel adventurously over the Great Plains. Gathering an army of women from among the "free fems" (escaped slaves), she becomes a chief and leader of her people.

In *The Female Man* women of the all-female utopia are farmers, artists, members of the police force, scientists, and so on, and: "there's no being out too late in Whileaway, or up too early, or in the wrong part of town or unescorted. . . . There is no one who can keep you from going where you please . . . no one who will follow you and try to embarrass you by whispering obscenities in your ear. . . . While here, where we live!"[21]

In *Les Guérillères* bands of strong women roam freely everywhere, run machinery and control production.

Sally Gearhart's characters, with their hard-won training in paraphysical powers, travel freely over forests and plains. But they avoid the cities, for men still rule there.

The physical freedom to travel safely and without money is emphasized also in the two-sexed societies, though *The Dispossessed* shows such freedom being enjoyed by a male character. Most of *The Shattered Chain* is taken up with the travels and adventures of bands of Free Amazons, who are twice taunted and attacked by groups of men (for no reason). Even *Triton*—urban, class-bound, money-economy that it is—is far freer physically than any American city; indeed Delany emphasizes that the "Unlicensed Sector" of Lux, the part of the city without laws, is safer than the rest. (This sort of unpoliced part of town is usually used in science fiction as a pretext for showing various kinds of violence.) It's hardly necessary to stress here that physical mobility without cultural restraints, without harassment or the threat of it, is denied women in the United States today (not to mention elsewhere) and that access to most professions and public activities is similarly restricted.

Careful inspection of the manless societies usually reveals the intention (or wish) to allow men in . . . if only they can be trusted to behave. *Les Guérillères*, the most lyrical of the group, has the women allowing men back into their society, but only after the women have won. *Motherlines* (the sequel to a previously published novel, *Walk to the End of the World*, which depicts the Holdfast society) has a sequel in which the escaped slaves return to the Holdfast as an army, though the Holdfast may have destroyed itself in the interval.[22] In *The Female Man* Whileaway is one of a number of possible societies, none of them in our future.

Whether tentative or conclusively pessimistic, the invented, all-female worlds, with their consequent lesbianism, have another function: that of expressing the joys of female bonding, which—like freedom and access to the public world—are in short supply for many women in the real world. Sexually, this amounts to the insistence that women are erotic integers and not fractions waiting for completion. Female sexuality is seen as native and initiatory, not (as in our traditionally sexist view) reactive, passive, or potential. (Earlier sexist views, which see women as insatiable, do not really contradict the later view. Both address themselves, in reality, to problems of male sexuality, i.e., the problems of controlling women, and both perceive female sexuality as existing in relation to male fears or needs.)

Along with physical mobility and the freedom to choose one's participation in the world goes a theme I shall call the rescue of the female child. This theme occurs in only three works under discussion here, but it also turns up in two recent, non-utopian science-fiction novels, both of them concerned with feminist themes and both written by women.

In *The Shattered Chain* occurs the clearest example of this event: Free Amazons rescue a twelve-year-old girl, Jaelle, and her mother from the gynocidal Dry Towns, in which pubertal girls' wrists are chained together and the chain fastened to their waists so that never again will they be able to extend both arms fully. Jaelle (her name echoes Jael in *The Female Man*) later becomes a Free Amazon.

In *Walk to the End of the World* the fem Alldera is pregnant when she flees slavery. Her daughter, born after her own rescue by the Riding Women, is adopted by them and eventually goes through an adolescent rite of passage. As Alldera puts it: "I really did it. I was no mother, I didn't know how to become one—I was just a Holdfast dam. But I got her away from the men and I found her a whole family of mothers, and saw her into a free life as a young woman."[23]

Woman on the Edge of Time also shows a serious rite of passage undergone by a female child at puberty. Connie Ramos, the heroic and abused woman of our own time, able to visit this future utopia, witnesses the beginnings of the rite (survival in the woods alone). At first disgusted by the future society, Connie finally wishes that her own daughter—taken away from her three years before by the state—could somehow be adopted by the people of the novel's utopia.

The two subsequent novels are my *The Two of Them*,[24] written before my acquaintance with these other examples, and Vonda McIntyre's *Dreamsnake*.[25] In *Two* a twelve-year-old girl living in a quasi-Islamic, misogynist society, who wants to be a poet, is taken off-planet at her own request by a man and woman from an interstellar espionage organization. In *Dreamsnake* the heroine rescues a pubertal girl from a brutal male guardian who beats and rapes her. The author of *Dreamsnake*, told of this paper, objected that the little girl's oppression did not come from the realities of the nonsexist society depicted in the novel. However, she then added that the character's oppression might very well come out of the conditions of the author's society.

Puberty is an awakening into sexual adulthood for both sexes. According to Simone de Beauvoir in *The Second Sex*, it is also the time when the prison bars of "femininity," enforced by law and custom, shut the girl in for good.[26] Even today entry into woman's estate is often not a broadening-out (as it is for boys) but a diminution of life. Feminist utopias offer an alternative model of female puberty, one which allows the girl to move into a full and free adulthood. All the novels described above not only rescue the girl from abuses that are patriarchal in character; they provide something for her to go to, usually an exciting and worthwhile activity in the public world: healer (*Dreamsnake*), Free Amazon (*The Shattered Chain*), Riding Woman and horse-raider (*Motherlines*), or poet (*The Two of Them*). We are used to envisioning puberty for girls as a sexual awakening, usually into reactive sexuality (Sleeping Beauty, q.v.). This is one aspect of puberty missing in the above examples; the children therein are sexual beings, certainly, but the last thing (say the tales) that matters for the adolescent girl is that she be awakened by a kiss; what is crucial is that she be free.

A discussion of these recent feminist utopias would be incomplete without some reference to their anti-feminist opposite numbers: the role-reversal (or battle of the sexes) science-fiction novel, which assumes as its given the sexist assumptions the feminist utopias challenge and attack. I have discussed this subject elsewhere.[27] Briefly, the battle-of-the-sexes stories present all-female or female-dominated worlds (of which there are none among the feminist utopias) that are returned to the normalcy of male dominance by male visitors from our own society or male renegades from the world of the story. These men overthrow a gynocracy that is both awesomely repressive and completely inefficient. The method of overthrow is some form of phallic display: flashing, a kiss, rape. The books are badly written, apolitical, and present women as only potentially sexual; they also present rape as either impossible or desired by the woman. These stories are not only strikingly violent; they are violent without feeling, and in contrast to the all-female, feminist utopias, never propose an all-male world as a solution to their problem. Their authors are not, it seems, willing to do without women. However the books are surprisingly non-erotic, sex being a matter of power in them and not pleasure.

It seems clear that the two kinds of novels are not speaking to the same conflict. That is, the battle-of-the-sexes stories envision what is essentially (despite science-fiction trappings) a one-to-one confrontation between one man and one woman, in which the man's sexual power guarantees his victory, while the feminist utopias, if they present a conflict at all, see it as a public, impersonal struggle. One might expect public war to be more violent than personal conflict; thus the relative gentleness of the feminist books is all the more surprising.

However, it may well be that the feminist books, because their violence is often directed *by women against men*, are perceived as very violent by some readers. For example, *The Female Man* contains only four violent incidents: a woman at a party practices judo on a man who is behaving violently toward her and (by accident) hurts him; a woman kills a man during a Cold War between the sexes after provocation, lasting (she says) twenty years; a woman shoots another woman as part of her duty as a police officer; a woman, in anger and terror, shuts a door on a man's thumb (this last incident is briefly mentioned and not shown). A male reviewer in *Mother Jones*[28] quoted at length from the second and fourth incidents (the only quotations from the novel he used), entirely disregarding the other two. Ignoring the novel's utopian society, which is one of four, he called the book "a scream of anger" and "a bitter fantasy of reversed sexual oppression," although the only fantasy of reversed sexual oppression in the novel appears to be the reviewer's. There is one scene of reversed sex roles in the book, and that involves not a woman and a man but a woman and a machine.

What are we to make of these books? I believe that utopias are not embodiments of universal human values, but are reactive; that is, they supply in fiction what their authors believe society (in the case of these books) and/or women lack in the here-and-now. The positive values stressed in the stories can reveal to us what, in the authors' eyes, is wrong with our own society. Thus if the stories are family/communal in feeling, we may pretty safely guess that the authors see our society as isolating people from one another, especially (to judge from the number of all-female utopias in the group) women from women.

If the utopias stress a feeling of harmony and connection with the natural world, the authors may be telling us that in reality they feel a lack of such connection. Or perhaps the dislike of urban environments realistically reflects women's experience of such places—women do not own city streets, not even in fantasy. Nor do they have much say in the kind of business that makes, sustains and goes on in cities. (For example, according to the popular culture fantasies about cities expressed on TV cop shows, cities are places where women and powerless men are threatened with bodily harm by powerful men and saved [if at all] by other powerful men. Since truly powerful men, one would think, don't need fantasies about being powerful, such fantasies must be addressed to ordinary, powerless men. They are certainly not addressed to women.)

The stories' classlessness obviously comments on the insecurity, competitiveness, and poverty of a class society.

Their relative peacefulness and lack of national war go hand in hand with the acceptance of *some* violence—specifically, that necessary for self-defense and the expression of anger, both of which are rare luxuries for women today.

The utopias' sexual permissiveness and joyfulness is a poignant comment on the conditions of sexuality for women: unfriendly, coercive, simply absent, or, at best, reactive rather than initiating.

The physical mobility emphasized in these books is a direct comment on the physical and psychological threats that bar women from physical mobility in the real world.

The emphasis on freedom in work and the public world reflects the restrictions that bar women from vast areas of work and experience.

The rescue of the female child speaks to an adolescence that is still the rule rather than the exception for women, one made painful by the closing in of sexist restrictions, sexual objectification, or even outright persecution.[29]

Some of the above is common to thoughtful people of both sexes, like the dislike of war and the insistence that violence has consequences, but most are specific to women's concerns. Noticeably absent are many wishes common in contemporary fiction and contemporary science fiction: material success, scientific triumph, immortality, being admired for one's exceptional qualities, success in competition, inherited status, and so on. In general, competitiveness and *the desire to be better than* are absent. Also absent is a figure who often appears in women's novels: the Understanding Man, a love affair with whom will solve everything.* There is only one Understanding Man in the group, and he is a spectacular failure, put into the story to illustrate the ineffectuality of undoubted good will and intelligence in dealing with great differences in power between groups. As the women's-movement slogan goes, there is no personal solution.[30] *The Shattered Chain* presents a nice young fellow for the Free Amazon, Jaelle, to fall in love with; he too is a spectacular failure, not (I suspect) because the author intended him to be one, but because having set the book's terms up so uncompromisingly in the first two-thirds of the novel, Bradley cannot make him a real character and still have her love affair even remotely workable.

Comparison of *Triton* with the other books is instructive; it seems to me that for better or worse the one male author in the group is writing from an implicit level of freedom that allows him to turn his attention, subtly but persistently, away from many of the questions that occupy the other writers. For example, *Triton* argues that no form of voluntary sexuality is privileged, while the other books deal with rape and the simple availability of sex that is neither coerced, exploitative, nor unavailable. *Triton* enjoys its sophisticated urban landscape, while the other stories are preoccupied with escape from an urban landscape that they do not own, do not enjoy, and in which they are not safe or happy. *Triton* makes a point of the financial discrimination suffered by children, while the other authors are busy saving their children from solitary imprisonment, madness, rape and beatings, or being chained for life.

In short, most of these utopias are concerned with the grossest and simplest forms of injustice. I do not believe that this fact detracts from their value any more than it detracts from the value of, say, *The Fear and Misery of the Third Reich*. And in these recent feminist utopias we certainly have part of the growing body of women's culture, at least available in some quantity (however small) to readers who need and can use it. I need not recommend *The Dispossessed* to anyone—it's already famous in the science-fiction community—nor does Samuel Delany lack readers. But it might not be amiss to mention that *Woman on the Edge of Time* is a

---

*For example, the unconventional, non-masculine lover, Duncan, in Margaret Atwood's *The Edible Woman* (New York: Popular Library, 1969).

splendid book in the tradition of nineteenth-century utopias, with all the wealth of realistic detail that tradition implies, and that women's studies classes might also tap the raw power of "Your Faces, O My Sisters!" to mention only two of the works discussed here. Here is Alice Sheldon's mad young woman, unable to stand our world and so by sheer imagination trying to inhabit another, the woman who will be killed because she thinks she's free:

> Couriers see so much. Some day she'll come back here and have a good swim in the lake, loaf and ramble around the old city. So much to see, no danger except from falling walls, she's expert at watching for that. Some sisters say there are dog-packs here, she doesn't believe it. And even if there are, they wouldn't be dangerous. Animals aren't dangers if you know what to do. No dangers left at all in the whole, free, wide world![31]

And here is Piercy's Consuelo Ramos, trapped for life in a big state mental hospital (a much worse place than a prison), later to be the subject of an experiment in brain control through surgery that is not in the least science-fictional but very much of the present.[32] Connie's longing for and assent to utopia states eloquently the suffering that lies under the utopian impulse and the sufferer's simultaneous facing of and defiance of pain, racism in this case, as well as class and sex:

> Suddenly she assented with all her soul. . . . For the first time her heart assented. . . . Yes, you can have my child, you can keep my child. . . . She will be strong there, well fed, well housed, well taught, she will grow up much better and stronger and smarter than I. I assent. I give you my battered body as recompense and my rotten heart. Take her, keep her!. . . She will never be broken as I was. She will be strange, but she will be glad and strong and she will not be afraid. She will have enough. She will have pride. She will love her own brown skin and be loved for her strength and her good work. She will walk in strength like a man and never sell her body and she will nurse her babies like a woman and live in love like a garden, like that children's house of many colors. People of the rainbow with its end fixed in earth, I give her to you![33]

NOTES

This essay first appeared in *Future Females: A Critical Anthology*, edited by Marleen Barr (Bowling Green, OH: Bowling Green University Popular Press, 1981).

1. Monique Wittig. *Les Guérillères* (Paris: Editions de Minuit, 1969), English trans. David Le Vay (New York: Viking Press, 1971).
2. Suzy McKee Charnas, *Motherlines* (New York: Berkley-Putnam, 1978).

3. Ursula Le Guin, *The Dispossessed* (New York: Harper & Row, 1974).

4. Joanna Russ, *The Female Man* (New York: Bantam, 1975).

5. Samuel Delany, *Triton* (New York: Bantam, 1976).

6. Marion Zimmer Bradley, *The Shattered Chain* (New York: Daw Books, 1976).

7. Marge Piercy. *Woman on the Edge of Time* (New York: Doubleday, 1976).

8. Sally Gearhart, *The Wanderground: Stories of the Hill Women* (Watertown, Mass.: Persephone Press, 1979).

9. Catherine Madsden, "Commodore Bork and the Compost," *The Witch and the Chameleon,* no. 5/6 (1976).

10. Raccoona Sheldon, "Your Faces, O My Sisters! Your Faces Filled of Light!" in *Aurora: Beyond Equality,* ed. Vonda N. McIntyre and Susan Janice Anderson (New York: Fawcett, 1976).

11. James Tiptree, Jr., "Houston, Houston, Do You Read?" in *Aurora: Beyond Equality.*

12. Carol Pearson, "Women's Fantasies and Feminist Utopias," *Frontiers* 2, no. 3 (1977).

13. Ibid., p. 50.

14. Joanna Russ, "The Image of Women in Science Fiction," in *Images of Women in Fiction: Feminist Perspectives,* ed. Susan Koppelman Cornillon (Bowling Green, Ohio: Bowling Green University Popular Press, 1972).

15. Theodore Sturgeon, *Venus Plus X* (Boston: G. K. Hall, 1976).

16. Russ, *The Female Man,* pp. 81–82.

17. Pearson, p. 52.

18. Madsden, p. 16.

19. Ibid., p. 16.

20. Tiptree, p. 97.

21. Russ, *The Female Man,* pp. 81–82.

22. Volume 3 is in progress. The author refuses to divulge what the free fems find at the Holdfast or what happens there.

23. Charnas, p. 234.

24. Joanna Russ, *The Two of Them* (New York: Berkley, 1978).

25. Vonda McIntyre, *Dreamsnake* (New York: Houghton Mifflin, 1978).

26. Simone de Beauvoir, *The Second Sex* (New York: Bantam, 1961), pp. 306–47.

27. Joanna Russ, "*Amor Vincit Foeminam:* The Battle of the Sexes in Science Fiction," Chapter 4, this volume.

28. Michael Goodwin, "On Reading: A Giant Step for Science Fiction," *Mother Jones I* (1976), 62.

29. "Persecution" may strike some readers as too strong a word. But surely father-daughter incest (which, to judge from the publicity recently given the problem is usually unwanted by the daughter and enforced by the father through threats of emotional blackmail) deserves to be called persecution, as do wife-battering and rape.

30. See Suzy McKee Charnas, *Walk to the End of the World* (New York: Ballantine, 1974).

31. Sheldon, p. 17.

32. See Peter Roger Breggin, "The Second Wave," in *Madness Network News Reader* (San Francisco: Glide Publications, 1974). Amygdalotomy, the operation with which Connie is threatened, is part of the contemporary repertoire of psychosurgery. So are the other operations described in Piercy's book.

33. Piercy, p. 141.

To Write "Like a Woman": Transformations of Identity in the Work of Willa Cather

*T*he following essay, first published in 1986, had a stormy career. I read all of Cather I could after a Colorado friend and colleague, Michele Barale, told me that Cather described Nebraska and the mountain West better than anybody and that her women were immensely attractive. I found that Barale was right and came up for air, thinking, "I know this woman and I know her life because it's mine." I thought that by the middle 1980s (when I finished the piece) Cather's lesbianism had certainly become an open secret, at least among feminist critics. I was wrong. The first (feminist) journal I sent this essay to gave it—with my name on it—to six readers, two of whom liked it and four of whom objected to it in the strongest terms, all denying that Cather was a lesbian, all insisting that I hadn't conclusive evidence of her gayness, and one calling my description of her an "accusation." In short, the documentation demanded to substantiate a description that still seems to me a very, very obvious one exceeded that of The Encyclopedia Britannica, all of it. I have since become familiar with this typical manifestation of homophobia (a chapter in the book I have just finished is called "She Isn't, She Wasn't, and Why Do You Keep On Bringing It Up"), but it was new to me then. I wrote an enraged letter, tore it up, wrote another, waited three days, wrote an even angrier one and sent it. The essay finally came out in 1986 in The Journal of Homosexuality. Since 1986 I have learned not only to expect homophobia from a good many feminists but also to dislike the whole courtly minuet of introductions, explanations, notes, bibliographies and so on which seems to have been devised largely to keep the peasants from bursting into the ballroom and clumping about with you know who. I do not mean that people should be allowed to invent their footnotes but one of the kinds of intelligent and knowledgeable critics discouraged by requirement for the right mannerisms are those who have disabilities *that limit their energy, their time, or their ability to produce copy quickly. I dictated the following essay, had it typed, and was able to correct it some time later; much of the polishing was done by editors at the journal in which it was published. All this took an enormous amount of energy and time and broke the habitual connection between writing and using a keyboard that I had established through decades of work. The requirements of scholarship ought, I think, and so do many others, be changed for those who cannot produce their ideas in the thirty-pages-with-footnotes form scholarly discourse demands. Scholarly discourse would benefit.*

How is a lesbian to write? Or to put the question more accurately, how can a lesbian novelist use her experiences and feelings, especially her sexual ones, in an era that doesn't permit her to be open about them?

Although Willa Cather's biographer, James Woodress, does not state openly that his subject was homosexual, her early life, as he describes it, very much resembled the lives of Alice Mitchell and Alberta Lucille Hart, who appear in Jonathan Katz's *Gay American History*.[1] By the age of fifteen, Cather had cut her hair "shorter than most boys" and was signing her name "William Cather, Jr." She had always played male roles in amateur theatricals, and even in college was "trying her best not to be a girl." She also still signed herself "William Cather," had a "masculine" voice, and made her entire elementary Greek class laugh when she first appeared in the college classroom because she looked like a boy from the waist up but was skirted from the waist down.[2] In adult life she was "obsessed with the desire for privacy"[3]—not surprising for a woman who "had no need for heterosexual relationships" (Woodress goes this far only to add "She was married to her art"), whose romances were with other women, and who called the death of one of her intimates, Isabelle McClung, "a thunderbolt." After McClung's death, according to Woodress, Cather hardly knew how to go on living, was in a comatose state, and was unable to feel anything. She also declared that all her novels had been written to Isabelle McClung.[4]

Even Cather's literary mentor, Sarah Orne Jewett, criticized her for adopting a man's point of view in her fiction, calling it a masquerade.[5]

Woodress himself complains about Cather's "masquerades," as does the critic Mary Ellmann.[6] According to Woodress, Cather also received a great deal of criticism on the publication of her novel *One of Ours,* a novel in which the central consciousness is that of a young man, Claude Wheeler, and in 1921 she told a reviewer, in Woodress's words, that she "always felt it presumptuous and silly for a woman to write about a male character."[7] However emphatic such a declaration was, I believe it to have been placatory and very likely insincere, since the "presumption" was one the novelist insisted upon in most of her work, including the novels *A Lost Lady, The Professor's House,* "Tom Outland's Story" (a self-contained part of *The Professor's House*), *Death Comes to the Archbishop, O! Pioneers, My Antonia,* and *One of Ours,* and short stories such as "Coming, Aphrodite," "Paul's Case," "A Wagner Matinee," "A Death in the Desert," and the marvelous "The Enchanted Bluff." If Willa Cather was masquerading, it was a masquerade she returned to again and again, despite Jewett's advice, despite reviewers' possible reactions, and despite her own belief, spoken if not felt, that such a masquerade was silly and presumptuous. What had been common, respectable behavior between women during most of Sarah Orne Jewett's lifetime—"romantic friendship," "the development of affection between friends to the point where it becomes indistinguishable from love," women's love poems written to women, and "a model 'Boston marriage' [to Annie Fields] which lasted for almost three decades"[8]—such was by Cather's time simply perversion. Lillian Faderman traces this change of social climate in the last two decades of the nineteenth century. Krafft-Ebings's *Psychopathia Sexualis,*[9] first published in 1882, when Willa Cather was nine years old, was the first widely influential text to establish the idea of female "inversion" as both morbid and a medical entity, and by the time Cather was in her early twenties any intellectual who had missed *Psychopathia Sexualis* in translation could find the same ideas in Havelock Ellis's also very influential *Studies in the Psychology of Sex* (1897).[10] The innocent rightness in feelings of love for and attraction to women that Jewett and her contemporaries enjoyed was not possible to Cather's generation; the social invention of the morbid, unhealthy, criminal lesbian had intervened. Indeed, when Annie Fields wanted to bring out a volume of Jewett's letters after Jewett's death, Mark DeWolfe Howe, Fields's friend and biographer, suggested that she omit four-fifths of the indications of the women's affection for each other, lest readers misinterpret it.[11] This event is very reminiscent of the recent publication of Eleanor Roosevelt's letters to Lorena Hickok, after which the excuse/ complaint the executor of the estate offered was that what seems to be so clear in the letters of course isn't, that readers just don't understand Roosevelt's effusive, old-fashioned style.[12] In view of the changed social climate in the early twentieth century (American popular concern with lesbianism's morbidity began in the 1920s, but any *au courant* intellectual must have known about such matters earlier), Willa Cather's "masquerade" was a necessity. Following Jewett's advice, specifically about an early story, "On the Gull's Road," and changing her heroes to heroines (Jewett wrote "a woman could love her—in the same protecting way—a woman could even care enough to—take her away from such a life"[13]) would have meant personal and professional disaster.

Cather's novels show distinct traces of this masquerade. In an earlier version of this paper I wrote that Cather's novels depict a world in which heterosexual relationships are impossible, but this is not really the case. Such relationships can appear in her work if they are described from a distance; they are impossible only to those of Cather's heroes who are at the center of the story's consciousness. And described over and over again is that these loves are not so much frustrating, enraging, or embittering as they are simply hopeless.

One of the things James Woodress chooses to find ridiculous in *One of Ours* is Claude Wheeler's wedding night, when his wife, Enid, literally locks him out of their train compartment, thus breaking Claude's heart. What is missing, says Woodress, is sexual frustration.[14] This is true. But there's more missing than that. What's missing is a whole complex of feelings that a real young man would feel under those circumstances, both in our day and in the era in which the novel occurs.

From literature, consciousness-raising groups, and psychotherapy groups, and from what men have told me, I have surmised what such a man would feel. First of all, he might not feel sexually frustrated in that particular scene, for Claude, after all, is a virgin and can easily be thought of as rather frightened. But as the situation evolves, Cather makes it clear that Enid remains distant and disgusted, however physically available she may be. Claude would most certainly feel first of all angry, and the anger would be born of a feeling of entitlement. After all, he might well think, what did she get married for? What did she think marriage was about? A sensitive man, Claude might well also feel the guilt that exists on the other side of the entitlement, that he was a cad for forcing himself on Enid, that he is bestial, that, given the era in which the novel is set, women really are more pure than men, and so on. What Cather creates instead is a kind of absolute heartbreak at the sheer untouchability of the woman and her rejection of Claude. In fact, one gets a very strong impression from the book that Enid might as well lock her bedroom door at night. They're married people living in the same house, and yet there's absolutely no sense of physical contact between them, not even in the negative forms of anger, bitterness, or frustration.

Even in *O! Pioneers*, where there is a tangible obstacle between the young couple—the young woman, Marie, is married to someone else— there are elements that simply do not make sense. Again, I doubt that a male writer would imagine the situation as Cather does, nor would a real man live it the same way. For one thing, Emil is not only in love with Marie, but remains so, monogamously and hopelessly, for several years, not even thinking of another woman during that entire time. (He certainly doesn't go and visit the local whorehouse, as he might very likely do in, say, a Hemingway story.) Again, it's not the specific physical frustration that's emphasized, but the emotional deprivation, the impossibility and hopelessness of the situation. Moreover, although she makes it clear that she will not become his lover, the woman responds with a great deal of affection. The two young people are surprisingly intimate, in a very unchaperoned way, which strikes me as extraordinary for that time and place, although it would certainly not be strange for such a friendship to develop between two young women, a relationship in which one of them could feel at once extremely affectionate while also totally secure from any sexual problems or sexual advances.

In *The Professor's House*, no tangible obstacle separates the couple since the professor and his wife have been married for some years, and yet they clearly have not really spoken with or touched each other in a long time. There is no open anger, only resolute detachment on his side and chilliness on hers. In this novel occurs the absolutely astonishing imagery that Ellen Moers points out in *Literary Women*: the dress dummies in the professor's study, intensely seductive and soft to the eye, yet which when touched astonish and repel by the extremely unpleasant hardness of their texture.[15] (One might note here that the professor's study is a converted sewing room in the attic of the family house and that Cather's own study, in which she wrote *O! Pioneers*, was a converted sewing room in the attic of the McClung family house.) Moers, in her passages on Cather's work, is coy about naming the "ancient very female view of the nature of love" expressed by Cather, but there is no doubt that the love in question is lesbian, as the other writers she discusses in this connection make clear, including Woolf, Stein, and Colette. Nor is Tom Outland, who appears in the middle of *The Professor's House*, more sexual than the Professor; indeed, he is about as non-sexual a young man as one can find in literature—not unsexed, but in some strange way set apart from the possibility of any sexual act or occasion. The atmosphere of his stay on the mesa is so intensely, so transcendentally imaginative that the preserved female corpse found there, which he, his friend, and the priest who is his teacher call "Mother Eve," is a shock. Even more shocking is the priest's rather risqué hint that this ancient Indian woman may have been killed for adultery. The event, its unexpectedness and its surprising ugliness, parallels the shock of touching those seemingly generous and lovely dress dummies, only to find them extremely unpleasant.

The longer one looks at these stories, the less the feelings of the characters seem to match the novelistic situations. The Professor, although his detachment from his wife is matched by his detachment from life itself as expressed finally by his almost-suicide, has no specifically sexual memories of the past, just as Marie in *O! Pioneers* feels only sadness that she must remain married to a man she no longer loves. She's afraid of him, yet Cather gives us no memory or fearful anticipation of his making sexual demands of her. Again, what Cather emphasizes is the impossibility of the whole situation, well expressed by Emil's desire for one look of love from Marie's eyes and nothing more. The prohibition against adultery is not enough to explain a love that can be satisfied only in death. Rather, in one of the strongest scenes in the book, love is made identical with death; only in death can anything happen between the two. In *The Professor's House*, the Professor's "original nature" returns to him at middle age after "his nature as modified by sex"[16] has somehow disappeared. The misogyny he expresses throughout the rest of the book results in an absolute lack of interest in family life, his children, and "especially" his wife, whose presence he cannot stand any longer and whom he describes as "chiselled . . . a stamp upon which he could not be beaten out any longer . . . a hand holding flaming arrows," that is, something unbearable.[17]

Death, impossibility, monogamy, heartbreak, untouchableness, loneliness, inevitable frustration—through these Cather is making the very strong statement that the desire for women, the love of women, is impossible to her protagonists. Other men may be entitled to it, as in

Emil's case in *O! Pioneers,* or achieve it, as in *A Lost Lady,* but never is it accessible to the male character at the center of the story. In *The Professor's House,* the Professor simply gives it up. Never explicitly described in her fiction, but probably very real to Cather, was the experience of living outside a lesbian circle in an essentially hetero-sexual world, where information about lesbianism did not exist, where she was the only one of her kind (or thought she was), and where the only women she could be attracted to were heterosexual women who would respond with friendship, with a great deal of affection and concern, even perhaps with the considerable non-sexual touching permitted between women, but with absolutely nothing more. In the face of such total deprivation, the sense of specific genital frustration Woodress complains of as missing in *One of Ours* simply gets lost in the general starvation, and the appropriate response becomes that of Claude Wheeler: heartbreak, hopelessness, and helplessness.

If one goes back and translates the situations in Cather's novels into lesbian situations, the fiction often makes clearer sense. If Claude and Enid were women setting up house together, one of them affectionate, the other passionate, then the horror of the affectionate one at the passionate one's passion and the consequent distance between them make perfect sense, as do the passionate one's helplessness and hope-lessness. The impossibility of Marie and Emil's love and his extraordi-nary monogamy make sense. (Emil's showing off his Mexican costume to all the town girls in one scene in the book recalls young Cather's taking male roles in local dramatic productions. The costumes and roles are possible; the reality is not.) The bitterness of the young man who finds out that the heroine in *A Lost Lady* is having an adulterous love affair also makes more sense. The lady is available, all right, *but to men.* Moers calls the novel "an Electra story, raw and barbarous."[18]

Willa Cather grew up in an extremely deprived situation, one that did not end with the nineteenth century, a truth to which much contempo-rary writing by openly lesbian artists attests. Like most lesbian artists, she did not have the protection of (for example) Natalie Barney's money. Apparently, she did not find an openly lesbian circle in which, for example, Renée Vivien could write openly of lesbian passion. She did not or could not risk her respectability. Such a situation is mitigated only somewhat by finding a partner; Jill Johnston has written very well of the "fearfully tenacious dependent isolated . . . déclassé, illegal and paranoid marriage"[19] in which one clings desperately to the other precisely because there is no assurance that either of them will ever be able to find another partner, and even if one does, she will never be socially entitled to her. As Johnston convincingly shows, everyone and everything conspire to separate lesbian lovers, from the isolation forced on them by society to deliberate attempts by parents, friends, institutions, or merely heterosexual men who feel challenged to break the couple up. In short, the sexual psychology depicted in so much of Cather's work is that of the lesbian in love with the heterosexual woman because she believes there is nobody else to be in love with. Lesbian writers who moved in a predominantly and openly lesbian society, like Radclyffe Hall or Djuna Barnes, did not seem to exhibit this psychology. (The misery of *The Well of Loneliness* was special pleading; Hall's *The Unlit Lamp* has no such deferring to prejudices.) I suspect many such writers face other phenomena, such as Renée Vivien's guilt or the ghetto problem because their community, rejected by the larger society, is far too closed in; however, deprivation per se is not the same kind of problem. It is, however, a problem for writers who live, or have lived, in the same social context as Cather—for example, Carson McCullers. Again, in McCullers's work one finds the emphasis on imaginary rather than real satisfactions, and the presentation of mutual love as inherently impossible. And in May Sarton's *Mrs. Stevens Hears the Mermaids Singing,* there is something of the same feeling, that loving a woman is somehow transcendentally wonderful but always transitory, in some sense unspeakable, if not actually impossible. The difference is always one of social context, of the possibility of honesty, and of the availability of sexual partners. Does this kind of ambiguous material in Cather make the work worse? I think not. If her male characters were in accord with either real male experiences or the literary traditions governing such things, we would merely have an addition (observed at second hand at that) to material which is in very long supply. Descriptions of female sexuality are rare, however, and rarer still are descriptions of lesbian sexuality. Nor does the "masquerade," the existence of lesbian feeling in Cather's work, seem to lessen the value of the work. Quite to the contrary, it was possible for Cather, in masquerade, to speak more completely, more clearly, and less self-consciously than could, for example, Djuna Barnes in *Nightwood*. The sense of alienation and the grotesque, which Bertha Harris finds admirable in lesbian literature,[20] is precisely what is missing in Cather. The male mask enabled her to remain "normal," American, public, and *also* lesbian. Even now, any openly lesbian writer is almost forced to be a self-conscious rebel, a position congenial to some, but one that can be constricting nonetheless; such a role Cather simply did not take or need.

I would suggest that, as an example, the character of Claude Wheeler is not one of Cather's greatest failures, as she and her biographer seem to think, but rather one of her greatest successes. The scene in which Claude imagines himself to be one of the world's "moon children" and his wife, Enid, to be one of the world's "sun children" is echoed in many fairly recent lesbian novels in which the protagonists feel themselves to be members of a world of darkness, not of the daily world of heterosexual social life. Yet how many of these characters have been able to do this kind of musing while lying on their backs under the moonlight on a Nebraska farm—and so un-self-consciously, so innocently, while so unaware of the presence of the moon in Western literature as a symbol of femaleness?

The innocence, of course, had to go. If the next state can be called guilty self-consciousness, and the stage after that self-conscious rebellion, no matter what aesthetic advantages they offer (and I believe they offer many not available to Cather, honesty being one of them), they do not have the same advantages as Cather's masquerade; they cannot possibly create the aesthetic completeness and richness of Cather's work. Under whatever disguise, Tom Outland, Claude Wheeler, and so many of the other male personae of the books Cather gave us are, in a very precious and irreplaceable way, records not of male but of female experience, indeed of lesbian experience. In a sense not thought of by contemporary reviewers, and even possibly by Cather herself, Claude Wheeler and many other nominally male characters in Cather's work are, for lesbians, truly *One of Ours*.

NOTES

1. J. Katz, *Gay American History: Lesbians and Gay Men in the U.S.A.* (New York: Avon Books, 1978), pp. 390–414.
2. J. E. Woodress, *Willa Cather: Her Life and Art.* (New York: Pegasus, 1970), pp. 45, 53.
3. Ibid., p. xi.
4. Ibid., p. 173.
5. Ibid., p. 132.
6. M. Ellmann, *Thinking about Women* (New York: Harcourt, Brace Jovanovich, 1968). Ellmann speaks of Cather's "bluff, middy-blouse suspicions of . . . sexuality" (p. 114) and calls Claude Wheeler in *One of Ours* an aspirant to the feminine in spirit (p. 192). Ellman appears to be annoyed at Cather's attributing

"male" virtues to her female characters, and "female" virtues to her male characters. I believe homophobia to have been at work here.

7. Woodress, p. 194.

8. L. Faderman, *Surpassing the Love of Men: Romantic Friendship and Love between Women from the Renaissance to the Present* (New York: William Morrow, 1981), pp. 197–199.

9. R. von Krafft-Ebing, *Psychopathia Sexualis* (New York: Surgeon's Book). Original work published 1886.

10. H. Ellis, *Studies in the Psychology of Sex: Sexual Inversion* (Philadelphia: F. A. Davis, 1911). Original work published 1897.

11. Faderman, p. 197.

12. "Was Eleanor Elesbian?" *Seattle Gay News,* November 23, 1979.

13. Faderman, p. 202.

14. Woodress, p. 194.

15. E. Moers, *Literary Women: The Great Writers* (Garden City, N.J.: Anchor Books, 1977), p. 359.

16. W. Cather, *The Professor's House* (New York: Vintage, 1973), p. 267.

17. Ibid., p. 274.

18. Moers, p. 363.

19. J. Johnston, *Lesbian Nation: The Feminist Solution* (New York: Simon & Schuster, 1973), p. 157.

20. B. Harris, "What We Mean to Say: Notes toward Defining the Nature of Lesbian Literature." *Heresies 3: Lesbian Art and Artists* (Fall 1977), pp. 5–8.

On "The Yellow Wallpaper"

*T*he following was originally written as a letter of commentary to the NWSA Journal 1:1, Autumn, 1988. The letter proved too long (the Journal had transformed itself into a newsletter in the interim) so its publication here is its first. The essay treated in the letter is Diane Price Herndl's "The Writing Cure: Charlotte Perkins Gilman, Anna O., and 'Hysterical' Writing." Literary critics' current fixation on psychoanalysis seems to me to be the result of several factors: political reaction, the desire for a job and publication in a very tight market, the narrowness of graduate school education, and intellectuals' tendency to over-interpret. I believe that the desire for system and completeness also plays a role here and the absolute ignorance of the sciences that afflicts so many humanists whose standards of what constitutes evidence is (unless they are historians) not good. Thus many accept an intellectual system that has never been proved to be true, or even demonstrated to be true, but merely assumed, which multiplies entities with a blitheness that would've astounded Thomas Ockham, which can explain anything after the fact but is useless for prediction, and which relies on badly contaminated evidence—Naomi Weisstein's feminist objections (1969) have never even been addressed, let alone countered. As Susan Koppelman has put it, when things are so bad that merely describing them accurately is a radical act, people retreat into paying arduous and jargonistic attention to imaginary matters. In this connection, Stephen Gould's The Mismeasure of Man is important reading. In an era when the feminism of even fifteen years ago has been buried or declared too "crude" or "passé," when medicine has abandoned all but Freud's quite early formulations and the economy is in a dreadful state, literary critics adopt whatever promises system, control, understanding without effort, and evasion of the hard questions. Literary criticism was very like this in the fifties. So narrow is humanistic

*education and so wholesale are its exclusions that many do not even
know that there are alternatives to the study of human subjectivity
other than psychoanalysis, and that assuming people to be totally
rational is not the only one. Like someone trying to push an unbal-
anced shopping cart round a corner (they go one way, the cart goes
the other) literary scholars try to use the received ideas of their
particular disciplines for feminist purposes, not having the guts (or
the sheer desperation) to simply throw them over and rely on the only
experts in the field: us and our experience. The result is a kind of
messed-up patchwork that retreats further and further from anything radical or useful. I do not mean to come down that hard on
Herndl's essay as a particularly bad example but to indict the
education given her and the models that have taught her that this is
the way to do feminism and criticism. In a world in which mystification is one of the most used ways of controlling intellectual activity,
there is seldom more to a phenomenon than meets the eye—usually
there is less—and over-interpretation (always easy for temperaments
like ours) becomes a plague. For such a muddle psychoanalysis is
perfectly designed. Depend upon it: the twentieth century is just as
stupid as the nineteenth and its received ideas are just as deadly.
Feminism has not yet been transformed into reaction but it will be,
and feminist psychoanalysis will be one of the forces that does the job.*

Dear Editors,

Why do so many scholars read so little? Diane Herndl's essay in your
Autumn 1988 issue is one of a number of critical analyses of "The Yellow
Wallpaper" written by feminists in the last ten years. Herndl misses a
good deal of what is in Gilman's story because (like so many others) she
is largely ignorant of women's literary traditions in particular and, in
general, of work outside the very restricted canon of English literature
still common today. A new restricted canon of (women's) literary
masterpieces is no improvement on the old restricted canon of (mostly
men's) masterpieces; both too often ignore the "paraliterary" traditions
from which many such works spring and the political, economic and
social context that is inseparable from such works' meaning and value.
Not all critics do this, of course, and of course Herndl is not the only one
who does it, but I have found far too much of such ignoring and such
ignorance in feminist criticism.

In analyzing "The Yellow Wallpaper" Herndl admits to her literary calculus a general statement of women's oppression, depth psychology of the Freud-via-Lacan sort—and nothing else. But "The Yellow Wallpaper" is a ghost story. To anyone at all familiar with the genre the signs are unmistakable: the large, beautiful house so mysteriously let at a low rent after standing long untenanted, the narrator's romantic wish for a ghost, her sensitivity to the evil influence that dwells in the house, her husband's fatuous ignorance of anything wrong and his belief in a limited and foolish rationality. These elements are conventions in a tradition that existed before Gilman wrote and that continues to exist today, a tradition in which a great many women have been active in both England and the United States. (The Feminist Press will shortly publish an anthology of ghost stories and stories of the supernatural written by feminist women.) The story, read in this context, takes on meanings quite different from those Herndl proposes.

First, to a reader of ghost stories and horror stories (I have been one for forty years) it is abundantly clear why the wallpaper has been picked off the walls, why the window is barred, why the bed has been fastened to the floor and why there are "rings and things" fastened to the wall. The identity of the strange woman behind the wallpaper is also clear. The room is haunted. It is neither gymnasium nor nursery but a private madhouse in which at least one other woman has been incarcerated. The ghost haunting the room is this woman, the one "behind" the wallpaper who lived (and probably died) in the room and who takes over the heroine's mind during the course of the story or at the very least merges her own mind with the heroine's. *She* is the evil secret of the "hereditary estate" (I certainly agree with Herndl's explication of that phrase), the patriarchal way of life which crushes active, ambitious women. The protagonist is not driven mad by her husband. He is merely an unwitting accomplice of The House (a powerful symbol in women's writing in English, as Ellen Moers and Gilbert and Gubar have noted) as is his sister. Husband and sister are both conventional people whose conventionality leads them to collaborate with the system. After all, woman's place is in the home even when*—as in Gilman's story—the home is literally a private madhouse, that "private" place in which women are driven mad by the most important institution of patriarchy, an institution that pretends to be private and is public and which

---

*or perhaps because

enforces women's obedience by confining them to the "personal" realm of home and family. (In this context it is important to note the narrator's relief that her baby—significantly, it's a girl—is free of the room with the yellow wallpaper. That is, the next generation may have more luck in escaping or changing the institution than this one has had.)

Nor is the above merely an enrichment of Herndl's interpretation. If the heroine is not driven mad but is haunted or possessed, then psychoanalysis (or any other strictly psychological explanation of her "madness") is out of place, Gilman's stated intentions to the contrary. "The Yellow Wallpaper" is not a realistic story, after all, and I do not believe it makes sense to diagnose a literary character's psychosis unless such a character is presented as a case study *in realistic or naturalistic fiction.* High culture is still dominated by realism—the dominant mode of fiction in the West for roughly the last two centuries—but surely the "paraliterary" genres exist to receive and express what can't easily be contained by realism. If we look at "The Yellow Wallpaper" not as a woman's descent into madness but *as a ghost story,* it becomes clear, I think, that the characters are almost faceless, including the narrator, who is barely characterized at all aside from her longing for "congenial work with excitement and change." The story is a feminist fable, the heroine Everywoman, the husband/doctor the Patriarch and the sister the patriarchy's Forewoman. Because this is a ghost story and not (say) *The Bell Jar,* there is a fourth character in it. Realistic stories cannot present institutions as literally part of the *dramatis personae* but ghost stories can—and that, I am sure, is why Gilman wrote the story *as* a ghost story and not as simple autobiography, memoir or case study.

But how are we, then, to take the character's madness? And why does it scare us half to death? (When I first read the story at age fifteen I couldn't bear to finish it because it frightened me so; when I taught it in the 1970s to a woman's studies class most of the young women in the class said that it had frightened them.)

Well, if we try to take the madness as a realistic account, we will have to call it schizophrenia, if we call it anything at all. But schizophrenia and other psychoses have little to do with regression to childhood ways of thinking: Freud was simply wrong about the nature of the psychoses. Nor was Gilman's own illness (if it was a genuine illness) schizophrenia. Her own account (in her note to "The Yellow Wallpaper") describes it as severe depression. I find the heroine's madness in "The Yellow Wallpaper" unconvincing as a clinical description of anything; rather it seems to be a lurid mixture of melodramatic nineteenth-century ideas about madness, some typical of Gilman's own time (like "hysteria") and some dating back farther (like the cunning of the insane). Herndl describes well the invalidation practiced on the protagonist and I agree with her that Gilman's heroine is confused, feels strangled, suffocated, and desperate, and half knows that the people who tell her they are doing her good are really doing her harm. But Gilman's character also gibbers nonsense, tries to bite pieces out of her bed, hallucinates and goes on all fours. (To understand the ghost story tradition of going on all fours, read Kipling's "The Mark of the Beast"—I suspect that the young Gilman, whose strenuous moral and physical self-cultivation recalls Teddy Roosevelt's, was much more likely to associate creeping with bestiality than with infantile behavior.) Now most women invalidated by the patriarchy do not display "insane cunning" or bite their furniture or fancy that the wallpaper is laughing at them. And if they do, they don't do it like Lucia di Lammermoor. What Gilman does in the story—and I think it is a mark of her creative genius that she does so—is put together the most vivid and dramatic images of "madness" she could find in the literary and medical traditions of her time and then link these to the invalidation "women" experience from a society in which they are always treated as somehow "in the wrong." Women (or feminists) do not usually go mad—but those women whose perceptions are at odds with socially imposed familial "truths" often fear they are—or may be—or must be going—or will go—mad. Consciousness-raising groups in the 1970s were full of women who called themselves and their reactions and perceptions "crazy" and who were enormously relieved to find others with the same "craziness." *The Feminist Mystique* describes such things very well and also describes the desperate courage it took to allow oneself to admit to such "crazy" feelings and thoughts. Gilman has created, out of our own fears of total invalidation, a state she calls madness, in which our worst fears come true. That is precisely why so many women (white women anyway) instantly know that "The Yellow Wallpaper" is about them and why we are so terrified by it. Like Gilman, who never had hallucinations despite her grinding depression, we feel our desperation—"near the borderline"—and imagine we can "see over" (Lane, 1980, 19).

I believe the school of feminist criticism to which Herndl belongs presents other serious problems besides its ignorance of literature outside the canon. There is the central focus on psychoanalysis, which draws attention away from social forces. There is the clinging to the issue of speech and silence as quintessentially *the* feminist issue, which draws attention away from all sorts of other issues and replaces other possible feminist activity with talk about talk about talk. (Herndl's little essay on *infans*—not her own creation—is a quintessential example of the silliness possible to those who consider the pun the major agency in human thought.) There is also the ahistoricity of treating human psychology—and hence human activity and human speech—as everywhere and always the same. Like far too many other critics, Herndl also assimilates literary criticism to the physical sciences, using literary critical constructs as if they could be applied deductively to all works of literature like Newton's laws of motion. I believe that many of the current followers of *Cixous et Cie.* like psychoanalysis because it *seems* systematic, rigorous and objective. In short it's a pseudo-science that gives literary humanists (the only people besides psychoanalysts who believe much in psychoanalysis nowadays) the pleasure of mastering a "complex" and "rigorous" body of thought without the real difficulties attendant on attempts to understand biochemistry or (God forbid) mathematics. Literary criticism is as good as the knowledge and sensitivity of those who do it and yes, we don't get paid enough, but making noises like crystallographers or fruit-fly geneticists won't help there either.

To get back to Gilman for a moment: transforming genre works by setting feminist meanings loose in them is a narrative strategy Gilman uses elsewhere. Of the fourteen stories published in Ann J. Lane's *Charlotte Perkins Gilman Reader* (1980) at least ten are genre pieces, while of the remaining four *Herland* is science fiction and *Unpunished* is described by Lane as a "detective story." Lane notes that "Gilman used the variously common fictional forms to propagandize for her humanist vision" (xxxix) and "Gilman used the common vocabulary of her time to convey her ideas in a popular mode." (xi) Characteristically, such pieces begin as the crudest and flattest kind of popular fiction—and then suddenly upset both the literary conventions of the genre and the social mandates from which the genre draws both its methods and its ruling ideas.

How do we criticize fiction that lays about it with a two-by-four? As Paul Lauter has pointed out, we have no contemporary critical language for describing this kind of art, nor do we have a contemporary critical theory for assessing it (Kampf and Lauter, 1972). The formal values of subtlety, complexity, richness, and allusion don't help us in reading works like Gilman's. The insistence on finding hidden depths in work that hasn't any can only distort the work and destroy its meaning. Much of the feminist literature of the last twenty years (like that often created by political radicals elsewhere) has been distinguished by its bareness and obviousness, from Susan Griffin's "You won't know the half of it, not in a million years" to Marge Piercy's "What can they do to you? Anything they like." Criticism like Herndl's can't handle such work. I have never met a criticism that can.

And of course we simply don't know enough about women's litera-ture to develop a decent critical theory about it. We haven't read enough of it. To name only a few American examples: half of Shirley Jackson's short stories of fantasy and horror have appeared only in magazines; little attention has been paid to Mary Wilkins Freeman's terse studies of New England women's heroism; and where are there reprints of Eliza-beth Stuart Phelps's novels *besides* her *Avis?*

I believe that the radical feminist challenges of the last twenty years are being transformed into a new version of super-subtilizing quietism. Those whose only knowledge of feminism is that of *Psych et Po* know little of our rich and daring feminist heritage, either in literature, literary theory, or action. I suspect that many young critics (I have met some of them) cling to the new-psychoanalytic school of feminist theory be-cause it's the only feminism they know. It may also attract some (like the graduate student I know who said she wanted to do "real" criticism) because it does not challenge or ignore male authority but rather assimilates itself to the very traditions feminists themselves used to challenge. Its jargon, its obfuscation of the plain truth that speech, however eloquent, usually remains ineffective in the face of power and money (and how we are intimidated if we have neither!), its pseudo-scientific air, its emphasis on personal transformation and its focus on female psychology (poor, tired female psychology, blamed for a century for everything from juvenile delinquency to "hysteria" to nail-biting), its assimilation of intellectual rebellion to intellectual authority—well, it certainly resembles no feminism I know. Riesman called this sort of thing "restriction by partial incorporation," sixties radicals called it "co-optation," and Marxists speak of it as "revisionism." What is happening now in the United States seems to me to resemble very much what happened during the 1920s in England, when feminism, still in the air, was quietly being replaced by what one critic has since called "social welfare feminism." I believe that the effect of essays like Herndl's is bad, bad critically and bad politically. When there is a respectable, academically acceptable "feminism" that has split completely from what women's studies used to be—Florence Howe once called us the academic arm of the women's movement—we will all be the losers. Once a radical politics (or literary criticism) is limited and diluted to the point where it can safely become part of the establishment, *it can also be dispensed with.* I have seen this kind of political tag played too many times in the last twenty years to want ever to see it again. Surely we can hope for more for ourselves, our students, and our discipline.

Sincerely,
Joanna Russ

13

Is "Smashing" Erotic?

Chrysalis *was one of the very good non-academic feminist magazines of the 1970s. Unfortunately it went out of business trying to make the difficult financial jump from being a very popular small periodical to a viable slick one. In its time it published some remarkably good things, one of them being Nancy Sahli's essay on some women's relations with each other in nineteenth-century Europe and North America and the way such relations were declared unnatural (that is, lesbian) as a way of containing the subversive social possibilities of such women's feminism or simply their attachment to one another. Sahli was right, of course; the accusation of lesbianism was indeed a way of defaming many women's independence and restricting the social space available to women in general. Nonetheless Sahli did not take the next step—so what if they were?— and I was moved to write the following letter. I don't know what Sahli's view of the matter would be now (both her essay and my comment were published in 1979) but at that time it was possible for an intelligent, dedicated, outspoken feminist like Sahli to be made so uneasy by the attribution "lesbian" that she actually argued that her examples weren't "lesbian"—using for the purpose a definition so narrow that nobody could possibly fit it without having been caught in flagrante by a blackmailer. (No one's heterosexuality is ever denied because of the lack of such evidence.) Although the specific disagreement between us is not important now, I think the issue is still important, i.e. the double standard of evidence that consigns homosexuality to nonexistence, keeps gay people isolated and makes the rate of teen-age suicide much higher for gay adolescents than for others. Hence the following.*

Dear Editors,

Nancy Sahli's essay was delightful. And yet there are things in it that present a real problem, one that has appeared recently in other women's publications: Judith Schwarz's article on Katharine Lee Bates and Katharine Coman, and Lee Chambers-Schiller's review of Miss Marks and Miss Woolley, *both* in *Frontiers* IV,1; and Judith Hallett's very peculiar essay on Sappho in *Signs* IV,3. To varying degrees, all these pieces present the appearance of uneasily backing into a subject that all of them are either soft-pedalling or (in the case of Hallett) denying outright.

Here is Sahli, insisting that "the" point is not "whether these relationships were sexual, even on an unconscious level," and protesting Krafft-Ebing's identification of a woman who dressed in men's clothing (in 1884), wrote "tender love-letters" to another woman, and disliked the idea of relationships with men as a Lesbian. Why? Because her affair was "Platonic." And again, Sahli protesting the identification of Olive Chancellor, in *The Bostonians*, as a Lesbian since "nowhere in the novel can one find evidence of any variant sexual behavior."

Explicit sexual activity seems some kind of Rubicon for Sahli, on the other side of which lies Heaven knows what. I'm reminded of the heterosexual teenage code of the 1950s, in which petting above the waist was O.K., while petting below the waist imperilled one's respectability—as if both activities weren't erotic. There is, in Sahli's essay, an obvious and very appealing delight in the all-female space she describes, a space that's innocent, emotional, free, and romantic. And yet it is perfectly clear that the motivational fuel for all this activity is erotic. Without genuinely erotic intensity between the women Sahli speaks of, there would be no motive, no point to all the courtship except as play-acting, i.e., a substitute or rehearsal for "real" sex, which is ("of course") heterosexual. This was not only the nineteenth-century attitude, the "girl friendship" stage of Josiah Holland; it persisted into the twentieth century, although the age at which this stage of attachment was supposed to end got earlier and earlier (from college age to puberty itself) as female solidarity was perceived as more and more threatening.

Why is genital activity such an absolute dividing line for Sahli, as well as the other writers I've mentioned, all of whom—to some degree—betray uneasiness with the subject? To apply Sahli's reasoning to heterosexual activity would lead to some strange results; are we not to call a nineteenth-century young woman heterosexual because, although she has experienced passionate attachments to young men, writes them "tender love-letters," and does not wish for close relationships with women, she nonetheless does not engage in specific sexual activity with these men? Surely not.

I'm not sure what the taboo really is here. Is "Lesbian" still so loaded a word that its very presence impugns the innocence, the emotionality, even the human decency of the relationships Sahli describes? Is sexual activity itself so guilty or so base or so frightening (heterosexual activity can certainly be unpleasant, frightening, or "base" for women in patriarchy) that it can't be allowed—even as a motive—into Sahli's paradise of freedom and innocence? (The title of the essay, "Before the Fall," is suggestive!)

The sexuality underlying these relationships is not "the" point, but it certainly is an important point. Some conclusions that can be drawn from this point, for example, are that people are more erotically various than they are supposed to be, that sexuality is more complex than it is supposed to be, and that splitting of erotic feeling into "sexual" and "emotional" is a product of male training, not female. (What we get is a general anti-genital training, which men don't.)

Trying to insist that women are not explicitly sexual or that our relationships with both sexes are "emotional" and not genital does not counter the exploitation and abuse of women's heterosexuality by patriarchy, and it certainly will not prevent the kind of labeling Sahli deplores in her article. There is no sense in colluding with the patriarchy in this area; our sexuality ought to be named for what it is, as it is our very great resource. Nor must we follow implicitly masculine definitions of what sex is (which is what Sahli may be doing) and refuse to acknowledge as sexual any motive or action that isn't explicitly physical. Acknowledging Lesbian sexuality (one's own or other women's) puts one into direct confrontation with the patriarchy and subjects one to danger and discomfort that the college girls of Sahli's essay didn't have to face.

Personal or not, the issue of Lesbianism, of erotic feeling between women, is a kind of Rubicon for feminism. It's not just that the issue can be used to divide women or that "Lesbian" is a code word for female solidarity (as used by anti-feminists, that is). There is something more at stake here, namely the fashion in which sexuality itself is controlled by patriarchy and the particular mystifications it undergoes in the contemporary form of patriarchy from binding women to the family and the economy to the repressive desublimation that occurs more subtly under late industrial capitalism—the reduction of sex to "only" sex, to a consumer good, to something mechanical, simple, and manipulable.

And the lack of real choice and autonomy for women in both situations.

What is crucial about woman/woman eroticism is that it (much more than man/man eroticism) stands completely outside both the heterosexual institution and the way human sexuality itself has been viewed and controlled by patriarchal societies. Historically, Lesbianism has been totally "wild," not only taboo but impossible, non-existent, in the West in a way that male homosexuality has not. Male homosexuality seems to be fairly easily culturally assimilable to a reductive, consumer-goods view of sex (read some of the male gay publications on sale at your neighborhood newsstand!). Lesbian sexuality, because it is neither male nor heterosexually institutionalized, resists such treatment.

One of the things this means is that we are forced to talk about female sexuality in general in an alien vocabulary. Stress the physical eroticism of woman/woman ties, and one is "progressing" into the seductive view of "only" sex (as well as the presumed ugliness and nastiness that accompany that view in this very anti-sexual society). Stress the emotional bond, and one is "regressing" into the view of women as asexual creatures who have plenty of emotions but no independent, real appetite.

It is striking that even in a work intending to demonstrate that women's love for women is called names only when it's perceived as a threat to the system, Nancy Sahli herself shies away from what seem to me the obvious erotic components of what she's describing. If you want examples of women's autonomy being slandered by being declared Lesbian, Krafft-Ebing's German lady and Henry James's Olive Chancellor are extraordinarily bad examples. (James's own homosexual temperament is something of an open secret, by the way.) What is so awful about recognizing the erotic intensity in such women's behavior?

Here is Harriet Desmoines in the latest issue of *Sinister Wisdom* (#9): "The partition of the body that patriarchy tries to effect does not work very well with [women] . . . it's not so easy to isolate the sexual from the nonsexual [with] . . . women. The word Lesbian points to the erotic tone of everything that happens between women . . . mothers and daughters . . . sisters . . . students and teachers . . . girl friends. And if . . . that makes you feel as nervous as it makes me feel, then I think we can agree that the energies we generate between ourselves . . . are tabooed in patriarchy because those energies are powerful—and scary—and it's about time we tapped into them."

This letter first appeared in *Chrysalis*, no. 9 (Fall 1979).

14

Letter to Susan Koppelman

ears ago at an MLA conference I saw a young man, a graduate student, read a paper on one of Ursula Le Guin's science-fiction novels. After he had finished and it was time for discussion, a handsome, middle-aged woman at the back of the room rose and said emphatically, "You're wrong. I didn't." It was Le Guin. Writers seldom have the opportunity to criticize the literary critics, so when my long-time friend Susan Koppelman sent me a paper on one of my stories, "The Autobiography of My Mother," that she had heard presented at (I think) a regional MLA meeting and asked me what on earth it was all about, I told her. Some writers do not analyze their own methods or other people's but some—like E. M. Forster, T. S. Eliot, Virginia Woolf, Henry James, George Bernard Shaw, or Bertolt Brecht (I am pulling names from the top of my memory here)—are very conscious artists indeed and write about their work or their fields in general. Nonetheless, literary critics assume they know better—possibly because they would find themselves unemployed if they didn't—and how often do you get a chance to take a swipe at one of them? I don't want to swipe too hard at the anonymous person talked about below, as she was a graduate student and, I suspect, more of a victim of her own education than an active agent in somebody else's, but (again) the issue is an important one. Anyone who seriously tries to make received ideas do feminist work will find that the received ideas end up making her feminism do their work, and anyone who really thinks that respectability will do us good in any field—well, I don't know what to say. I am not against people lying their heads off when they have to, to make a living, but believing the junk you may be forced to practice is another matter. I can only refer readers to Stephen Jay Gould again; "the barrel of theory is always full"—full of the most unusable, even stupid, stuff—and knowledge does not proceed simply by accretion. What is striking here (as elsewhere) is how little

knowledge and how little sense of history go into a view of literature
that sees it still—still!—now, after the New Criticism is dead and
gone—as being produced by a narrowly literary tradition and The
Unconscious. Especially in a field like science fiction, in which you
have to know a great deal. Unless you are making movies, of course.
(I remember Harlan Ellison recounting how he nearly throttled a
producer who insisted he could get a character out of a tight spot by
having him climb a laser beam.*) Enough. I'll end up writing*
another *letter.*

November 23, 1984

Dear Susan,

Yes, I got ———'s paper on my story and yes, I don't wonder that you couldn't follow it. If you hadn't read the story, you would have had an easier time of it. The conclusion the writer comes to, that the story subverts patriarchal ideology, i.e., its version of women and of the world creates feminist space, is surely true, but the rest is jargon, wrong-headedness, and the kind of arbitrary assumptions that either stupefy a reader or make her want to shake ———. Alas, the assumptions don't come from feminist theory or experience but from several gentlemen whose version of women's lives are, as you'd expect, more than a little peculiar. (Once or twice ——— seems to be quoting Hélène Cixous, but no citation is given.)

She misses a great deal in the story, usually the most straightfor-wardly feminist statements—which is heartbreaking for a graduate student who *is* a feminist. She may also expect a writer not to be conscious of her (the writer's) intent. Oh yes I was. For example, the passage she calls "pre-symbolic" (I think she means what we used to mean by "pre-verbal") and to which she assigns "sexual confusion" (!) while also stating that this "strain" represents the difficulty, for a woman, of "uttering her truth" is of course parody. Parody is perfectly conscious *criticism;* it is neither pre-symbolic nor strained (nor sexually confused; it's the myths that are sexually confused). Of course in order to use cultural inventions that aren't intended to be ours, we must do things like parody, and so far I agree with her. But little of it is as "deep" and so on as that sort of critic likes to imagine. Here the "little summer-camp maedchen" (she misses *Mädchen in Uniform*) "disemboweled the myth" and "passed it from hand to hand." *That's* the model for the story, if you please! They are tearing the gender myths to pieces (oh, those savage little girls!) and it makes as much sense that way as the other. *Parody is contempt;* it is also an assertion that something is senseless and absurd. And it is right on the surface. And ———'s assumption that "traditional" narrative is always linear is simply not true. Shall we send her Chekhov? But she doesn't know literature outside a very limited canon.

Or look at her assertion that the story is "broken into segments." Why on earth shouldn't it be? You caught it right away; the segments are dramatic scenes, followed by "lyrical" passages of commentary. But ——— — doesn't seem to know theatre (including modern, post-realistic theatre, which was the new thing when I was in New York City in my twenties and saw *Mann ist Mann* and other Living Theatre productions) or post-realistic fiction. Modernism has been around for some time now also. She is also heartbreakingly ignorant of feminist theory. I am really annoyed at this attempt to play with the big boys (I mean the recent stuff in feminist criticism)—real theory always looks "crude" and "obvious" and "simple" next to gussied-up patriarchal theory, first because most of us refuse to mess up our communication or our language with the sort of reifying, mystifying garbage so many theoreticians love; and second because we are dealing with issues so extremely obvious and grossly plain that it takes enormous social forces (as with racism) to make these phenomena seem "invisible" or "natural." So everybody looks for "deep" causes and fancy ways of talking about what is not nearly as complex as they think.

To see ——— finding acceptable feminist theory, which she obviously needs and loves (bless her), in two or three white men is very painful to me. If only she had Dale Spender's overview of Gage's *Woman, Church and State* or a real history of the Pankhursts or anything at all!

But here she is, heaven help us, quoting Freud—of all people!—and Lacan and Lévi-Strauss.

Of course she doesn't know anything about fantasy either. For one thing she misses the arrogance of the title and its allusion to Stein, and since the first few lines suggest to her Chodorow's highly speculative and rather faulty theory of boundary confusion between mother and daughter (not what Chodorow said, actually, but it's turned into that lately), after that she gallops off mightily in the wrong direction.

In the actual text, there is never confusion between the identity of mother and daughter. It is their *roles* that keep switching. It is character-istic of ———, like the Freudians *and* the New Criticism (quite an affinity there, no?), that she dwells on selected details but does not seem to notice the plot. (Fiction has those embarrassing gaucheries, doesn't it? Oh my!) As the story says outright, echoing (I might add) a VERY famous passage in you-know-where, "Am I my mother's mother?" This isn't guilt at ruining one's mother's life (I certainly don't find that there and it was a miserable life before the daughter arrived on the scene) but what one early feminist called "the compassion trap"—remember? It's the quintessential feminist situation. Tillie Olsen and Alta both wrote about it. Both mother and daughter live in a world which oppresses both of them; how far can mother or child *or any woman* claim for herself the nurturant energies so obviously needed for others? Daughter didn't get enough from mother because (says the story) mother was always waiting for The Man; ——— seeth not. Do you give "unselfishly" to daughter (or mother) and perpetuate this wretched vicious circle or do you "selfishly" claim such energies for yourself and thus deprive mother/daughter/others of what they quite genuinely need and what they won't get from anyone else?

Why does ——— adopt male authorities, like so many other feminist literary critics? Is it genuine ignorance? Or do men still seem so worthy, so central, so important, so normative, that "Freudian" feminism *via* we know who plus Lacan plus whoever *allows her to be a feminist at all,* while all our recent (and current) classics look simple-minded or non-authori-tative? Her being a graduate student predisposes me to theory I. Maybe time will cure it. If it's a tactic, it won't work. The men around her will say "yes, dear" (if they notice anything) and will then go on as before. This kind of conciliatory behavior—see, we'll prove to them that femi-nists fit into the existing disciplines—isn't heard and doesn't get pre-served in the discipline; it will simply be ignored and lost. Since the conflict feminists have with the patriarchal establishment and its theory isn't about what's right or wrong but about who's boss (like Humpty Dumpty), the only tactics that work are open confrontation and active non-cooperation. Play by the rules and you may get an immediate pat on the head but ten minutes later (sometimes it takes longer but as we know, seldom) you'll try to enter the conversation and you know what? Nobody will hear you.

This attempt to be respectable is lost, lost, lost—unless it is used consciously and wilily as pure camouflage. And if ——— were doing that, she wouldn't be writing about feminism or women's work at all.

I wonder if the other story ——— analyzes was that sad and guilty— maybe it was, but all this insistence on the difficulty of expressing female truths, the guilt of daughters for ruining mothers' lives &c. adds up to (for me) a kind of proto-feminist misery. The Freudian concentration on intra-personal deep causation, established in infancy, seems to dis-hearten every woman I know. It smears the social-political truth that most of this "deep" causation *is political*—i.e., it is right on the surface. We learn it and it is reinforced every day. But none of that sounds fashionable. The power of sheer jargon! The utter thingifying-ness of Freudian talk! (I hear that Freud himself never did it; I wouldn't be surprised.) There seems to be an odd idea around that art should be easy—or authenticity likewise—and otherwise it is such a terrible "strain" that no woman can do it! Art was never easy; originality always meant stating the truth in a foreign language, and if you're not happy doing that, you're in the wrong business. What about Melville? I am losing my patience. These folks are advancing backwards with all possible speed and calling themselves feminists as they do so. I ache for ——— because she's young but *where is her anger?* I think from now on, I will not trust anyone who isn't angry. Hopelessness is not a first step. It may be the prelude to finding out where one is, but that's all. Nothing really good is ever easy—but it's worth it. The other sort of thing is merely the old feminine (not feminist) game of Ain't It Awful. And of course someone like ——— (who knows neither real feminism nor real psychology) thinks Freudian stuff is psychology *per se* because they've no notion that other psychology exists. Like Nancy Henley's. Like simple learning theory. Like biochemistry. Like neurology. C. P. Snow is prob-ably spinning in his grave, like a lathe. Gage is merely dampening hers, with tears.

Anyone who wants to do the bi-cultural tightrope act has my blessing—but you can't quote the "proper" authorities and hide away enough feminism just to get some of it expressed. The "authorities" are anti-feminist, period. Better do two kinds of work: something fairly technical which few will understand, but which will make them feel stupid, and then—in different periodicals—write what you really feel and want and believe. The technical stuff does have to interest you, of course, but then technical stuff *is* interesting.

The sort of culture English Departments produce is dreadful. They know so little and leave out so much out of sheer ignorance; and then there's the stuff they leave out because it's in their interest to do so. It's an unbelievably narrow education. Also (P.S.) some Freudians get this weird idea that Freud knew everything. He didn't. Henry Ford's joke about the color of car his customers could get (i.e. *they had no choice*) can be found studying mass production, industrialization, the automobilization of the United States, &c. &c. Actually my father (who once owned a Model A) told me the joke. —— says it's a *hearse?!* Heck, I *rode* in the Model A. My father (earlier) owned a Model T. My mother told me about riding in a Model T. So much for the memory of the younger generation! Does this person think Freud contains all of history and human culture? Thus it is to study English and never American history or the history of technology, in short, nothing but the Great Works and outdated psychology. I have a callus on my forehead from banging it against the wall. (It was Ford, by the way, who said, "History is bunk," a saying most graduate students—and professors—in English seem bent on embodying. Not so!) I will go read G. B. S. and feel sympathetic with his plight, which is mine. We are surrounded by nonsense.

Love,
Joanna

P.S. Like most Freudians, —— does not understand that there is a difference between *interpreting* human motives and *proving* them. Henley takes up some of this, as part of her investigation of social psychology. Because behavior more or less fits one psychological scheme doesn't mean it can't fit others as well—and then parsimony and completeness and all the other means used to choose one theory over another must be applied. But these people generally know nothing of real scientific theory and think that if an idea strikes you or looks nice, it must be true. Nor do they realize that all theories are merely models. No sophistication, actually. Let 'em read Gould.

INDEX

JOANNA RUSS has published science-fiction novels, short stories, and criticism for thirty-five years and has been active as a feminist for twenty-five. Her books include *The Female Man, The Two of Them, How to Suppress Women's Writing,* and *Magic Mommas, Trembling Sisters, Puritans and Perverts: Feminist Essays.*